Lecture Notes in Artificial Intelligence   12871

Subseries of Lecture Notes in Computer Science

More information about this subseries at http://www.springer.com/series/1244

Troels Andreasen · Guy De Tré ·
Janusz Kacprzyk · Henrik Legind Larsen ·
Gloria Bordogna · Sławomir Zadrożny (Eds.)

Flexible Query Answering Systems

14th International Conference, FQAS 2021
Bratislava, Slovakia, September 19–24, 2021
Proceedings

 Springer

Editors
Troels Andreasen 🆔
Roskilde University
Roskilde, Denmark

Janusz Kacprzyk 🆔
Systems Research Institute
Polish Academy of Sciences
Warsaw, Poland

Gloria Bordogna 🆔
CNR - IREA
Milan, Italy

Guy De Tré 🆔
Ghent University
Ghent, Belgium

Henrik Legind Larsen 🆔
Legind Technologies A/s
Esbjerg, Denmark

Sławomir Zadrożny 🆔
Systems Research Institute
Polish Academy of Sciences
Warsaw, Poland

ISSN 0302-9743 ISSN 1611-3349 (electronic)
Lecture Notes in Artificial Intelligence
ISBN 978-3-030-86966-3 ISBN 978-3-030-86967-0 (eBook)
https://doi.org/10.1007/978-3-030-86967-0

LNCS Sublibrary: SL7 – Artificial Intelligence

This Springer imprint is published by the registered company Springer Nature Switzerland AG
The registered company address is: Gewerbestrasse 11, 6330 Cham, Switzerland

Preface

This volume is the proceedings of the 14th International Conference on Flexible Query Answering Systems 2021 (FQAS 2021) held during September 19–24, 2021 in Bratislava, Slovakia, and organized jointly with the 19th World Congress of the International Fuzzy Systems Association and the 12th Conference of the European Society for Fuzzy Logic and Technology (IFSA-EUSFLAT 2021), along with International Summer School on Aggregation Operators (AGOP 2021) and the International Joint Conference on Rough Sets (IJCRS 2021).

The international conferences on Flexible Query Answering Systems (FQAS) are a series of premier conferences focusing on the key issue in an information society of providing easy, flexible, and intuitive access to information and knowledge to everybody, even people with a very limited computer literacy. In targeting this issue, the conference draws on several research areas, such as information retrieval, database management, information filtering, knowledge representation, soft computing, management of multimedia information, data mining, and human-computer interaction.

Moreover, in many papers presented at the conference and included in this proceedings volume, explicit and implicit relations to elements of the broadly perceived data science and artificial intelligence are included which are shown to yield an added value. The conference provides a unique opportunity for researchers, developers, and practitioners to explore new ideas and approaches in a multidisciplinary forum.

The previous FQAS conferences, which have always attracted a large audience from all parts of the world, include FQAS 2019 (Amantea, Italy), FQAS 2017 (London, UK), FQAS 2015 (Cracow, Poland), FQAS 2013 (Granada, Spain), FQAS 2011 (Ghent, Belgium), FQAS 2009 (Roskilde, Denmark), FQAS 2006 (Milano, Italy), FQAS 2004 (Lyon, France), FQAS 2002 (Copenhagen, Denmark), FQAS 2000 (Warsaw, Poland), FQAS 1998 (Roskilde, Denmark), FQAS 1996 (Roskilde, Denmark), FQAS 1994 (Roskilde, Denmark).

An important contribution of the conference has also been the fact that it has greatly facilitated a deeper discussion on the papers presented which, as a rule, has resulted in new collaborative works and research further progress in the areas.

We hope that the collection of main contributions presented at the conference, completed with plenary talks by leading experts in the field, will provide a source of much needed information and inspiration on recent trends in the topics considered.

Besides the accepted papers, to encourage the audience to engage in discussions at the event, we have included in the proceedings a perspective paper, written by ourselves, on the views of challenges of flexible query answering and six invited papers on hot research topics written by well-known researchers in the field: Antoon Bronselaer, Fabio Crestani, Allel Hajali, Peter Vojtas, Henri Prade, and Adnan Yazici.

Unforeseeable COVID-19 circumstances made the organization of this year's edition challenging. We are glad that quite a large number of the regular paper submissions were of high quality. This indicates that researchers who submitted a paper were well motivated and put a lot of effort into their work. Out of the 11 regular papers submitted, 10 were accepted after a rigorous two-stage revision process where each paper has been reviewed by at least three members of the International Program Committee, who were carefully chosen based on their knowledge and competence. This corresponds to an exceptional acceptance rate of 90.9%. The invited papers, all written by authorities in their research field, have been reviewed by two members chosen from the general chairs and Program Committee chairs.

The contributions included in the proceedings of FQAS 2021 have been grouped into two broad categories: model-based flexible query answering, intended as representation-based approaches, and data-driven flexible query answering, intended as approaches exploiting data to train a model based on machine learning principles. Among the first category of approaches we find the following papers:

- The paper by Henri Prade and Gilles Richard entitled "Analogical Querying?" proposes a new way of exploiting examples of items that are known to be liked and counter-examples of items that are known to be disliked, in case-based querying. This relies on analogical proportions, that is, statements that compare pairs of items laying bare the similarities and the differences between items.
- The paper by Gregory Smits et al., entitled "Flexible Querying Using Disjunctive Concepts" addresses end users querying relational databases by exploiting the query by example paradigm and proposes a translation extracting from the examples complex search conditions materialized by fuzzy disjunctive concepts.
- The paper by Sebastien Ferre entitled "Analytical Queries on Vanilla RDF Graphs with a Guided Query Builder Approach" describes an approach aimed to make the expression of analytical queries over RDF data more user-friendly than when using SPARQL. The core of the approach is to 'bridge the gap between natural languages and formal languages'.
- The paper by Troels Andreasen et al., entitled "Realization of a Natural Logic in a Database System" aims at ensuring explainability of query inferences suited for ontology-structured knowledge bases, which constitutes an important advantage with respect to embedding approaches.
- Horacio Tellez Perez and Jef Wijsen authored a paper entitled "Generalized Weighted Repairs" dealing with the problem of repairing inconsistent relational database instances in which facts are qualified by truthfulness scores. This decision problem is central in consistent query answering.
- Guy De Tré and Jozo Dujmović contributed with a paper entitled "Dealing with Data Veracity in Multiple Criteria Handling: An LSP-Based Sibling Approach" that investigates the impact of data veracity on criterion handling and proposes a novel LSP-based evaluation approach to explicitly cope with this issue.
- The paper by Allel Hajali entitled "On Controlling Skyline Query Results: What Does Soft Computing Bring?" proposes flexible skyline queries modeled within soft computing in order to solve the two well-known problems occurring when retrieving either an insufficient number of objects or too many skyline objects. To face insufficiency it relaxes the skyline query by introducing a fuzzy preference. To reduce the number of retrieved objects it proposes a refined skyline query based on fuzzy formal concept analysis.

- The paper by Sinan Keskin and Adnan Yazici entitled "Management of Complex and Fuzzy Queries Using a Fuzzy Spatial OLAP-Based Framework" tackles the inability of OLAP to flexibly query and analyze multidimensional uncertain and fuzzy data, which are very common in existing complex contexts such as multimedia and spatiotemporal applications. They propose a fuzzy spatiotemporal query framework with Multi-Dimensional Extension (MDX) query types on a SOLAP for a meteorological database, which inherently contains fuzzy spatial objects and relationships.
- Antoon Bronselaer, in his paper entitled "Data Quality Management: an Overview of Methods and Challenges", reflects on current approaches to modeling and assessing the quality of data in different disciplines, and organizes the techniques on two levels, the macro level and micro level, by providing a general methodology for both of them. Finally, he identifies open issues and challenges for future research.
- The paper entitled "J-CO, a Framework for Fuzzy Querying Collections of JSON Documents" by Paolo Fosci and Giuseppe Psaila is a demonstration paper describing a flexible language to query large collections of JSON documents stored in NoSQL databases.

In the second category, comprising data-driven approaches, we grouped the following six papers:

- The paper entitled "Detecting ESG Topics Using Domain-Specific Language Models and Data Augmentation" by Tim Nugent et al., investigates two approaches that can help mitigate the issues that prevent the applicability of deep learning-based language models, typically the case of paucity of appropriately labelled data, and the use of specialized language and symbols in the financial domain.
- Alfredo Cuzzocrea et al. in their paper entitled "A Novel Approach for Supporting Italian Satire Detection Through Deep Learning" tackle the novel issue of automatic satire detection by applying deep learning that has shown to be useful for modeling sarcasm and irony.
- The paper entitled "DocTalk: Combining Dependency-Based Text Graphs and Deep Learning into a Practical Dialog Engine" by Yifan Guo et al. describes a software tool allowing for summarizing and question answering textual documents by exploiting a hybrid approach combining graph-based representation of documents with deep learning using BERT.
- The paper by Angel Diaz-Garcia et al. "A Comparative Study of Word Embedding for the Construction of a Social Media Expert Filter" aims at ranking reliable sources of information to filter expert users in social networks according to a certain topic of interest by a comparative study of the results of the application of different word embedding (as well as different representation) models.
- The paper by Samuel Brezani and Peter Vojtas entitled "Aggregation for Flexible Challenge Response" considers real-world recommender systems based on Fagin-Lotem-Naor data models with aggregation and the main interest is to test the challenge-response framework in several real settings in which data-driven models are available. The paper shows how data-driven models can be flexibly combined to achieve greater accuracy.

– The paper entitled "The Impact of User Demographics and Task Types on Cross-App Mobile Search" by Mohammad Aliannejadi et al. reports a behaviour study of users when accessing information from their mobile phones as a preliminary phase for designing a unified mobile search and recommendation framework. The results of this study outline the dominant influencing factors that the design of a metasearch engine on mobile devices should take into account.

We wish to thank all the authors for their excellent contributions and their collaboration during the editing process of the volume. We look forward to the same fruitful collaboration during future FQAS conferences that are planned for the years to come. Special thanks are due to the peer reviewers, whose excellent and timely work has significantly contributed to the quality of the volume.

Last but not least, we wish to thank Miriam Costales, Anna Kramer, and Christine Reiss for their dedication and help to implement and finish this publication project on time whilst maintaining the highest publication standards.

August 2021

Troels Andreasen
Guy De Tré
Janusz Kacprzyk
Henrik Legind Larsen
Gloria Bordogna
Sławomir Zadrożny

Organization

General Chairs

Troels Andreasen   Roskilde University, Denmark
Guy De Tré   Ghent University, Belgium
Janusz Kacprzyk   Polish Academy of Sciences, Warsaw, Poland

Program Committee Chairs

Gloria Bordogna   National Research Council (CNR), Italy
Sławomir Zadrożny   Polish Academy of Sciences, Warsaw, Poland

Steering Committee

Henrik Legind Larsen   Legind Technologies A/S, Denmark
Troels Andreasen   Roskilde University, Denmark

FQAS International Advisory Board

Troels Andreasen   Roskilde University, Denmark
Jesús Cardeñosa   Universidad Politécnica de Madrid, Spain
Panagiotis Chountas   University of Westminster, UK
Henning Christiansen   Roskilde University, Denmark
Guy De Tré   Ghent University, Belgium
Jørgen Fischer Nilsson   Technical University of Denmark, Denmark
Norbert Fuhr   University of Duisburg-Essen, Germany
Hélène Jaudoin   Université de Rennes, France
Janusz Kacprzyk   Polish Academy of Sciences, SRI, Poland
Donald H. Kraft   Louisiana State University, USA
Henrik Legind Larsen   Legind Technologies A/S, Denmark
Maria J. Martin-Bautista University of Granada, Spain
Gabriella Pasi   Università degli Studi di Milano, Italy
Frederick E. Petry   Stennis Space Center, USA
Olivier Pivert   Université de Rennes, IRISAUMR, France
Roman Slowinski   Poznań University of Technology, Poland
Sotir Sotirov   Burgas "Prof. Dr. Assen Zlatarov" University, Bulgaria
Nicolas Spyratos   Université Paris-Sud, France
Ronald R. Yager   Iona College, USA
Adnan Yazici   Middle East Technical University, Turkey
Sławomir Zadrożny   Polish Academy of Sciences, SRI, Poland

Program Committee

Troels Andreasen	Roskilde University, Denmark
Ignacio J. Blanco	University of Granada, Spain
Gloria Bordogna	National Research Council (CNR), Italy
Antoon Bronselaer	Ghent University, Belgium
Patrice Buche	INRAE, France
Henning Christiansen	Roskilde University, Denmark
Alfredo Cuzzocrea	ICAR-CNR and University of Calabria, Italy
Ernesto Damiani	University of Milan, Italy
Bernard De Baets	Ghent University, Belgium
Guy De Tré	Ghent University, Belgium
Sébastien Ferré	Université de Rennes, CNRS, IRISA, France
Jørgen Fischer Nilsson	Technical University of Denmark, Denmark
Allel Hadjali	LIAS/ENSMA, France
Petr Hurtik	IRAFM, University of Ostrava, Czech Republic
Helene Jaudoin	IRISA-ENSSAT, France
Etienne Kerre	Ghent University, Belgium
Donald D. Kraft	Louisiana State University, USA
Marie-Jeanne Lesot	Sorbonne Université, LIP6UPMC, France
Antoni Ligeza	AGH University of Science and Technology, Poland
Nicolás Marín	University of Granada, Spain
Trevor Martin	University of Bristol, UK
Grzegorz J. Nalepa	AGH University of Science and Technology, Poland
Andreas Nuernberger	Otto-von-Guericke-Universität Magdeburg, Germany
Jose Angel Olivas	Universidad de Castilla-La Mancha, Spain
Frederick E. Petry	Stennis Space Center, USA
Olivier Pivert	Université de Rennes, IRISAUMR, France
Henri Prade	Université Paul Sabatier, IRITCNRS, France
Giuseppe Psaila	University of Bergamo, Italy
Zbigniew Ras	University of North Carolina at Charlotte, USA
Guillaume Raschia	University of Nantes, LINA, France
Marek Reformat	University of Alberta, Canada
Francisco P. Romero	Universidad de Castilla-La Mancha, Spain
Miguel-Angel Sicilia	University of Alcala, Spain
Andrzej Skowron	Warsaw University, Poland
Dominik Slezak	University of Warsaw, Poland
Grégory Smits	Université de Rennes, IRISA, France
Umberto Straccia	ISTI-CNR, Italy
Peter Vojtas	Charles University in Prague, Czech Republic
Jef Wijsen	University of Mons, Belgium
Adnan Yazici	Middle East Technical University, Turkey
Slawomir Zadrożny	Polish Academy of Sciences, SRI, Poland
Wlodek Zadrożny	University of North Carolina at Charlotte, USA

Additional Reviewers

| Jorge Galicia | LIAS/ENSMA, France |
| Seethalakshmi Gopalakrishnan | University of North Carolina at Charlotte, USA |

Contents

xiv   Contents

Data-Driven Approaches

Detecting Environmental, Social and Governance (ESG) Topics Using
Domain-Specific Language Models and Data Augmentation   157
  Tim Nugent, Nicole Stelea, and Jochen L. Leidner

A Novel Approach for Supporting Italian Satire Detection Through
Deep Learning   170
  Gabriella Casalino, Alfredo Cuzzocrea, Giosué Lo Bosco,
  Mariano Maiorana, Giovanni Pilato, and Daniele Schicchi

DocTalk: Combining Dependency-Based Text Graphs and Deep Learning
into a Practical Dialog Engine   182
  Yifan Guo, Weilun Sun, Ali Khan, Tam Doan, and Paul Tarau

A Comparative Study of Word Embeddings for the Construction of a Social
Media Expert Filter   196
  Jose A. Diaz-Garcia, M. Dolores Ruiz, and Maria J. Martin-Bautista

Aggregation for Flexible Challenge Response   209
  Samuel Brezani and Peter Vojtas

The Impact of User Demographics and Task Types on Cross-App
Mobile Search   223
  Mohammad Aliannejadi, Fabio Crestani, Theo Huibers,
  Monica Landoni, Emiliana Murgia, and Maria Soledad Pera

Author Index   235

Perspective Paper

Perspectives and Views of Flexible Query Answering

Troels Andreasen[1] ⓘ, Guy De Tré[2] ⓘ, Janusz Kacprzyk[3] ⓘ,
Henrik Legind Larsen[4] ⓘ, Gloria Bordogna[5(✉)] ⓘ, and Sławomir Zadrożny[3] ⓘ

[1] Computer Science, Roskilde University, Roskilde, Denmark
troels@ruc.dk
[2] Department of Telecommunications and Information Processing, Ghent University,
St.-Pietersnieuwstraat 41, B9000 Ghent, Belgium
Guy.DeTre@UGent.be
[3] Systems Research Institute, Polish Academy of Sciences, Warsaw, Poland
{Janusz.Kacprzyk,zadrozny}@ibspan.waw.pl
[4] Legind Technologies A/S, Esbjerg, Denmark
henrik@legind.com
[5] CNR - IREA, via A. Corti 12, 20133 Milan, Italy
bordogna.g@irea.cnr.it

Abstract. Flexible Query Answering Systems (FQAS) is a multidisciplinary research field at the crossroad of Information retrieval, databases, data mining, multimedia and geographic information systems, knowledge based systems, social networks, Natural Language Processing (NLP) and semantic web technologies, whose aim is to improve human ability to retrieve relevant information from databases, libraries, heterogeneous archives, the Web and the Web 2.0. The present paper has the objective to outline the perspectives and challenges offered by the heterogeneous panorama of current techniques.

Keywords: Perspectives of flexible query answering · Model based approaches · Data driven approaches

1 Introduction

Query Answering Systems (QASs) have the main objective of satisfying the needs of end users to retrieve information contents they are interested in, including structured data typically managed in databases, unstructured and semi-structured texts in natural language such as Web documents typically managed by information retrieval systems and search engines, documents containing spatial and/or temporal information, multimedia documents containing audio, image and videos files, structured RDF data in the Semantic Web, social posts within social networks and, last but not least, natural language processing and knowledge based answers [1, 27–30]. In such a varied context, formulating queries that can be flexibly interpreted by the systems is an essential objective in order to satisfy users' needs.

© Springer Nature Switzerland AG 2021
T. Andreasen et al. (Eds.): FQAS 2021, LNAI 12871, pp. 3–14, 2021.
https://doi.org/10.1007/978-3-030-86967-0_1

The International Conference on Flexible Query Answering Systems (FQAS), firstly organized in 1994 in Roskilde, Denmark, has been the premier conference concerned with this up-to-date issue of improving user systems interaction when searching for information, by investigating the proposals of flexible querying facilities and intuitive access to information. This was before the first question-answering (Q/A) evaluations track started in 1999 as part of the Text Retrieval Conference (TREC) [2].

Traditionally, FQAS has been a multidisciplinary conference gathering research contributors at the crossroad of different disciplines, such as Information retrieval, databases, data mining, multimedia information systems, geographic information systems, knowledge based systems, social network querying and mining, Question Answering (Q/A), Natural Language Processing (NLP) and semantic web technologies, in order to aid retrieval from information repositories such as databases, libraries, heterogeneous archives, the Web and the Web 2.0.

Traditional flexible querying has been strongly related to human-computer interaction (HCI) defined by the Association for Computing Machinery (ACM) as "...a discipline that is concerned with the design, evaluation and implementation of interactive computing systems for human use and with the study of major phenomena surrounding them". It is easy to see that this has human and machine aspects. From the machine point of view, issues exemplified by computer graphics or development environments are relevant, while from the human point of view, issues related to communication, argumentation, graphic design, natural language, cognitive and psychological analyses, to just mention a few, are important.

More recently, it has become more and more obvious that virtually all problems related to flexible querying, as well as many other related areas, are plagued by uncertainty, imprecision, vagueness, incompleteness, etc. which should be reflected in analyses, designs and implementations.

It has become obvious that the traditional widely employed logical, probabilistic and statistical tools and techniques that have been used for decades cannot cope with those problems with the omnipresent broadly perceived imperfect information. Luckily enough, progression in view of both more sophisticated logics and probabilistic and statistical tools and techniques, including fuzzy logic, rough sets theory and their extensions exemplified by intuitionistic fuzzy sets theory, possibilistic analyses, fuzzy rough/rough fuzzy sets theory, etc. have made it possible to deal with many more aspects of the imperfection of information, notably uncertainty, imprecision, vagueness, incompleteness etc. A high potential of these new fields has been recognized by the flexible querying community, and reflected in the list of topics considered, of the FQAS Conferences since the very beginning.

Within elective frameworks to make human interaction flexible using such diverse techniques, model-based approaches are defined with the main shared characteristics to be representation based and human interpretable in the first place, i.e., "explainable by design" ex-ante to their use. Furthermore, they are also ex-post explainable in the second place, i.e., the criteria that yield results can be understandable to humans since they accurately describe model behaviour in the entire feature space [3].

These methods are increasingly competing with data-driven approaches based on Machine Learning, mainly Deep learning (DL) and Embedding technologies, which indeed exhibited high accuracy in many contexts, such as IR, NLP, speech to text, etc.

These approaches have polarized the landscape of papers presented in recent editions of ACM SIGIR, ECIR, ACM CIKM just to cite the most renowned international venues on the topics of IR, databases and knowledge based systems.

This dynamic is also reflected in the types of contributions submitted to FQAS in recent years. In fact, in the case of FQAS being a traditional venue for model-based approaches, the change of paradigm from model-based to data-driven, is also reflected in the lower number of contributions submitted to the FQAS conference in the last years and in a growing number of contributions proposing data driven approaches.

In an attempt to promote and stimulate the interest for the research on Flexible QAS and possibly to pave the way to renewed editions of future FQAS Conferences, in the following section we trace some challenges for future perspectives and views of the research on Flexible QA and QAS.

2 Challenges for Research on Flexible Query Answering Systems

During the last editions of the FQAS Conference, an increasing number of contributions applying data driven approaches is starting to appear, mainly exploiting Deep Learning (DL) and Embedding techniques. Such approaches investigate the applicability of deep learning and their comparison with representation based models for query answering tasks. In the following we discuss some possible perspectives of the research on FQAS that spring from the panorama of the techniques in use.

2.1 Coping with an Insufficient Effectiveness of Data Driven Models by Model Based Approaches to FQAS

There are domain contexts in which the performance of deep learning approaches need to be re-assessed since these can hardly be applied in the case of scarcity of training data and in highly specialized contexts.

As an example, [4] reports that the state-of-the-art data driven approaches can only achieve about 28% accuracy on the largest open question answering dataset in the legal domain (JEC-QA), collected from the National Judicial Examination of China [5], while skilled humans and unskilled humans can reach 81% and 64% accuracy, respectively. This huge gap between humans and machines on this domain indicates that FQAS is a current challenge in specialized domains.

Another issue of ML approaches is the fact that it can be unfair to rely on black box approaches when the training was done using data affected by some systematic bias [6], like for instance when using word embedding created from training texts expressing discrimination and unfairness towards women, disabled, black people, or when recognizing objects in images based on properties of the background [7, 8].

A current challenge is defining flexible query answering methods for mining possible bias affecting training collections: before training a DL approach for a given task it can be useful to evaluate the data suitability by querying the training collection for identifying biased opinions and detecting unbalanced polarity relatively to facts, people, genre, etc., cf. also a recent growing interest in countering disinformation/fake-news spreading.

Besides, fairness, reliability and interpretability are also important properties of QASs since to capture users' trust, the connection between the query and the retrieved documents should be understandable. This is a requirement in many contexts of high risk such as the medical and legal domains and more generally in safety-critical tasks, in which both retrieving relevant documents and answering questions require the ability of logical reasoning that must be understood by humans to obtain fidelity and trust [9].

Here comes the problem of defining what an explanation should be provided by a QAS, that we can regard as a decision making activity, whose objective is to retrieve a pertinent answer by evaluating a request expressing criteria for contents' selection.

There are two fundamental types of explanations: the first one is an ex-ante explanation relative to the system's general logic, and functionality. On the other hand, the second one is an ex-post explanation that unveils the specific answer taken by the system, which means explaining the rationale and individual circumstances of a specific answer.

We argue that this second type of explanation is what matters in a FQAS context in order to explain "why" a given document/item/piece of information has been retrieved as an answer to a query. To this end, since model-based FQASs are ex-ante explainable by their very nature, ex-post explanations of their answers to a query can be easily derived by knowing their logic.

Conversely, data driven DL query answering approaches, being mostly opaque mechanisms, need to be translated into, or approximated by, model-based FQASs mechanisms to generate ex-post explanations of their results.

In this respect we envisage a synergic role of DL and model-based FQAS approaches, where the first type of systems is used to yield answers to the queries so as to exploit their high accuracy for many tasks, while their translated/approximated version by a model-based FQAS is used to derive explanations of the answers.

Indeed, it is a current issue to provide DL FQAS with the desirable characteristics of ex-post explainability, which are also considered essential aspects of the European Union's way to Artificial Intelligence [10, 11], in line with the European General Data Protection Regulation (GDPR) that restricted the use of black box machine learning and automated decision-making concerning individuals [12]. Specifically, GDPR promotes transparency of automated systems, by requiring that systems provide meaningful information about the used logic, and a justification of outcomes in order to enable understanding and, possibly, to contest their results [9]. As an example, microblogging platforms such as Twitter have been used by many systems to report information about natural disasters since real-time posts are useful in identifying critical events and planning aids [31, 32]. Such systems need to be interpretable so that decision-makers can use them in real operational contexts. Nevertheless, they use NLP and DL methods to classify tweets, and explaining the rationale of the classification of short, noisy tweets is still questionable and has not been explored enough yet.

Methods for "transforming" DL approaches trained for a given QA task, for example by exploiting classified query logs, into transparent models are then a current challenge.

To qualitatively explain the criteria justifying the answer to a query, the "transformations" can approximate the network's behaviour [13].

Besides that, making a model behind DL-based FQAS explicit can be useful to assess if transfer learning of the models for new query intents can be applied without the need of re-training the network. This predictive ability has great practical impact since re-training a FQAS model for each new class of queries may be inefficient and costly.

There may be several kinds of explanations depending on several contextual factors such as:

- The knowledge of the user who formulated the question; for example, data scientists, domain experts, and decision makers need different explanations taking into account their knowledge, history and profiles.
- The query intent, i.e., if it is informational, navigational, or transactional [15]; for example, the results of a spatial query searching for restaurants may be explained with different geographic granularity depending on the fact that the query was formulated by a user in a specific location, who wants the best suitability possible in order to reach the restaurant, in this case the explanation can be "*it is the closest restaurant to your current location*". For a travel agency that needs to identify areas with many restaurants in a given city, the explanation can be "*it is the densest area of restaurants in the city*".
- The kind of information: for example, in the healthcare domain there are basically three main applications of FQASs: medical imaging interpretation in which explanations can be visual by showing similar cases, FQAS in huge collections of health documents in natural language, and FQAS for medical diagnosis in classic databases.
- Finally, also the level of the risks of the decision regarding fundamental rights, health, privacy demands different explanations.

Depending on the context, the "explanation" should be evaluated by considering its interpretability, describing the criteria used by the system in a way that is understandable to humans, its completeness and fidelity, assessing to which extent the model is able to imitate the black-box predictor by describing the functions of the system in an accurate way [13], and its accuracy, assessing to which extent the model can correctly predict unseen instances [14]. Nevertheless, accurate and complete explanations, for example by mathematical formalization of all the operations performed by the system, are hardly human interpretable for non-experts. Thus matching these evaluation criteria at the same time may lead to design persuasive systems rather than transparent systems. A persuasive system may be unethical if it oversimplifies the description of a complex system by hiding its undesirable characteristics in an attempt to attract trust of the user [13].

In this context, explanations of opaque FQAS mechanisms for example based on decision trees and fuzzy rules providing a description of the functions executed in each neuron of a DL configuration, or based on neuron clustering and summarizing their functions, have the advantage of offering hierarchical explanations, where each level reflects a distinct degree of complexity and interpretability: a high level qualitative explanation using linguistic terms is human interpretable; a lower level quantitative explanation based on fuzzy sets, allows to "*precisiate*" the semantics of linguistic terms. This way both interpretable and transparent QA systems can be designed.

2.2 Coping with Big Data

Other research challenges relate to the increasing use of big data. On the one hand, novel technologies and applications like social media, sensors and Internet of Things generate tremendous amounts of data. On the other hand, technologies for managing textual documents evolved a lot, bringing along a demand for a seamless integration of textual data in database and information management systems.

Data management of big data is generally recognized to be subject to challenges related to, among others, volume, variety, velocity and veracity [33]. NoSQL and more recently NewSQL database systems have been proposed as solutions for managing data that cannot be (easily) transformed to fixed tabular structured data formats. Such systems have the common characteristics to rely on a horizontal scaling, with distributed (cloud) data storage and these are meant to (co)operate as components of a polyglot database system architecture also containing conventional database systems. Hence, one system is longer fitting everything, bringing along new system and data integration challenges.

Volume. QA being an essential component of any data management system also faces new challenges when applied in a big data context. Querying large data volumes that are subject to horizontal scaling [34] requires efficient distributed querying facilities and indexing mechanisms. QA processing should efficiently cope with "sharding" [35], distributed bitmap indexing and other horizontal scaling techniques. Querying heterogeneous data sources often involves (transparent) query decomposition and data integration techniques being applied to query answers.

Variety. Due to the lack of fixed database schemes QA in NoSQL in general only supports limited querying facilities (usually not supporting join operations). In NoSQL systems data availability is usually a higher priority than data consistency and reflecting the so-called eventual consistency in QA results is challenging. NewSQL [36] tries to solve this problem with advanced distributed transaction processing, bringing along new query answering challenges as NewSQL currently only works under specific conditions (i.e., simple predictable transactions that are not requiring full database scans). Sensor data and multimedia data require advanced content-based querying and indexing techniques, which implies interpreting, processing and retrieving data not relying on metadata, but on the content itself. Information retrieval in textual document collections has to cope with data semantics and context. This should lead to better interconnections between texts and novel query answering facilities.

Velocity. NoSQL systems are designed giving priority to fast data insertion. This implies that no time is wasted on data transformations (to a fixed database schema format), nor on data integrity checks and transaction processing. A disadvantage is that query processing in general becomes more complex and time consuming. However, modern Internet of Things and social media applications might also be demanding with respect to query execution times. Hence, the demand for faster query execution techniques in distributed, heterogeneous data environments.

Veracity. Large distributed heterogeneous data collections can only guarantee data consistency under limited circumstances. Moreover, trust in data is an important issue as bad data propagates to bad data analyses and querying results [37, 38]. A lot of research is spent on quality driven QA [39, 40] and on data quality frameworks being able to assess and handle data quality in order to better inform users on the quality of data processing results [41, 42]. Informing the users on the quality of QA or information retrieval results and improving data quality where possible and relevant is considered to be an important research challenge.

Last, but not least there are also the legal aspects of data management. General Data Protection Regulation (GDPR) [43] requirements demand for techniques like anonymization and pseudonymisation in order to guarantee the privacy of users and can be quite challenging to develop in case of textual data or multimedia data [44].

2.3 Emerging FQAS Topics

For a human being the most convenient way of communication is using natural language. Thus, the flexibility of man-machine interaction, notably in the context of query answering, may be achieved via the use of natural language. This has been a point of departure for the related domain of Question answering (Q/A), which aims at answering requests in natural language on data sources and, therefore, combines methods from NLP, IR and database processing. This is one of the traditional areas of interest within classical artificial intelligence [27, 29].

In the global world, a large number of Q/A systems have been developed for various languages. Some Q/A systems, specifically in English and Latin languages, have better performances than systems using Arabic, Semitic and Sino Tibetan languages in general. This may depend on the characteristics of the language and the different level of maturity of the research. Cross-lingual text classification and retrieval methods working on different language-dependent feature spaces and exploiting class-class correlations can be a direction to explore to design more effective Q/A systems in different languages [16].

As far as the types of systems are concerned, there is a current increasing trend of asking queries within community based systems: this reflects the increasing popularity of social networks and online communities in the acquisition of knowledge. Nevertheless, in evaluating queries in community based systems, a major issue is to assess the quality and veracity of the answers by estimating the trust of the information sources. Model-based FQA applying multi criteria decision making and aggregation operators can be a potential promising approach.

As stated in [17], the most crucial and ambitious goal of Semantic Web research for user's information needs is Q/A over Knowledge Graphs (KGQA). Users express their information needs by a question using their own terminology and retrieve a concise answer generated by querying an RDF knowledge base. This relieves them from the need to know both a formal language like SPARQL and the domain terminology of the knowledge base they are querying. This goal poses the problem of filling the lexical gap: different users with the same information needs may use different words to query a knowledge graph; on the other hand, answers to the same query with the same semantics may differ from a lexical point of view.

Besides, in distributed knowledge based systems, in which local domain ontologies coexist to represent heterogeneous domains, alignments must be defined to interpret knowledge from a given peer's point of view. Queries may be expressed by selecting terms from a local ontology, and the retrieved answers extracted from different knowledge based systems have to be translated into terms of the same ontology [24].

In KGQA, several approaches tackled the issues of answering queries asking for facts, list of resources/documents and yes/no answers, since these queries can be mapped into SPARQL queries using SELECT and ASK with distinct levels of complexity.

A novel issue is answering procedural queries, closely related to the one very well known in the area of expert systems, involving "why", asking for reasons, and "how", asking for instructions to solve a task. For example, people describe their disease symptoms by queries to search engines and want to know the reason why they experience such illness, and how to solve their problem. One may ask "How to relieve back pain preferably while sleeping" or "how to wrap a gift quickly". Furthermore, procedural queries may involve geography and time such as in requesting "how to reach a skiing area on the Alps by passing near a picturesque lake where to stop for lunch around midday", or asking "why severe floods caused huge damages in North West Germany during July 2021" [18].

Current research follows template based and natural language interfaces approaches which aid non-technical users to formulate formal queries using natural language by mapping input questions to either manually or semi-automatically created SPARQL query templates [25]. Other approaches exploit procedural knowledge automatically extracted from textual documents, i.e. by classifying procedural documents, by applying neural networks and language models. Finally, some approaches aid users in carrying out a specific task by responding to the query interactively, step by step, such as in a Chatbot mechanism [19]. A possible alternative approach to answer procedural queries is to retrieve multimedia documents in the form of images, audio files and videos illustrating or exemplifying the requested procedures by leveraging on neural systems' ability of modeling multimodal information sources [26]. Finally, since procedural queries generally involve vague and imprecise conditions, such as in the above queries "near a lake district", "around midday" and preferences "while sleeping" model based FQA approaches are a promising solution.

An emerging topic of Question Answering is Visual QA (VQA) in which a system takes as input both an image and a question about the image content, expressed in natural language, and produces a natural language answer as the output [20]; for example to aid visually-impaired users recognize the content of an image. To solve such tasks, VQA attention based approaches have been proposed in which a deep neural network, typically a CNN, is trained to recognize objects in the images so that the attention mechanism chooses from a predefined list of possible answers, the one that responds to the question. Nevertheless, till now, a few approaches proposed to combine Visual QA with word attention models, typically based on RNN [21]. To this end, flexible querying combined with VQA attention models can be a viable alternative to RNN word attention in order to highlight the different importance of the words in the questions on which the system must place its attention.

Finally, an important topic is answering queries which involve geographic entities or concepts and that require evaluating spatial operations. The importance of geographic searches is outlined by a Google survey reporting that four out of five people used search engines to conduct local searches [22]. Currently, geographic questions are still difficult to answer due to several limitations of QA systems that generally lack proper geographic representations of both entities and spatial relationships, whose meaning is generally vague. There are many entities with unsharp, imprecise or varying and context dependent boundaries: for example, in winter and summer time the river's border may change and the boundary of a forest may be vague. Spatial relationships are costly to evaluate in real time, and their meaning is strongly vague and dependent on both the user's context and the query intent. For example, the meaning of "near" changes if one is moving on foot or by car, if one is young and healthy or a disabled person, and if one is looking for either a restaurant "near" my hotel, or a small medieval town "near" Milano. Moreover, the uncertainty affecting the geometries of spatial entities makes it difficult to answer factoid queries, such as "how many lakes are there in Finland" or "how long is the coast of Norway?", "how far is downtown Paris?". Thus, current challenges are the ability to deal with the variability and context dependent meaning of linguistic terms; the ability to exploit several sources of data with distinct resolution; and, finally, the ability to be robust in handling the vagueness and uncertainty of geographic information and relationships [23].

Context plays an important role in QA, not only with respect to the geographic searches. Admittedly it is not a new topic in QA (cf., e.g., [45, 46]) but there are surely new avenues which should be explored, in particular with the use of a more flexible understanding of the very notion of context. Relevance of a search result may depend on *external* factors such as *location* of the user, *time* a query is posed, the *history* of other queries posed within the same *session* etc. It may, however, also non-trivially depend on the *internal* aspects of the search, i.e. on the content of the data source. In the database querying framework, a good example of an approach providing means for taking into account such an internal context are queries with the *skyline operator* [47] or, a more general approach related to Chomicki's *preference queries* [48]. A newer example of such an approach are *contextual bipolar queries* [49]. Some new approaches in this vein include [50] where some more flexible understanding of the sophisticated context considered within analytic queries is proposed and [51] where a new idea of *searching for a context* is proposed.

We believe that the cross fertilization of data-driven approaches with model-based ones can offer more interpretable and explainable solutions to Flexible QA systems. Investigating hybrid Flexible QA models can be a fruitful direction of research to design more transparent systems.

3   Conclusions

This paper is motivated, first of all, by a long time experience of the authors and their active and intensive involvement in research and practical applications in the field of QA and related areas, hence a deep familiarity with the field. This has been amplified by the involvement of the editors in the organization and running of practically all FQAS conferences which have always provided a premiere forum for the presentation of novel developments by the whole research community in the respective areas. Moreover, the FQAS have always provided a venue for the presentation of many new proposals and solutions, often of a visionary type. This has made the FQAS one of those scientific gatherings that have always inspired the community. This paper, on the perspectives and views of the research on FQASs was written with the intention of further stimulating the interest towards the synergic and hybrid application of two paradigms for FQAS, the model-based and the data driven approach. We are aware that the identified challenges and the described topics offer only a partial view of the research on FQASs, filtered by our own expertise. However, we hope that it will help to reflect on the current situation, to outline the limitations and vocations of the single FQAS conference.

References

1. Hirschman, L., Gaizauskas, R.: Natural language question answering: the view from here. Nat. Lang. Eng. Spec. Issue Quest. Answer. **7**(4), 275–300 (2001)
2. Voorhees, E.M.: The TREC-8 question answering track report. In: Proceedings of TREC-8, pp. 77–82 (1999)
3. Markus, A.F., Kors, J.A., Rijnbeek, P.R.: The role of explainability in creating trustworthy artificial intelligence for health care: a comprehensive survey of the terminology, design choices, and evaluation strategies. arXiv (2020). arXiv:2007.15911
4. Zhong, H., Xiao, C., Tu, C., Zhang, T., Liu, Z., Sun, M.: JEC-QA: a legal-domain question answering dataset. In: Proceedings of the AAAI Conference on Artificial Intelligence (2020), vol. 34, no. 05, pp. 9701–9708. https://doi.org/10.1609/aaai.v34i05.6519
5. Zhong, H., Xiao, C., Tu, C., Zhang, T., Liu, Z., Sun, M.: 1JEC-QA: a legal-domain question answering dataset. https://arxiv.org/pdf/1911.12011.pdf. Accessed 24 May 2021
6. Buhrmester, V., Münch, D., Arens, M.: Analysis of explainers of black box deep neural networks for computer vision: a survey. arXiv:1911.12116v1 [cs.AI], 27 November 2019
7. Hirschberg, J., Manning, C.D.: Advances in natural language processing. Science **349**(6245), 261–266 (2015)
8. Angwin, J., Larson, J., Mattu, S., Kirchner, L.: Machine bias. https://www.propublica.org/art icle/machine-bias-risk-assessments-in-criminal-sentencing. Accessed 24 May 2021
9. Hamon, R., Junklewitz, H., Malgieri, G., De Hert, P., Beslay, L., Sanchez, I.: Impossible explanations? Beyond explainable AI in the GDPR from a COVID-19 use case scenario. In: Proceedings of ACM FAccT 2021 (2021)
10. European Commission 2020. White Paper: On Artificial Intelligence - A European approach to excellence and trust. European Commission. https://ec.europa.eu/info/sites/default/files/ commission-white-paper-artificial-intelligence-feb2020_en.pdf. Accessed 24 May 2021
11. European Commission High Level Expert Group on Artificial Intelligence 2019. Ethics Guidelines for Trustworthy AI. https://digital-strategy.ec.europa.eu/en/library/ethics-guidelines-tru stworthy-ai. Accessed 24 May 2021
12. European Parliament and Council of the European Union 2016. Regulation (EU) 2016/679 of the European Parliament and of the Council of 27 April 2016 on the protection of natural persons with regard to the processing of personal data and on the free movement of such data, and repealing Directive 95/46/EC (General Data Protection Regulation)
13. Gilpin, L.H., Bau, D., Yuan, B.Z., Bajwa, A., Specter, M., Kagal, L.: Explaining explanations: an overview of interpretability of machine learning. In: IEEE 5th International Conference on Data Science and Advanced Analytics (DSAA), pp. 80–89 (2018)

14. Guidotti, R., Monreale, A., Ruggieri, S., Turini, F., Giannotti, F., Pedreschi, D.: A survey of methods for explaining black box models. ACM Comput. Surv. **51**(5), 1–42 (2019). Article no. 93
15. Broder, A.: A taxonomy of web search. In: Proceedings of SIGIR Forum, vol. 36, no. 2, pp. 3–10 (2002)
16. Moreo, A., Pedrotti, A., Sebastiani, F.: Heterogeneous document embeddings for cross-lingual text classification. In: Proceedings of ACM SAC 2021, IAR track, pp. 685–688 (2021)
17. Trotman, A., Geva, S., Kamps, J.: Report on the SIGIR 2007 workshop on focused retrieval. SIGIR Forum **41**(2), 97–103 (2007)
18. Höffner, K., Walter, S., Marx, E., Usbeck, R., Lehmann, J., Ngonga Ngomo, A.C.: Survey on challenges of question answering in the semantic web. Semant. Web **8**(6), 895–920 (2017)
19. Maitra, A., Garg, S., Sengupta, S.: Enabling interactive answering of procedural questions. In: Métais, E., Meziane, F., Horacek, H., Cimiano, P. (eds.) NLDB 2020. LNCS, vol. 12089, pp. 73–81. Springer, Cham (2020). https://doi.org/10.1007/978-3-030-51310-8_7
20. Antol, S., et al.: VQA: visual question answering. In: Proceedings of ICCV 2015 (2015)
21. Lu, J., Yang, J., Batra, D., Parikh, D.: Hierarchical question-image co-attention for visual question answering. In: Proceedings of the 30th International Conference on Neural Information Processing Systems, pp. 289–297 (2016)
22. https://www.searchenginewatch.com/2014/05/07/google-local-searches-lead-50-of-mobile-users-to-visit-stores-study/
23. Maia, G., Janowic, K., Zhua, R., Caia, L., Lao, N.: Geographic question answering: challenges, uniqueness, classification, and future directions. arXiv:2105.09392v1 [cs.CL] 19 May 2021. Accessed 24 May 2021
24. Hosseinzadeh Kassani, S., Schneider, K.A., Deters, R.: Leveraging protection and efficiency of query answering in heterogenous RDF data using blockchain. In: Alhajj, R., Moshirpour, M., Far, B. (eds.) Data Management and Analysis. SBD, vol. 65, pp. 1–15. Springer, Cham (2020). https://doi.org/10.1007/978-3-030-32587-9_1
25. Affolter, K., Stockinger, K., Bernstein, A.: A comparative survey of recent natural language interfaces for databases. VLDB J. **28**, 793–819 (2019)
26. Kafle, S., de Silva, N., Dou, D.: An overview of utilizing knowledge bases in neural networks for question answering. In: Proceedings of the 20th International Conference on Information Reuse and Integration in Data Science (IRI), pp. 326–333 (2019)
27. Lehnert, W.: Human and computational question answering. Cogn. Sci. **1**(1), 47–73 (1977)
28. Wolfram Research, Inc., Wolfram|Alpha Notebook Edition, Champaign, IL (2020)
29. Simmons, R.F.: Natural language question-answering systems. Commun. ACM **13**(1), 15–30 (1969)
30. Ferrucci, D., et al.: Building Watson: an overview of the DeepQA project. AI Mag. **31**(3), 59–79 (2010)
31. Nguyen, D.T., Ali Al Mannai, K., Joty, S., Sajjad, H., Imran, M., Mitra, P.: Robust classification of crisis-related data on social networks using convolutional neural networks. In: Proceedings of the 11th International AAAI Conference on Web and Social Media (ICWSM 2017) (2017)
32. Verma, S., et al.: Natural language processing to the rescue? Extracting "situational awareness" tweets during mass emergency. In: Proceedings of the Fifth International AAAI Conference on Weblogs and Social Media (ICWSM) (2011)
33. De Mauro, A., Greco, M., Grimaldi, M.: A formal definition of big data based on its essential features. Libr. Rev. **65**, 122–135 (2016)
34. Cattell, R.: Scalable SQL and NoSQL data stores. ACM SIGMOD Rec. **39**(4), 12–27 (2010)
35. Bagui, S., Nguyen, L.T.: Database sharding: to provide fault tolerance and scalability of big data on the cloud. Int. J. Cloud Appl. Comput. **5**(2), 36–52 (2015)
36. Pavlo, A., Aslett, M.: What's really new with NewSQL? SIGMOD Rec. **42**(2), 45–55 (2016)

37. Lukoianova, T., Rubin, V.L.: Veracity roadmap: is big data objective, truthful and credible? Adv. Classif. Res. Online **24**(1), 4–15 (2014)
38. Berti-Equille, L., Lamine Ba, M.: Veracity of big data: challenges of cross-modal truth discovery. ACM J. Data Inform. Qual. **7**(3), art.12 (2016)
39. Mihaila, G.A., Raschid, L., Vidal, M.E.: Using quality of data metadata for source selection and ranking. In: Proceedings of the Third International Workshop on the Web and Databases, WebDB 2000, Dallas, USA, pp. 93–98 (2000)
40. Naumann, F.: Quality-Driven Query Answering for Integrated Information Systems. Springer, Berlin (2002). https://doi.org/10.1007/3-540-45921-9
41. Batini, C., Scannapieco, M.: Data Quality: Concepts, Methodologies and Techniques Data-Centric Systems and Applications). Springer, New York (2006)
42. Cichy, C., Rass, S.: An overview of data quality frameworks. IEEE Access **7**, 24634–24648 (2019)
43. Voigt P., von dem Bussche A.: The EU General Data Protection Regulation (GDPR): A Practical Guide. Springer, Cham (2017). https://doi.org/10.1007/978-3-319-57959-7
44. Bolognini, L., Bistolfi, C.: Pseudonymization and impacts of Big (personal/anonymous) Data processing in the transition from the Directive 95/46/EC to the new EU General Data Protection Regulation. Comput. Law Secur. Rev. **33**(2), 171–181 (2017)
45. Martinenghi, D., Torlone, R.: Querying context-aware databases. In: Andreasen, T., Yager, R.R., Bulskov, H., Christiansen, H., Larsen, H.L. (eds.) FQAS 2009. LNCS (LNAI), vol. 5822, pp. 76–87. Springer, Heidelberg (2009). https://doi.org/10.1007/978-3-642-04957-6_7
46. Bordogna, G., Ghisalberti, G., Psaila, G.: Geographic information retrieval: modeling uncertainty of user's context. Fuzzy Sets Syst. **196**, 105–124 (2012)
47. Börzsönyi, S., Kossmann, D., Stocker, K.: The skyline operator. In: Proceedings of the 17th International Conference on Data Engineering, pp. 421–430 (2001)
48. Chomicki, J.: Preference formulas in relational queries. ACM Trans. Database Syst. **28**(4), 427–466 (2003)
49. Zadrożny, S., Kacprzyk, J., Dziedzic, M., De Tré, G.: Contextual bipolar queries. In: Jamshidi, M., Kreinovich, V., Kacprzyk, J. (eds.) Advance Trends in Soft Computing. SFSC, vol. 312, pp. 421–428. Springer, Cham (2014). https://doi.org/10.1007/978-3-319-03674-8_40
50. Zadrożny, S., Kacprzyk, J.: Fuzzy analytical queries: a new approach to flexible fuzzy queries. In: Proceedings of the 29th IEEE International Conference on Fuzzy Systems, FUZZ-IEEE 2020, pp. 1–8. IEEE, Glasgow (2020)
51. Zadrożny, S., Kacprzyk, J., Dziedzic, M.: A concept of context-seeking queries. In: Proceedings of the 30th IEEE International Conference on Fuzzy Systems, FUZZ-IEEE 2021, pp. 1–6. IEEE, Luxembourg (2021)

Model-Based Flexible Query Answering Approaches

Analogical Querying?

Henri Prade$^{(\boxtimes)}$ and Gilles Richard

IRIT - CNRS, Université Paul Sabatier,
118 route de Narbonne, 31062 Toulouse Cedex 09, France
{prade,richard}@irit.fr

Abstract. This short paper suggests a new way of exploiting examples of items that are known to be liked and counter-examples of items that are known to be disliked, in case-based querying. This relies on an extrapolation mechanism using analogical proportions. Analogical proportions are statements that compare pairs of items laying bare the similarities and the differences between items. They provide a tool that enables a comparative use of examples and counter-examples in order to build appropriate answers to a user query.

1 Introduction

Querying is not always made explicit by specifying through a generic description what kind of items we are looking for. It may be based on examples of items we like and items we dislike. Still the relevant attributes for judging the items may be available or not. Indeed one may have at our disposal some cases of preferred items and maybe some cases of items that are rejected; then the cases may have a description in terms of attribute values. But one may also think of querying by means of images for which no high level description is available [2].

In this paper, we assume that the items are described in terms of attributes, and that the user has provided some information, through examples and counter-examples suggesting what she/he is looking for and what does not fit her/his expectations respectively. This information may arise from the observation of past choices or past judgements of the user as in a recommendation system, and the aim is to propose her/him new items that she/he may like.

In a previous work to which one of the authors contributed two decades ago, one was taking advantage of past cases by looking for new items that are similar on all important attributes with at least one example of prized items and that are dissimilar to all rejected items on at least one important attribute [9]. Here we suggest another way to take lessons from examples, which is based on analogical proportions [20] that are statements of the form "a is to b as c is to d". Such proportions take into account how pairs of items (a, b) and (c, d) are similar and how they differ (the items being described in terms of attribute values); then this may be exploited for extrapolating d (or a part of it) from (a, b, c) and predict if such a d may be liked or not from the positive or negative appreciations associated with a, b and c.

© Springer Nature Switzerland AG 2021
T. Andreasen et al. (Eds.): FQAS 2021, LNAI 12871, pp. 17–28, 2021.
https://doi.org/10.1007/978-3-030-86967-0_2

The paper is organized as follows. Section 2 recalls how examples and counter-examples can be used in case-based querying on the basis of similarities between attribute values. Section 3 explains how examples and counter-examples can be exploited through analogical proportions for proposing new items of interest to the user, while providing the necessary background on analogical proportions. Section 4 briefly surveys some related work, before concluding.

2   Case-Based Querying

Examples of what the user likes, as well as counter-examples of what she/he dislikes, are supposed to be described in terms of precisely known attribute values for attributes $i = 1, \cdots, n$. These attributes are assumed to be relevant and sufficient for describing their main features from a user's point of view. To support the intuition, in an AirBnb-like perspective, attributes such has "has-a-dishwasher", "has-a-microwave", "distance-from-the-sea", "number-of-bedroom", etc. could be considered. Examples (resp. counter-examples) are just a list of accommodations that the user has liked (resp. not liked).

An example j is denoted with $\overrightarrow{a_j} = (a_{1j}, \cdots, a_{nj})$ and a counter-example k with $\overrightarrow{b_k} = (b_{1k}, \cdots, b_{nk})$. Thus a_{ij} is the value of attribute i for example j, b_{ik} the value of attribute i for counter-example k.

It should be clear for the reader that here we have two distinct databases, one $\mathcal{C}$ gathering the cases – examples and counter-examples – associated to a user, and the database $\mathcal{T}$ of available items among which one looks for items suitable for the user. Then a request (such as "I look for an accommodation this summer"), based on examples $j = 1, \cdots, J$ and counter-examples $k = 1, \cdots, K$ should look for the items t that are similar to at least one example (w.r.t. all the attributes) and which are dissimilar to all the counter-examples (each time w.r.t. at least one attribute), as proposed in [9]. Another way to put it in our AirBnB context, is to say that we look for an accommodation very "similar" to *one* the user has liked in the past and "dissimilar" to *all* the ones the user has disliked in the past.

Thus, the more similar an item t is w.r.t. (at least) one representative example and the more dissimilar t is w.r.t. all representative counter-examples, the more suitable t is for the user.

Let us assume we have at our disposal, for each attribute i, a fuzzy similarity relation S_i on the domain of i (S_i is supposed to be reflexive and symmetrical). Similarities are graded in $[0, 1]$.

Given t a vector of attribute values $a_1(t), \ldots, a_n(t)$,

- $\min_i S_i(a_i(t), a_{ij})$ provides the minimum of agreement between t and example j over all attributes i
- then $\max_{j=1,\cdots,J} \min_i S_i(a_i(t), a_{ij})$ gives the agreement of the best matching example to t in the set of examples. This provides a measure of how t matches with the examples.

– a dual reasoning shows that $\min_{k=1,\cdots,K} \max_i 1 - S_i(a_i(t), b_{ik})$ estimates the agreement of worst matching counter-examples to t in the set of counter-examples. This provides a measure of how t mismatches with the counter-examples.

The items t in $\mathcal{T}$ can then be rank-ordered in terms of the function:

$$c(t) = \min[\max_{j=1,\cdots,J} \min_i S_i(a_i(t), a_{ij}), \min_{k=1,\cdots,K} \max_i 1 - S_i(a_i(t), b_{ik})]$$

Clearly, $S_i(., a_{ij})$ defines a fuzzy set of values close to a_{ij}, while $1 - S_i(., b_{ik})$ defines a fuzzy set of values not similar to b_{ik}, for each attribute i. As can be seen, $c(t)$ is all the larger as there exists an example j very similar to t on all attributes, and all counter-examples k are very dissimilar to t on at least one attribute. In a way, $c(t)$ is a measure of the quality of the match between t and the user preferences described as examples and counter-examples. If $c(t)$ is large, then t is a candidate answer for the user. Obviously, this is a way to give the same informative value to each example and counter-example. But we can also take into account the extent to which each example or counter-example is highly *representative*; in other words, to what extent the example (resp. counter-example) is satisfactory (resp. unsatisfactory) from the user's point of view. Let $\lambda_j \in [0,1]$ and $\rho_k \in [0,1]$ be the extent to which example j and counter-example k respectively are highly representative. Besides, we may also consider the *importance* of the attributes. Let $w_i \in [0,1]$ be the level of importance of attribute i in a description. We assume that at least one attribute is fully important, i.e., $\exists i, w_i = 1$ (normalization condition). Then, we get

$$c(t) = \min[\max_j \min(\lambda_j, \min_i \max(1 - w_i, S_i(a_i(t), a_{ij})),$$
$$\min_k \max(1 - \rho_k, \max_i \min(w_i, 1 - S_i(a_i(t), b_{ik})))]$$

As can be seen, if $\lambda_j = 0$ (resp. $\rho_k = 0$), example j (resp. counter-example k) is not taken into account. When $w_i = 0$, attribute i is ignored. When all the importance and representativeness weights are equal to 1, we recover the previous formula.

These formulas may be effective for rank-ordering items on the basis of a small number of examples and counter-examples, the larger $c(t)$, the higher the plausibility that t is of interest for the user [6].

3   Analogical Proportion-Based Answering

In the approach recalled in the previous section, the candidate item t is compared to each example and to each counter-example. Then the extent to which t is similar to at least one example and the extent to which t is dissimilar with all counter-examples are just aggregated by the conjunctive operation min in $c(t)$. Thus, no comparison between examples, between counter-examples, or between an example and a counter-example takes place. In some sense, we are not fully taking lesson from both examples and counter-examples, trying to understand why this item is an example and why this other one is a counter-example. This is what the analogical proportion-based approach could help to do. We start with an analysis of what we can learn from such comparisons.

Moreover, we start with the simple cases of nominal attribute values, i.e., the attribute domains are finite, with two or more elements. When the domain has two elements only, this is referred as the Boolean case.

3.1   Comparing Items

Let us consider a pair of vectors describing examples, or counter-examples, say $\overrightarrow{a}$ and $\overrightarrow{b}$, with n components. We suppose that the components are the values of n *nominal* attributes.

Their comparison yields a partition of the n attributes in two subsets: the subset $\mathcal{A}^{=}_{\overrightarrow{a},\overrightarrow{b}} = \{i \mid a_i = b_i\}$ where the two vectors agree, and the subset $\mathcal{D}^{\neq}_{\overrightarrow{a},\overrightarrow{b}} = \{i \mid a_i \neq b_i\}$ for which they are different. This state of fact can be interpreted differently depending on what is being compared:

- an example from $\overrightarrow{a}$ and a counter-example $\overrightarrow{b}$. Then the change of values $\mathcal{D}^{\neq}_{\overrightarrow{a},\overrightarrow{b}}$ from $\overrightarrow{a}$ to $\overrightarrow{b}$ "explains" why we move from an example to a counter-example.
- two examples $\overrightarrow{a}$ and $\overrightarrow{a'}$. Then the change of values $\mathcal{D}^{\neq}_{\overrightarrow{a},\overrightarrow{a'}}$ from $\overrightarrow{a}$ to $\overrightarrow{a'}$ does not affect the example status: $\overrightarrow{a'}$ remains satisfactory for the user.
- two counter-examples $\overrightarrow{b}$ and $\overrightarrow{b'}$. Similarly to the previous case, the change of values $\mathcal{D}^{\neq}_{\overrightarrow{b},\overrightarrow{b'}}$ from $\overrightarrow{b}$ to $\overrightarrow{b'}$ does not affect the counter-example status: $\overrightarrow{b'}$ remains unsatisfactory for the user.

At this step, we can already mention a first benefit that can be drawn from the last two dashes above. Indeed assume that some attribute i has a domain $\mathcal{D}_i$ with at least 3 elements, *ordered* in a meaningful way (e.g., $\mathcal{D}_i = \{\texttt{one-star}, \texttt{two-stars}, \cdots, \texttt{five-stars}\}$), then we have a natural notion of "*betweenness*" in domain $\mathcal{D}_i$ (e.g., $\texttt{three-stars}$ is between $\texttt{two-stars}$ and $\texttt{five-stars}$). This "betweenness" relation can be readily extended to vectors: $\overrightarrow{a^\circ} = (a_1^\circ, \cdots, a_n^\circ)$ is between $\overrightarrow{a} = (a_1, \cdots, a_n)$ and $\overrightarrow{a'} = (a'_1, \cdots, a'_n)$, if i) a_r° is between a_r and a'_r for all ordered domains $\mathcal{D}_r$, and ii) $a_s^\circ = a_s = a'_s$ for non ordered domains or domains with two elements $\mathcal{D}_s$. Then one may plausibly infer that a° is an example if a and a' are examples. Similarly, one may plausibly infer that b° is a counter-example as soon as b° is between two counter-examples. This provides an *interpolative* way to increase the number of examples and the number of counter-examples. See [13,21,22] for the use of the betweenness idea in other settings (case-based reasoning, interpolation between default rules, completion of knowledge bases made of if-then rules).

3.2   Boolean and Nominal Analogical Proportions: A Background

When pairing two pairs having "aligned" disagreement sets, one obtains an analogical proportion, as we are going to see. We first recall their modeling in the Boolean case before extending them to nominal attribute values.

Analogical proportions are statements of the form "a is to b as c is d", which is denoted $a : b :: c : d$. Their origin dates back to Aristotle [1] (at least), and was inspired by a parallel with (geometric) numerical proportions, namely $\frac{a}{b} = \frac{c}{d}$; see [17]. In agreement with this parallel, they are supposed to obey the following postulates: Given a set of items X (items could be Booleans, real numbers, Boolean vectors, real-valued vectors, words or even sentences in natural language, etc.), analogical proportions form a quaternary relation supposed to obey the 3 following postulates (e.g., [11]): for $a, b, c, d \in X$,

1. $a : b :: a : b$ (*reflexivity*);
2. if $a : b :: c : d$ then $c : d :: a : b$ (*symmetry*);
3. if $a : b :: c : d$ then $a : c :: b : d$ (*central permutation*).

The unique minimal Boolean model [19] obeying these 3 postulates is a quaternary propositional logic connective when X is the Boolean set $\mathbb{B} = \{0, 1\}$ [15]:

$$a : b :: c : d = ((a \wedge \neg b) \leftrightarrow (c \wedge \neg d)) \wedge ((\neg a \wedge b) \leftrightarrow (\neg c \wedge d))$$

where $\leftrightarrow$ denotes the equivalence connective. It makes explicit that "a differs from b as c differs from d and that b differs from a as d differs from c". It is easy to check that this formula is only valid for the 6 following valuations (among 16 candidate valuations) shown in Table 1.

Table 1. Valid valuations for Boolean analogical proportion.

$$0 : 0 :: 0 : 0$$
$$1 : 1 :: 1 : 1$$
$$0 : 1 :: 0 : 1$$
$$1 : 0 :: 1 : 0$$
$$0 : 0 :: 1 : 1$$
$$1 : 1 :: 0 : 0$$

It can be seen that 1 and 0 play a symmetrical role, which makes the definition *code-independent*. This is formally expressed with the negation operator as: if $a : b :: c : d$ then $\neg a : \neg b :: \neg c : \neg d$. To deal with items represented by *vectors* of Boolean values, the analogical proportion definition is extended componentwise from X to X^n:

$$\overrightarrow{a} : \overrightarrow{b} :: \overrightarrow{c} : \overrightarrow{d} \quad \text{iff} \quad \text{for all } i \in \{1, \ldots, n\}, a_i : b_i :: c_i : d_i$$

It can be easily checked that $\overrightarrow{a} : \overrightarrow{b} :: \overrightarrow{c} : \overrightarrow{d}$ holds if and only if $\mathcal{A}^{=}_{\overrightarrow{a},\overrightarrow{b}} = \mathcal{A}^{=}_{\overrightarrow{c},\overrightarrow{d}}$, $\mathcal{D}^{01}_{\overrightarrow{a},\overrightarrow{b}} = \mathcal{D}^{01}_{\overrightarrow{c},\overrightarrow{d}}$ and $\mathcal{D}^{10}_{\overrightarrow{a},\overrightarrow{b}} = \mathcal{D}^{10}_{\overrightarrow{c},\overrightarrow{d}}$ where $\mathcal{D}^{01}_{\overrightarrow{a},\overrightarrow{b}} = \{i \mid a_i = 0, b_i = 1\}$ and $\mathcal{D}^{10}_{\overrightarrow{a},\overrightarrow{b}} = \{i \mid a_i = 1, b_i = 0\}$, see, e.g., [18].

When a, b, c, d take their values in a finite set $\mathcal{N}$ (with more than 2 elements), we can derive three patterns of analogical proportions in the nominal case, from the six possible assignments for analogical proportions in the Boolean case. This generalization, which still agrees with the postulates, is thus defined by:

$$a : b :: c : d = 1 \text{ iff } (a, b, c, d) \in \{(u, u, u, u), (u, v, u, v), (u, u, v, v) \mid u, v \in \mathcal{N}\} \tag{1}$$

$$a : b :: c : d = 0 \text{ otherwise.}$$

This leads to $|\mathcal{N}| + 2|\mathcal{N}|(|\mathcal{N}| - 1) = |\mathcal{N}|(2(|\mathcal{N}| - 1))$ valid patterns as can be checked; for, e.g., $|\mathcal{N}| = 3$, it yields 15 distinct patterns. Then $\mathcal{D}^{01}_{\overrightarrow{a},\overrightarrow{b}}$ has to replaced by $\mathcal{D}^{uv}_{\overrightarrow{a},\overrightarrow{b}} = \{i \mid a_i = u, b_i = v\}$ and then the analogical proportion $\overrightarrow{a} : \overrightarrow{b} :: \overrightarrow{c} : \overrightarrow{d}$ holds if and only if $\mathcal{A}^{=}_{\overrightarrow{a},\overrightarrow{b}} = \mathcal{A}^{=}_{\overrightarrow{c},\overrightarrow{d}}$ and $\forall u, v \; \mathcal{D}^{uv}_{\overrightarrow{a},\overrightarrow{b}} = \mathcal{D}^{uv}_{\overrightarrow{c},\overrightarrow{d}}$.

This is the basis of an inference principle, first proposed in [16] for nominal values, that can be stated as follows:

$$\frac{\forall i \in \{1, ..., n\}, \quad a_i : b_i :: c_i : d_i \text{ holds}}{\forall j \in \{n+1, ..., m\}, \quad a_j : b_j :: c_j : d_j \text{ holds}}$$

As can be seen, knowledge from some components of source vectors is transferred to their remaining components, implicitly assuming that the values of the n first components determine the values of the others.

This requires to find x such that $a : b :: c : x$ holds. The solution may not exist (e.g., for $0 : 1 :: 1 : x$). It is solvable if and only if $a = b$ or $a = c$ in the Boolean case. Then, the *unique* solution in the nominal case is given by $x = c$ if $a = b$ and $x = b$ if $a = c$.

Lastly, let us observe that given three vectors $\overrightarrow{a}, \overrightarrow{b}, \overrightarrow{c}$, one can compute a new vector $\overrightarrow{d}$ such that $\overrightarrow{a} : \overrightarrow{b} :: \overrightarrow{c} : \overrightarrow{d}$ holds, *provided that* all the componentwise equations $a_i : b_i :: c_i : x_i$ are solvable, for $i = 1, \cdots, n$.

The above remark means that it provides another way to enlarge the set of examples and counter-examples in the case-based querying process by *extrapolating* them in the following manner. Let us attach to each vector, say $\overrightarrow{a}$, a $(n + 1)$th binary attribute $qual(\overrightarrow{a})$ with value 1 if $\overrightarrow{a}$ is an example and 0 if it is a counter-example. Then three vectors $\overrightarrow{a}, \overrightarrow{b}, \overrightarrow{c}$, if the equations are solvable will yield a new example if $qual(\overrightarrow{a}) : qual(\overrightarrow{b}) :: qual(\overrightarrow{c}) : 1$ holds (it is the case if the three vectors are examples (since $1 : 1 :: 1 : x$ yields $x = 1$ as a solution), or if $\overrightarrow{b}$ is an example and the two other vectors are counter-examples ($0 : 1 :: 0 : x$ yields $x = 1$), or if $\overrightarrow{c}$ is an example and the two other vectors are counter-examples ($0 : 0 :: 1 : x$ yields $x = 1$). The process yields a new counter-example if $qual(\overrightarrow{a}) : qual(\overrightarrow{b}) :: qual(\overrightarrow{c}) : 0$ holds, i.e., in case of three counter-examples (since $0:0::0:x$ yields $x=0$), or if $\overrightarrow{b}$ is a counter-example and the two other vectors are examples ($1:0::1:x$ yields $x=0$), or if $\overrightarrow{c}$ is a counter-example and the two other vectors are examples ($1:1::0:x$ yields $x=0$).

Table 2 exhibits how a plausible example $\overrightarrow{d}$ can be obtained from an example $\overrightarrow{b}$ and two counter-examples $\overrightarrow{a}$ and $\overrightarrow{c}$. As can be seen, each of the 4 vectors can be divided into three sub-vectors which correspond respectively to i) a subpart *common* present in each vector, ii) a subpart where $\overrightarrow{a}$ and $\overrightarrow{b}$ agree, as well as $\overrightarrow{c}$ and $\overrightarrow{d}$, but differently, iii) a subpart referring to attributes on which the example and the counter examples differ. Note that $\overrightarrow{d}$ should differ from $\overrightarrow{c}$ as $\overrightarrow{b}$ from $\overrightarrow{a}$. It is clear that $\overrightarrow{a}:\overrightarrow{b}::\overrightarrow{c}:\overrightarrow{d}$ holds in a componentwise manner, that $\overrightarrow{d}$ is unique and that $\overrightarrow{d}$ is different from $\overrightarrow{a}$, $\overrightarrow{b}$, $\overrightarrow{c}$ as soon as $\overrightarrow{a}$ and $\overrightarrow{c}$ are distinct.

Table 2. Inducing example $\overrightarrow{d}$ from example $\overrightarrow{b}$, and counter-examples $\overrightarrow{a}$ and $\overrightarrow{c}$

Item	General context	Sub-context	Distinctive features	Qual
$\overrightarrow{a}$	common	common-1	absent	0
$\overrightarrow{b}$	common	common-1	present	1
$\overrightarrow{c}$	common	common-2	absent	0
$\overrightarrow{d}$	common	common-2	present	1

3.3   Analogical Querying

Let us go back to our querying problem. We may use two different strategies for taking advantage of the analogical proportion-based approach.

- A first strategy consists in enlarging the collection $\mathcal{C}$ of examples and counter-examples using the betweenness relation and/or the extrapolation method described at the end of the previous subsection. Then the approach described in Sect. 2 can be applied to this enlarged collection to order the generated candidate answers $t \in \mathcal{T}$ with regard to the function value $c(t)$.
- Another quite different strategy consists in applying analogical inference directly to the initial collection $\mathcal{C}$ of examples and counter-examples, viewing the assessment of each item $t \in \mathcal{T}$ as a classification problem. We detail this idea below.

Analogical inference has been successfully applied to classification [5,14]. Here we are going to classify each candidate answer t in the database either as a satisfactory item, i.e., a plausible example, or not. As in the enlargement procedure, a vector $\overrightarrow{a}$ is completed by a $(n+1)$th binary attribute $qual(\overrightarrow{a})$ with value 1 if $\overrightarrow{a}$ is an example and 0 if it is a counter-example. Then, a database item t will be considered as satisfactory if the analogical proportion

$$\overrightarrow{a} : \overrightarrow{b} :: \overrightarrow{c} : \overrightarrow{t}$$

holds, where $\overrightarrow{t}$ is the vector extracted from t that corresponds to the restriction of t to the n attributes used in the description of the examples and counter-examples.

This means that for each t, we are looking for triples $\overrightarrow{a}, \overrightarrow{b}, \overrightarrow{c}$ in the set of examples and counter-examples such that the above proportion holds and $qual(\overrightarrow{a}) : qual(\overrightarrow{b}) :: qual(\overrightarrow{c}) : 1$ holds. If no triple is found, t is not selected. If a triple is found, t may be selected. However it may happen that while a triple fulfilling the conditions exists, there exists another triple $\overrightarrow{a'}, \overrightarrow{b'}, \overrightarrow{c'}$ such that $\overrightarrow{a'} : \overrightarrow{b'} :: \overrightarrow{c'} : \overrightarrow{t}$ holds, but the solution of $qual(\overrightarrow{a'}) : qual(\overrightarrow{b'}) :: qual(\overrightarrow{c'}) : x$ is $x = 0$. Then if there are more triples like $\overrightarrow{a'}, \overrightarrow{b'}, \overrightarrow{c'}$ than like $\overrightarrow{a}, \overrightarrow{b}, \overrightarrow{c}$, the item t should not be selected. This basic procedure may be improved in different ways taking lessons from other classification applications [5, 12].

This classification approach departs from the case-based querying approach in several respects. Observe that no degree is attached to a selected t in the analogical classification approach (since analogical proportion is an all-or-nothing notion in the Boolean and in the nominal cases), while the degree $c(t)$ in the case-based evaluation reflects the similarity to some example (and the dissimilarity with all counter-examples). Moreover, a t selected by the classification approach may be such that $c(t)$ is quite low, since when $\overrightarrow{a} : \overrightarrow{b} :: \overrightarrow{c} : \overrightarrow{t}$ holds, $\overrightarrow{t}$ may be quite different from the three other tuples (which ensures a form of serendipity).

Note that the prediction power of the classification approach depends on the possibility of finding triples $(\overrightarrow{a}, \overrightarrow{b}, \overrightarrow{c})$ for a sufficiently large number of t's, such that $\overrightarrow{a} : \overrightarrow{b} :: \overrightarrow{c} : \overrightarrow{t}$ holds, which requires a number of examples and counter-examples larger than the case-based querying method of Sect. 2 where half a dozen examples and counter-examples may be enough for getting some results [6].

3.4   Extension with Graded Analogical Proportions

Items may also be described by means of numerical attributes. Analogical proportions have been extended to handle them. Then each numerical attribute value has to be normalized in the unit interval $[0, 1]$ (i.e., changing the value a_i into $\frac{a_i - a_{i,\min}}{a_{i,\max} - a_{i,\min}}$ where $a_{i,\min}$ and $a_{i,\max}$ are the minimal and maximal possible values for attribute i).

Then the analogical proportion $a : b :: c : d$ becomes a matter of degree. The following expression A associates a degree of validity $A(a, b, c, d)$ to $a : b :: c : d$

for any 4-tuple of normalized attribute values:

$$A(a,b,c,d) = a : b :: c : d = \begin{cases} 1 - |(a-b) - (c-d)|, \\ \quad \text{if } (a \geq b \text{ and } c \geq d) \text{ or } (a \leq b \text{ and } c \leq d) \\ 1 - \max(|a-b|,|c-d|), \\ \quad \text{if } (a \leq b \text{ and } c \geq d) \text{ or } (a \geq b \text{ and } c \leq d) \end{cases}$$

$$(2)$$

When a,b,c,d are restricted to $\{0,1\}$, this expression coincides with the Boolean case definition. We can also check that the three patterns that make true $a : b :: c : d$ in the nominal case, applied to numbers, yield $A(a,b,c,d) = 1$. This highlights the agreement between the numerical extension and the original idea of analogical proportion. See [7] for more justifications of this expression as a meaningful extension of the expressions in the Boolean and nominal cases. We have $A(a,b,c,d) = 1$ if and only if $a - b = c - d$, as can be expected (then a differs from b as c differs from d and vice-versa). Note that in general $A(a,b,c,d)$ yields a degree in $[0,1]$, which evaluates to what extent the analogical proportions holds. For instance, we get a high value for the 4-tuple $(1,0,1,0.1)$, indeed $1 : 0 :: 1 : 0.1 = 0.9$, since 0.1 is close to 0. $A(a,b,c,d) = 0$ if and only if the change inside one of the pairs (a,b) or (c,d) is maximal (e.g., $a = 0$ and $b = 1$), while the other pair shows either no change (the two values are equal) or any change in the opposite direction.

Moreover, it is easy to check that the *code independence* property still holds, namely: $a : b :: c : d = (1-a) : (1-b) :: (1-c) : (1-d)$. Code independence here means that not only 0 and 1, but more generally a and $1-a$ play symmetric roles, and thus it is the same to encode a numerical attribute positively or negatively.

Then, the degree to which an analogical proportion between four vectors holds is computed as the average of componentwise validity degrees with:

$$A(\overrightarrow{a}, \overrightarrow{b}, \overrightarrow{c}, \overrightarrow{d}) = \frac{\sum_{i=1}^{n} A(a_i, b_i, c_i, d_i)}{n} \tag{3}$$

In practice, the resulting degree $A(\overrightarrow{a}, \overrightarrow{b}, \overrightarrow{c}, \overrightarrow{d})$ is rarely equal to 1, but should be close to 1 when $\overrightarrow{a} : \overrightarrow{b} :: \overrightarrow{c} : \overrightarrow{d}$ is not far from being a perfect analogical proportion. Therefore the inference principle recalled in Subsect. 3.2 has to be adapted for a proper implementation as:

$$\frac{A(\overrightarrow{a}, \overrightarrow{b}, \overrightarrow{c}, \overrightarrow{d}) \geq \theta}{\forall j \in \{n+1, ..., m\}, \quad a_j : b_j :: c_j : d_j \text{ holds}} \tag{4}$$

where θ is a given threshold. Then the two procedures of analogical querying described in Subsect. 3.3 can be readily adapted, taking lesson from application to classification problems in case of numerical attributes [5]).

Besides, in Sect. 2, we have mentioned that examples and counter-examples could be associated with a degree of representativeness. Then this can be handled by dealing with the $(n+1)$th attribute $qual(\cdot)$ as a nominal attribute if we use a finite scale for representativeness. If we want to handle degrees of representativeness directly in $[0, 1]$, then one could use a graded extension of the binary evaluation for nominal attributes which evaluates to what extent we are close to one of the three patterns that make an analogical proportion true for nominal values. This extension (see [7] for its presentation) is equal to 1 *only for* these patterns (which is not the case with the expression of $A(\overrightarrow{a}, \overrightarrow{b}, \overrightarrow{c}, \overrightarrow{d})$) given in Subsect. 3.4.

4   Related Work

As already emphasized in [8], querying is closely related to decision issues. Besides, classification is a special kind of decision problem. Thus, each time we have at our disposal a collection of items, with their class or a label, represented by tuples of attributes values, one may apply an analogical proportion-based approach for completing the collection, or for predicting the label of a new item. This has been applied to machine learning [5,14], case-based reasoning [13], or case-based decision (e.g., for predicting the expected value of a decision) [4]. This paper is the first to propose such an approach to database querying.

There are some works dealing with "analogical database queries" [3], but they are devoted to a new type of database query, the general idea being to retrieve tuples that validate a relation of the form "a is to b as c is to d". Finding such quadruplets may serve explanation needs, as suggested in [10]. In this paper, the problem is different: namely we have a collection $\mathcal{C}$ of examples and counter-examples (reflecting the preferences of a user) on the one hand, and a database $\mathcal{T}$ of items on the other hand, where one has to find items that may be of interest for the user.

5   Concluding Remarks

We have outlined a new approach to case-based querying which goes beyond the simple exploitation of similarity relations. It relies on an extrapolation mechanism based on analogical proportions that enables us to generate new examples or counter-examples with respect to the preferences of a user, and select, and possibly rank-order items that may fit these preferences.

Much remains to be done for developing such querying systems. In particular, implementations and experiments have to be made. It may for instance help determining the order of magnitude of number of examples and counter-examples we start with that are necessary to make the approach effective in practice. And also to estimate the average complexity of the method, as it is strongly linked to this number.

References

1. Aristotle. Nicomachean Ethics. University of Chicago Press (2011). Trans. by Bartlett, R.C., Collins, S.D

2. Bartolini, I.: Image querying. In: Liu, L., Tamer Özsu, M. (eds.) Encyclopedia of Database Systems, pp. 1368–1374. Springer, Boston (2009). https://doi.org/10.1007/978-0-387-39940-9_1440

3. Beltran, W.C., Jaudoin, H., Pivert, O.: Analogical database queries. In: Flexible Query Answering Systems 2015. AISC, vol. 400, pp. 201–213. Springer, Cham (2016). https://doi.org/10.1007/978-3-319-26154-6_16

4. Billingsley, R., Prade, H., Richard, G., Williams, M.-A.: Towards analogy-based decision - a proposal. In: Christiansen, H., Jaudoin, H., Chountas, P., Andreasen, T., Legind Larsen, H. (eds.) FQAS 2017. LNCS (LNAI), vol. 10333, pp. 28–35. Springer, Cham (2017). https://doi.org/10.1007/978-3-319-59692-1_3

5. Bounhas, M., Prade, H., Richard, G.: Analogy-based classifiers for nominal or numerical data. Int. J. Approx. Reason. 91, 36–55 (2017)

6. de Calmès, M., Dubois, D., Hüllermeier, E., Prade, H., Sèdes, F.: Flexibility and fuzzy case-based evaluation in querying: an illustration in an experimental setting. Int. J. Uncertain. Fuzziness Knowl. Based Syst. 11(1), 43–66 (2003)

7. Dubois, D., Prade, H., Richard, G.: Multiple-valued extensions of analogical proportions. Fuzzy Sets Syst. 292, 193–202 (2016)

8. Dubois, D., Hüllermeier, E., Prade, H.: Fuzzy methods for case-based recommendation and decision support. J. Intell. Inf. Syst. 27(2), 95–115 (2006)

9. Dubois, D., Prade, H., Sèdes, F.: Fuzzy logic techniques in multimedia database querying: a preliminary investigation of the potentials. IEEE Trans. Knowl. Data Eng. 13(3), 383–392 (2001)

10. Hug, N., Prade, H., Richard, G., Serrurier, M.: Analogical proportion-based methods for recommendation - first investigations. Fuzzy Sets Syst. 366, 110–132 (2019)

11. Lepage, Y.: Analogy and formal languages. Electr. Not. Theor. Comput. Sci. 53, 180–191 (2002). Moss, L.S., Oehrle, R.T. (eds.) Proceedings of the Joint Meeting of the 6th Conference on Formal Grammar and the 7th Conference on Mathematics of Language

12. Lieber, J., Nauer, E., Prade, H.: Improving analogical extrapolation using case pair competence. In: Bach, K., Marling, C. (eds.) ICCBR 2019. LNCS (LNAI), vol. 11680, pp. 251–265. Springer, Cham (2019). https://doi.org/10.1007/978-3-030-29249-2_17

13. Lieber, J., Nauer, E., Prade, H., Richard, G.: Making the best of cases by approximation, interpolation and extrapolation. In: Cox, M.T., Funk, P., Begum, S. (eds.) ICCBR 2018. LNCS (LNAI), vol. 11156, pp. 580–596. Springer, Cham (2018). https://doi.org/10.1007/978-3-030-01081-2_38

14. Miclet, L., Bayoudh, S., Delhay, A.: Analogical dissimilarity: definition, algorithms and two experiments in machine learning. J. Artif. Intell. Res. (JAIR) 32, 793–824 (2008)

15. Miclet, L., Prade, H.: Handling analogical proportions in classical logic and fuzzy logics settings. In: Sossai, C., Chemello, G. (eds.) ECSQARU 2009. LNCS (LNAI), vol. 5590, pp. 638–650. Springer, Heidelberg (2009). https://doi.org/10.1007/978-3-642-02906-6_55

16. Pirrelli, V., Yvon, F.: Analogy in the lexicon: a probe into analogy-based machine learning of language. In: Proceedings of the 6th International Symposium on Human Communication, Cuba (1999)

17. Prade, H., Richard, G.: From analogical proportion to logical proportions. Log. Univers. 7(4), 441–505 (2013)

18. Prade, H., Richard, G.: Analogical proportions and analogical reasoning - an introduction. In: Aha, D.W., Lieber, J. (eds.) ICCBR 2017. LNCS (LNAI), vol. 10339, pp. 16–32. Springer, Cham (2017). https://doi.org/10.1007/978-3-319-61030-6_2

19. Prade, H., Richard, G.: Analogical proportions: from equality to inequality. Int. J. Approx. Reason. **101**, 234–254 (2018)
20. Prade, H., Richard, G.: Analogical proportions: why they are useful in AI. In: Proceedings of the 30th International Joint Conference on Artificial Intelligence (IJCAI 2021), Montreal, 21–26 August, pp. 4568–4576 (2021). www.ijcai.org
21. Schockaert, S., Prade, H.: Interpolative reasoning with default rules. In: Rossi, F. (ed.) Proceedings of the 23rd International Joint Conference on Artificial Intelligence (IJCAI 2013), Beijing, 3–9 August, pp. 1090–1096. IJCAI/AAAI (2013)
22. Schockaert, S., Prade, H.: Completing symbolic rule bases using betweenness and analogical proportion. In: Prade, H., Richard, G. (eds.) Computational Approaches to Analogical Reasoning: Current Trends. SCI, vol. 548, pp. 195–215. Springer, Heidelberg (2014). https://doi.org/10.1007/978-3-642-54516-0_8

Flexible Querying Using Disjunctive Concepts

Grégory Smits[1]([✉]), Marie-Jeanne Lesot[2], Olivier Pivert[1],
and Ronald R. Yager[3,4]

[1] University of Rennes – IRISA, UMR 6074, Lannion, France
`{gregory.smits,olivier.pivert}@irisa.fr`
[2] Sorbonne Université, CNRS, LIP6, 75005 Paris, France
`marie-jeanne.lesot@lip6.fr`
[3] Faculty of Science, King Abdulaziz University, Jeddah, Saudi Arabia
[4] Machine Intelligence Institute, Iona College, New Rochelle, NY, USA
`yager@panix.com`

Abstract. A DB querying system is said to be flexible if it adapts to
the end user expectations and expertise. This paper introduces a novel
strategy to fuzzy querying that reduces the gap between complex search
conditions end users have in mind and formal queries understood by the
underlying DB system. In the Flexible Querying By Example paradigm,
the proposed strategy, called DCQ standing for Disjunctive Concept
Querying, extends a flexible querying system with subjective disjunctive concepts: it proposes two stored procedures that can be embedded
in any relational database management system to build a formal query
from a few user-given examples that represent the diversity of what the
user is looking for. The first procedure infers the membership function of
the implicit imprecise concept underlying the provided examples, with
the specificity of allowing for complex disjunctive concepts: it is able to
both capture properties shared by most of the selected representative
tuples as well as specific properties possessed by only one specific representative tuple. The second procedure allows to exploit the resulting
fuzzy concept in a query.

Keywords: Fuzzy querying · Disjunctive fuzzy concept · Fuzzy
measure · Choquet integral

1 Introduction

End users expect a lot from their stored data and from querying systems that
make the link between users and data. As a first interaction with a querying
system, users have *in fine* to express their information need using a formal query
language: SQL in our case as relational data are considered. Faithfully translating
concrete information needs into SQL queries is however a difficult task, and, to be
considered as smart, a DataBase (DB) querying system should help users express
what they are looking for. The Querying By Example (QBE) paradigm alleviates

© Springer Nature Switzerland AG 2021
T. Andreasen et al. (Eds.): FQAS 2021, LNAI 12871, pp. 29–40, 2021.
https://doi.org/10.1007/978-3-030-86967-0_3

Table 1. Accommodation DB: excerpt of the *housing* relation extension housing: {loan INT, surf INT, nbR INT, loc TEXT, outSurf INT}

	loan	surf	nbR	loc	outSurf
t_1	500	25	2	historical center	0
t_2	500	30	2	center	0
t_3	475	40	3	center	0
t_4	400	80	4	suburb	10
t_5	450	60	3	suburb	100
t_6	400	100	5	outskirts	500
t_7	800	25	3	historical center	0
t_8	500	20	1	center	10
...	...	...	...	...	...

Table 2. User given examples of *ideal housing*

	loan	surf	nbR	loc	outSurf
ih_1	400	30	2	center	0
ih_2	450	40	3	center	10
ih_3	400	80	4	suburb	10
ih_4	400	100	5	outskirts	500

the user task, only requiring he/she provides a few input tuple examples or the evaluation of a few data instances. The difficulty is then to understand the underlying user need, which often corresponds to imprecise, complex, context-dependent and subjective concepts.

As an illustrative example, consider a DB about accommodations for rent described by precise attribute values as surface, number of rooms, distance to center, loan, etc., and illustrated in Table 1, and a user looking for an *ideal housing* to start a professional life, for which he/she provides the instances given in Table 2. Several very different accommodations may satisfy this vague subjective concept of an ideal housing. The user may indeed be interested in a small flat without garden nor balcony if it is located close to the central and vibrant part of the city, or in a larger flat close to his/her office in the suburb or may even be willing to live in a small house with garden in the outskirts.

Other examples of such complex concepts are for instance: *atypical holidays*, *safe investment*, *promising student*, *good employee*, etc. Such complex searches are generally disjunctive by nature as very different tuples may satisfy a given concept, for various reasons. The key issue is then to infer automatically the definition of the concept underlying the provided representative examples and to retrieve the data instances satisfying it.

To the best of our knowledge, this issue of extending a flexible querying system with subjective disjunctive concepts using a QBE strategy has not been studied so far.

This paper introduces a cooperative querying strategy, called DCQ that stands for Disjunctive Concept Querying, to help users define fuzzy queries to retrieve from a relational DB tuples that best satisfy such complex concepts of a disjunctive nature. More precisely, we devise a Fuzzy Querying By Examples (FQBE) strategy that eases the concept definition step as it only requires the user to give a few representative examples of what he/she could be interested in. From these examples, a membership function describing the associated imprecise underlying concept is automatically inferred exploiting the CHOCO-LATE method [9]: a fuzzy measure is first built to quantify the extent to which combinations of attribute values match the underlying concept, as well as a measure quantifying the relevance of each attribute value individually. These two quantities are then aggregated using a Choquet integral, to determine the degree to which a point satisfies the concept. The paper proposes two stored procedures that can be embedded into any Relational DataBase Management System (RDBMS, PostgreSQL in our case). These two procedures, dedicated respectively to the definition of complex disjunctive fuzzy concepts and their use to fuzzy querying, can then serve as technical tools to develop enhanced DB querying or recommendation systems that better integrate the end user in data to knowledge translation processes.

The paper is structured as follows. Section 2 discusses related works and provides a reminder about the CHOCOLATE method the paper proposition exploits. Section 3 describes the proposed DCQ method and Sect. 4 a Proof-Of-Concept implementation of this strategy within a RDBMS.

2   Related Works

This section briefly reminds the main existing approaches to address the task of answering Query by Examples in data bases. It then describes some general works in the AI community regarding the definition and automatic learning of concepts based on some examples. It finally presents in more details the CHOCOLATE concept modeling approach on which the proposed DCQ strategy relies.

2.1   Flexible Querying and FQBE

Query by Example is a paradigm (initially introduced by M. Zloof [13] in the 70's) that makes it possible to interact with a data base and acquire results based on: i) one or several input tuples provided by the user or ii) the positive or negative evaluation of prototypical examples reflecting the content of the database.

To the best of our knowledge, three types of fuzzy QBE approaches can be found in the literature. The first one, by De Calmès et al. [3], presented by the authors as a case-based reasoning approach, looks for those items in the database that are similar to at least one example (wrt. all the attributes) and dissimilar to all counter-examples (wrt. at least one attribute). The goal of this approach is not to infer an interpretable fuzzy query expressing the preferences of the user but just to retrieve items based on a measure that combines similarity (with positive examples) and dissimilarity (with counter-examples).

In [12], Zadrozny et al. present a clustering-based approach that provides items iteratively until the user is satisfied. The new items to be assessed are selected with a k-NN algorithm. Positive and negative evaluations are used to find association rules determining whether some fuzzy predicates (from a list of predefined linguistic terms) are relevant to the user. Then for each attribute, at best one linguistic term is selected to express the user preferences for this attribute, only if the support, confidence and lift for the association rule that found it are "high enough." As can be seen, this approach resorts to an iterative evaluation of examples until the user is satisfied, without ever evaluating a fuzzy query.

In [6], the authors propose an approach that infers a fuzzy query from user-assessed prototypical examples, based on an algorithm determining the fuzzy predicates that best represent the positive examples (and at the same time discards the negative ones). As in [12], they consider a fuzzy vocabulary for each attribute domain in the database. This vocabulary makes it possible to formulate, in a linguistic way, descriptions of the attribute values shared by positive examples that are not shared by counter-examples (defined as *characterizations*).

All these approaches aim to infer simple *conjunctive* fuzzy queries, sometimes not even explicitly. The DCQ technique we propose in the present paper makes it possible to build a fuzzy query involving complex fuzzy concepts that cannot be easily expressed by a conjunctive/disjunctive combination of atomic fuzzy terms. Moreover, it does not require the user to provide counter-examples but only a limited number of positive examples.

2.2 Concept Modeling

The issue of concept modelling, at the core of the QBE paradigm, has been widely studied from a general perspective in artificial intelligence and data management, for instance in the framework of Formal Concept Analysis [11], as well as its fuzzy extensions [2], or as fuzzy prototypes [5,8]. In both cases, concepts are based on a conjunctive view, imposing that all members of the concept have common attribute values. Only a few works during the 70's and the 80's consider disjunctive concepts, both in the cognitive science [1] and the AI fields [4,7]. Whereas the conjunctive normal form seems to be the most appropriate way to model knowledge taxonomies, it is also clear that more sophisticated aggregation operators have to be defined to infer complex search conditions from a tiny set of user-provided prototypical examples that roughly illustrate what he/she is looking for.

This corresponds to the underlying principle of the CHOCOLATE approach [9] that allows to relax this classical constraint, as detailed in the next subsection.

Another axis of discussion regarding concept modelling and learning relates to the relations between concepts, depending whether they are defined in opposition one to another or independently. The first case is considered when building prototypes or performing a classification task, it requires the availability of both examples and counter-examples. It is also applied in most QBE approaches, as discussed in the previous section. Dealing with each concept individually, as is the case for FCA or CHOCOLATE, means that only representatives of the current concept are required. CHOCOLATE in particular alleviates the requirements on the user, as it considers that only very few representative examples are available.

2.3   The CHOCOLATE Approach

The CHOCOLATE method [9] is a procedure to infer a membership function to describe a concept C from a user-provided set $\mathcal{E}_C$ of representative examples: $\mathcal{E}_C$ constitutes a partial extent for the underlying and implicit concept C. This section summarises CHOCOLATE three steps (see [9] for a detailed description).

Throughout the paper, the following notations are used: R is a universal relation or the result of a join query, whose schema is $R : \{A_1, A_2, \ldots, A_m\}$, each attribute, categorical or numerical, $A_i \in R$ is associated with a definition domain D_i. Each tuple $t \in R$ ($t \in A_1 \times A_2 \times \ldots A_m$) is defined by the values it takes on the m attributes, $t.A_i$ denotes the value taken by t on attribute A_i. A *property* is defined as a couple made of an attribute and a value, denoted (A_i, p). A tuple t is said to possess a property (A_i, p) if $t.A_i = p$ and a set of properties s if $\forall (A_i, p) \in s, t.A_i = p$. Reciprocally, the properties of t are all the couples $(A_i, t.A_i)$ for $i = 1 \ldots m$.

Relevance of Individual Attribute Values. The importance of a property (A_i, p) wrt. a partial concept extension $\mathcal{E}_C$ serves to determine whether p is representative of the values taken by A_i in $\mathcal{E}_C$: the more p is shared, for attribute A_i, by representative elements of the concept, the more important it is. It is thus measured as

$$\delta_i(p) = \frac{|\{x \in \mathcal{E}_C / x.A_i = p\}|}{|\mathcal{E}_C|}. \tag{1}$$

The strict comparison imposed by the binary matching condition $x.A_i = p$ can be replaced by a relaxed comparison, considering the condition $sim_i(p, x.A_i) \geq \eta_i$, where sim_i is an appropriate similarity measure on the domain of attribute A_i and η_i a similarity threshold.

Representativity of Attribute Value Sets. Once the properties have been individually evaluated, the importance of *sets* of such properties is quantified. Whereas an individual value is considered important if it frequently appears in the partial concept extent, the importance of a subset of values depends on its size and whether it appears at least once in the partial concept extent. The fuzzy measure μ thus serves to quantify the extent to which the subset of attribute values matches one of the representative data points in $\mathcal{E}_C$. The μ score is maximal if the assessed set of properties exactly corresponds to one of the representative data points in $\mathcal{E}_C$. Denoting $s = \{(A_i, p_i), i = 1 \ldots |s|\}$ such a set of properties, the binary approach defines μ as:

$$\mu(s) = \max_{x \in \mathcal{E}_C} \frac{1}{m} |\{(A_i, p_i) \in s / x.A_i = p_i\}|, \tag{2}$$

where m denotes the number of attributes. As for the δ_i functions, the strict comparison $t.A_i = p_i$ can be relaxed as $sim_i(p, x.A_i) \geq \eta_i$.

Aggregation. The final step combines the evaluations of atomic properties and set of properties. CHOCOLATE uses the Choquet integral to perform this aggregation of the δ_i and μ evaluations. It especially takes into account, when comparing a set of properties wrt. representative data points (using the μ function), if these evaluated properties are individually specific to one data point or shared by many. This makes it possible to differentiate between a set of properties possessed by only a single representative data point and another set of properties of the same size but shared by several representative data points.

The candidate sets of properties are defined as the set of the most promising ones, according to their individual δ values: let H_j denote the subset of the j properties that best match the representative data points from $\mathcal{E}_C$, i.e. the j properties with maximal δ values. Let $\kappa_j(x)$ denote the jth value among the δ_i, i.e. the matching degree of the jth most representative property possessed by x wrt. concept C. CHOCOLATE defines the membership degree of a data point x to concept C based on the set of representative examples $\mathcal{E}_C$ as

$$\mathcal{S}_C(x) = \sum_{j=1}^{m} (\mu(H_j) - \mu(H_{j-1}))\,\kappa_j(x). \tag{3}$$

3 Proposed DCQ Method for Querying by Example Disjunctive Concepts

This section explains how to build a fuzzy QBE approach based on the CHOCO-LATE strategy, so as to extend a classical RDBMS with disjunctive fuzzy concept querying capabilities. An implementation of DCQ in a RDBMS (PostgreSQL in our case) is then presented, describing in turn the two stored procedures: the first one infers the membership function of a concept from a set of user-selected examples, implementing the CHOCOLATE strategy. The second one can be integrated into a selection statement to retrieve the tuples that best satisfy the concept.

3.1 Underlying Principles of DCQ

DCQ initiates the definition of a concept with the few user-given representative tuples. Identifying these representative tuples directly from the concerned relation extension is not conceivable in terms of system usability. DCQ is thus based on a user interface where some selected tuples are suggested to the user who just has to select those of interest. An illustration of such a graphical interface is provided Fig. 3 in the Proof-of-Concept section. From the whole relation extension, choosing which tuples to suggest is a research topic in itself that is outside the scope of this paper.

Once a few tuples of interest have been selected by the user, he/she can then ask the system to infer a membership function that best covers the properties

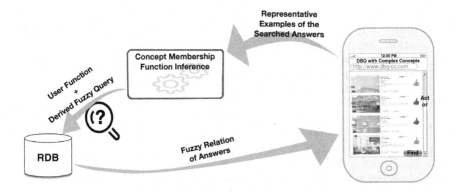

Fig. 1. Fuzzy QBE system handling complex search concepts

they possess. The user only has to name his/her concept, for instance *idealHousing* for the example mentioned in the introduction. A query is then executed on the DBMS to retrieve the tuples that best satisfy the concept. Tuples are then returned to the user in a decreasing order of their satisfaction degree wrt. the search concept. Figure 1 sketches the components of the query architecture.

3.2 Concept Definition Inference

Once the few representative tuples of the fuzzy concept to define have been selected by the user, the procedure that builds it membership function can be triggered. This procedure has the following prototype:

CREATE PROCEDURE infer_concept(label TEXT, rel_name TEXT, rep_ex HSTORE []);

where the parameters are respectively the label given to the concept to infer, the name of the considered relation, that can even be a view to the result of a join query and an array of dictionaries where each dictionary represents a user-selected representative example.

Example 1. The following example shows how to call the *infer_concept* procedure that builds the membership function of the concept *idealHousing* from the user-selected representative examples introduced in Table 2[1].

CALL infer_concept('idealHousing', 'housing_ads', {

    ' "loan"=>400, "surf"=>30, "nbR"=>2, "loc"=>"center", "outSurf"=>0 ',

    ' "loan"=>450, "surf"=>40, "nbR"=>3, "loc"=>"center", "outSurf"=>10 ',

    ' "loan"=>400, "surf"=>80, "nbR"=>4, "loc"=>"suburb", "outSurf"=>10 ',

    ' "loan"=>400, "surf"=>100, "nbR"=>5, "loc"=>"outskirts", "outSurf"=>500 '});

The procedure infer_concept creates a user function that implements the inferred membership function. This user function, that can then be integrated into the selection statement of a query, has the following prototype:

---

[1] The *hstore* module of Postgresql is used to store key/value pairs using the syntax "key"=>"value".

Input: $t, \mathcal{E}_C$ $\triangleright t \in R, \mathcal{E}_C \subset R$
Output: $\mu_C(t)$ $\triangleright \in [0,1]$

```
1  Function concept_name():
2  |   μC(t) ⟵ 0; ds ⟵ [];
3  |   foreach (Ai, pi) ∈ t do
4  |   |   ds[i] ⟵ δi(pi);
5  |   end
6  |   sortDesc(ds);
7  |   foreach j ∈ 1..m do
8  |   |   Hj ⟵ ds[1 : j];
9  |   |   Hj−1 ⟵ ds[1 : j − 1];
10 |   |   μ(Hj) ⟵ maxt'∈εC 1/m × |{(Ai, pi) ∈ Hj, t'.Ai = pi}|;
11 |   |   μ(Hj−1) ⟵ maxt'∈εC 1/m × |{(Ai, pi) ∈ Hj−1, t'.Ai = pi}|;
12 |   |   μC(t) ⟵ μC(t) + (μ(Hj) − μ(Hj−1)) × ds[j];
13 |   end
14 |   return μC(t);
15 End Function
```

Algorithm 1: Pseudo-code of the proposed function to implement the CHOCO-LATE strategy

$$\text{CREATE FUNCTION } concept\_name() \text{ RETURNS DECIMAL ;}$$

where $concept\_name$ is the name given to the concept by the user, $idealHousing$ for the considered example.

The function $concept\_name$ implements the CHOCOLATE strategy [9], reminded in Sect. 2.3. The implementation of this function, that returns the satisfaction degree of a tuple to evaluate wrt. the considered search concept, is given in Algorithm 1 in pseudo-code (its implementation in the pl/python language contains technical tricky aspects that do not help for its understanding).

3.3 Querying with Disjunctive Fuzzy Concepts

The user functions representing the inferred disjunctive fuzzy concepts can then be embedded into SQL queries in the following way:

```
SELECT *, get_mu() as mu
FROM rel_name
WHERE concept_name() > 0;
```

As underlined in [10], relying on user functions to implement fuzzy predicates and their direct use in selection statements may lead to a significant computation cost overhead. Query engines do not leverage existing indexes when a selection statement involves a user-function, and therefore perform a sequential search on the whole relation to identify tuples satisfying the predicate. A way to avoid this extra-cost is to perform a so-called *derivation* of the fuzzy query so as to translate it into a Boolean query whose execution can be natively optimised by the RDBMS query engine. A derived query aims at retrieving the tuples that may somewhat satisfy the initial fuzzy query. The membership degree within the concerned fuzzy predicate is then computed only for these tuples. As shown in the prototype query given hereafter, the selection clause now contains the Boolean condition, whose execution can be optimized by the query engine, and the user function to compute the concept membership degree is involved in the projection statement only:

```
SELECT *, concept_name() as mu
FROM rel_name
WHERE (derivedConditionOn_A₁) OR
      (derivedConditionOn_A₂) OR
      ...
      (derivedConditionOn_Aₘ);
```

where derivedConditionOn_A_i is the derived Boolean condition regarding attribute A_i. The derived condition aims at selecting the tuples whose value on attribute A_i is shared with at least one of the representative examples.

To obtain a derived condition, two aspects have to be taken into account, the nature of A_i (numerical vs. categorical), and the type of comparison used (binary strict one or similarity-based relaxed one).

When a strict comparison is used then the derived condition is of the form:

$(A_i$ IN $V)$

where $V = \{x.A_i, x \in \mathcal{E}_C\}$, C being the involved concept and $\mathcal{E}_C$ its partial extent. When A_i is numerical and a relaxed comparison is used, the derived condition is of the form:

$(A_i$ BETWEEN v^- AND $v^+)$

where $v^- = \inf_{v \in D_i, t \in \mathcal{E}_C} \mathrm{sim}_i(t.A_i, v) \geq \eta_i$
and $v^+ = \sup_{v \in D_i, t \in \mathcal{E}_C} \mathrm{sim}_i(t.A_i, v) \geq \eta_i$.

Example 2. The user query looking for *idealHousing* is thus translated into the following fuzzy query:

```
SELECT *, get_mu() as mu
FROM housing
WHERE idealHousing() > 0;
```

whose derived version is:

```
SELECT *, idealHousing() as mu
FROM rel_name
WHERE (loan IN (400, 450) ) OR
      (surf BETWEEN 30 AND 100) OR
      (nbR IN (2, 3, 4, 5) ) OR
      (loc IN ('center', 'suburb', 'outskirts') );
```

Considering, for a sake of clarity, a strict equality comparison between values of the tuple to evaluate and those of the representative tuples used to infer the concept membership function, Table 3 gives a very short excerpt of the fuzzy relation returned by the previous query. Applied on a toy example, the extract of the fuzzy relation given in Table 3 shows the interesting behaviour of the CHOCOLATE approach to quantify the satisfaction of a tuple regarding a

Table 3. Excerpt of the returned fuzzy relation containing the retrieved *idealHousing* instances associated with their membership degrees (column *mu*)

loan	surf	nbR	loc	outSurf	mu
...	...	...	...	...	...
500	25	2	historical center	0	0.15
500	30	2	center	0	0.25
400	40	3	center	0	0.3
400	80	4	suburb	40	0.3
650	80	4	outskirts	1000	0.1
...	...	...	...	...	...

complex disjunctive concept. One can indeed remark that the second and third tuple match the concept (with respective score of 0.25 and 0.3) for different reasons. For the second tuple, it is due to the fact that it shares 4 properties with one of the representative tuples (Table 2) and one of the them (*loc* = *center*) is possessed by two representative examples of the concept. For the third evaluated tuple, despite the fact that it shares 3 properties (*surf*, *nbR* and *loc*) with one of the representative example, it also possesses a property (*loan* = *400*) that seems to be important as it is possessed by 3 of the 4 representative examples. The Choquet-based approach thus captures and aggregates the importance of properties taken individually and combined conjunctively.

4   Proof-of-Concept of DCQ

A Proof-Of-Concept (POC) has been implemented[2] for a database containing 1,200 descriptions of accommodations to rent, each accommodation being described on 11 attributes. This POC aims at comparing the proposed strategy with two classical distance-based approaches.

4.1   Selection of the Suggested Tuples

The first question to address is to identify the tuples from the database to be suggested to the user. The idea is to cover as much as possible the diversity of the available data. It has been empirically decided to suggest up to 40 tuples. To do so a clustering algorithm based on affinity propagation has been employed to build 40 clusters whose centroids constitute the suggested examples. Figure 2 illustrates the use of this algorithm on two attributes (distance to center and loan) to show how centroids are identified.

4.2   Answers Retrieval

The user then peruses the suggested tuples to select those illustrating what he/she is looking for. Once five tuples have been selected (Fig. 3) to represent

---
[2] It is available at the url http://51.210.243.246:8081/fuzzy_queries/.

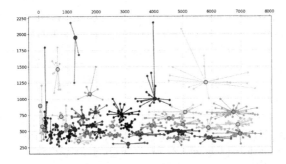

Fig. 2. Illustration of the clustering-based identification of the tuples to suggest

Fig. 3. QBE user interface showing the five tuples selected to initiate the search

his/her concept of ideal housing, the infer_concept function is called to infer the membership function of the search concept and to store it so that it can be latter reused.

A derived fuzzy query involving the user concept, as described in the previous section, is then submitted to retrieve the tuples that best satisfy the user requirements.

5 Conclusion and Perspectives

This paper introduces a technical solution to allow end users query relational data using complex search conditions materialized by fuzzy disjunctive concepts and their associated membership function. Functionalities have been first added to a classical RBMS so that it handles selection statements involving the satisfaction of such complex concepts. To ease the definition of complex search concepts, a query by example principle is envisaged. End users just have to select a few tuples that represent the diversity of what they are looking for. The approach then learns the important atomic properties as well as combinations of them possessed by at least one user-given representative example. A prototype has been developed to compare the proposed strategy to concept learning with two others based on the distance wrt. the closest or all the representative examples. Ongoing works aim at collecting and analysing the results of the ongoing experimentation with end users to have a subjective assessment of the proposed system on a real use case. An implementation of the approach to movie recommendation is also in progress and may constitute an interesting solution to the cold-start problem.

References

1. Anisfeld, M.: Disjunctive concepts? J. Gen. Psychol. **78**(2), 223–228 (1968)
2. Bělohlávek, R., Vychodil, V.: What is a fuzzy concept lattice? In: Proceedings of the 3rd International Conference on Concept Lattices and Their Applications, CLA05, pp. 34–45 (2005)
3. De Calmès, M., Dubois, D., Hullermeier, E., Prade, H., Sedes, F.: Flexibility and fuzzy case-based evaluation in querying: an illustration in an experimental setting. Int. J. Uncertainty Fuzziness Knowl.-Based Syst. **11**(01), 43–66 (2003)
4. Iba, G.A.: Learning disjunctive concepts from examples (1979)
5. Lesot, M.J., Rifqi, M., Bouchon-Meunier, B.: Fuzzy prototypes: from a cognitive view to a machine learning principle. In: Bustince, H., Herrera, F., Montero, J. (eds.) Fuzzy Sets and Their Extensions: Representation, Aggregation and Models. Studies in Fuzziness and Soft Computing, vol. 220, pp. 431–452. Springer, Heidelberg (2008). https://doi.org/10.1007/978-3-540-73723-0_22
6. Moreau, A., Pivert, O., Smits, G.: Fuzzy query by example. In: Proceedings of ACM Symposium on Applied Computing, SAC 2018, pp. 688–695 (2018)
7. Murray, K.S.: Multiple convergence: an approach to disjunctive concept acquisition. In: Proceedings of the International Joint Conference on Artificial Intelligence, IJCAI, pp. 297–300 (1987)
8. Rifqi, M.: Constructing prototypes from large databases. In: Proceedings of the International Conference on Information Processing and Management of Uncertainty in Knowledge-Based Systems (IPMU 1996), pp. 300–306 (1996)
9. Smits, G., Yager, R.R., Lesot, M.-J., Pivert, O.: Concept membership modeling using a choquet integral. In: Lesot, M.-J., et al. (eds.) IPMU 2020. CCIS, vol. 1237, pp. 359–372. Springer, Cham (2020). https://doi.org/10.1007/978-3-030-50146-4_27
10. Smits, G., Pivert, O., Girault, T.: Reqflex: fuzzy queries for everyone. Proc. VLDB Endow. **6**(12), 1206–1209 (2013)
11. Wille, R.: Restructuring lattice theory: an approach based on hierarchies of concepts. In: Rival, I. (ed.) Ordered sets. NATO Advanced Study Institutes Series (Series C – Mathematical and Physical Sciences), vol. 83, pp. 445–470. Springer, Dordrecht (1982). https://doi.org/10.1007/978-94-009-7798-3_15
12. Zadrozny, S., Kacprzyk, J., Wysocki, M.: On a novice-user-focused approach to flexible querying: the case of initially unavailable explicit user preferences. In: Proceedings of the 2010 10th International Conference on Intelligent Systems Design and Applications, ISDA 2010, pp. 696–701 (2010)
13. Zloof, M.M.: Query-by-example: a data base language. IBM Syst. J. **16**(4), 324–343 (1977). https://doi.org/10.1147/sj.164.0324

Analytical Queries on Vanilla RDF Graphs with a Guided Query Builder Approach

Sébastien Ferré[(⊠)]

Univ Rennes, CNRS, IRISA, Campus de Beaulieu, 35042 Rennes Cedex, France
`ferre@irisa.fr`

Abstract. As more and more data are available as RDF graphs, the availability of tools for data analytics beyond semantic search becomes a key issue of the Semantic Web. Previous work require the modelling of data cubes on top of RDF graphs. We propose an approach that directly answers analytical queries on unmodified (vanilla) RDF graphs by exploiting the computation features of SPARQL 1.1. We rely on the N<A>F design pattern to design a query builder that completely hides SPARQL behind a verbalization in natural language; and that gives intermediate results and suggestions at each step. Our evaluations show that our approach covers a large range of use cases, scales well on large datasets, and is easier to use than writing SPARQL queries.

1 Introduction

Data analytics is concerned with groups of facts whereas search is concerned with individual facts. Consider for instance the difference between *Which films were directed by Tim Burton?* (search) and *How many films were produced each year in each country?* (data analytics). Data analytics has been well studied in relational databases with data warehousing and OLAP [2], but is still in its infancy in the Semantic Web [3,9,15]. Most of the existing work adapts the OLAP approach to RDF graphs. Typically, data administrators first derive data cubes from RDF graphs by specifying what are the observations, the dimensions, and the measures [4]. End-users can then use traditional OLAP-based user interfaces for cube transformations and visualizations. More recently, other kinds of user interfaces have been proposed to ease analytical querying: natural language interfaces [1,9,16]; guided query construction, for instance based on pre-defined query templates [11]; and high-level query languages that can be translated to SPARQL [13]. The main drawback of using data cubes is that end-users have no direct access to the original RDF graphs, and can only explore the cubes that have been defined by some data administrator. This drawback is mitigated in [3] by an Analytical Schema (AnS), from which end-users can derive themselves many different cubes. However, there is still the need for a data administrator

---

This research is supported by ANR project PEGASE (ANR-16-CE23-0011-08).

T. Andreasen et al. (Eds.): FQAS 2021, LNAI 12871, pp. 41–53, 2021.
https://doi.org/10.1007/978-3-030-86967-0_4

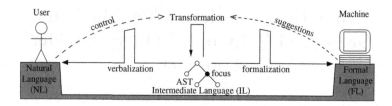

Fig. 1. Principle of the N<A>F design pattern

to define the AnS. A consequence of the lack of direct access is a limited expressivity for the end-user, compared to the direct use of SPARQL 1.1 [10]. Indeed, every OLAP view can be expressed as a SPARQL aggregation query (where each SPARQL result corresponds to a cube cell), while each data cube allows for a limited range of questions. Each new question may require the definition of a new data cube, which can generally be done by the data administrator only. The counterpart of SPARQL's expressivity is that it is much more difficult for an end user to write SPARQL queries than to interact with an OLAP user interface. Another drawback is that SPARQL engines are not optimized for data analytics like OLAP engines. However, they are already usable in practice as we show in this work, their optimization is out of the scope of this paper.

In this paper, we propose an alternative approach that exploits the computation features of SPARQL 1.1 (aggregations, expressions) to directly answer analytical queries on *vanilla* RDF graphs, i.e. RDF graphs *not* customized to data analytics. We rely on the N<A>F design pattern [5] to design a query builder user interface that is *user-friendly* and *responsive*. In particular, it is user-friendly by completely hiding SPARQL behind a verbalization of the built queries in natural language. It is also made responsive by giving intermediate results and suggestions for refining the query, at each step, not only at the end of the building process. Therefore, the user interface of our approach shares features with QA (verbalization of queries and suggestions in natural language), and OLAP (interactive visualization of results).

The paper is organized as follows. Section 2 shortly explains and illustrates the N<A>F design pattern, which serves as a formalization framework for this work. Section 3 formalizes the building of analytical queries as a new instance of N<A>F. Section 4 presents an evaluation of the expressivity, responsiveness, and usability of our approach. A Web application[1] is available online, and includes the permalinks of about 70 analytical queries, and some screencasts.

2   The N<A>F Design Pattern

The purpose of the N<A>F design pattern [5] is to bridge the gap between natural languages (NL) and formal languages (FL, here SPARQL), as summarized in Fig. 1. The user stands on the NL side, and does not understand the FL. The

---

[1] http://www.irisa.fr/LIS/ferre/sparklis/.

machine, here a SPARQL endpoint, stands on the FL side, and does not understand the NL. The design pattern has already been instantiated to three tasks
with different FLs [5]: (a) semantic search with SPARQL basic graph patterns
(including cycles), and their combination with UNION, OPTIONAL, and MINUS (hereafter called *simple graph patterns* (SGP)) [7], (b) semantic authoring with RDF
descriptions [8], and (c) ontology design and completion with OWL class expressions [6]. The central element of the bridge is made of the Abstract Syntax Trees
(AST) of an Intermediate Language (IL), which is designed to make translations
from ASTs to both NL (*verbalization*) and FL (*formalization*) as simple as possible. IL has no proper concrete syntax, NL and FL play this role, respectively for
the user and the machine. ASTs are tree structures where the nodes represent
query components and subqueries. Each node $X = \mathbf{C}(X_1, \ldots, X_n)$ is characterized by a *construct* $\mathbf{C}$, the type of the node, and a tuple of nodes $X_1, \ldots, X_n$,
the children of X. N<A>F follows the query builder approach, where the structure
that is incrementally built is precisely an AST. Unlike other query builders, the
generated query (FL) and the displayed query (NL) may strongly differ in their
structure thanks to the mediation of IL. The AST is initially the simplest query,
and is incrementally built by applying *transformations*. A transformation may
insert or delete a query component at the *focus*. The *focus* is a distinguished
node of the AST that the user can freely move to control which parts of the
query should be modified. Transformations are suggested by the machine based
on query semantics and actual data, and controlled by users after they have been
verbalized in NL.

We illustrate N<A>F on simple graph patterns (SGP). The AST

$$\mathbf{That}(\mathbf{A}(:\texttt{Film}), \mathbf{Has}(:\texttt{director}, \mathbf{Term}(:\texttt{Spielberg})))$$

is a nesting of constructs inspired by NL syntactic constructs, with RDF terms
as atomic components (e.g., class :Film, term :Spielberg). The tree structure of
the AST is traversed recursively to generate its translations to FL and NL.

- SPARQL: `?x a :Film. ?x :director :Spielberg.`
- English: `'a film whose director is Spielberg'`

The AST is built through the following sequence of transformations and ASTs
(the current focus is underlined):

(0) initial AST   : **Something**
(1) class :Film   : **A**(:Film)
(2) prop. :director : **That**(**A**(:Film), **Has**(:director, **Something**))
(3) term :Spielberg: **That**(**A**(:Film), **Has**(:director, **Term**(:Spielberg)))
(4) move focus   : **That**(**A**(:Film), **Has**(:director, **Term**(:Spielberg)))

The transformations are suggested according to the focus and actual results
of the current query. For example, at step (2) only properties having a film as
subject or object are suggested, and at step (3) only film directors are suggested
as terms. At each step, the user interface shows: (a) the verbalization of the current query with the focus highlighted, (b) the results of the generated SPARQL
query, and (c) the lists of suggested transformations.

3   Guided Building of Analytical Queries on RDF Graphs

The contribution of this paper is to fill the gap between the end-user and the computation features of SPARQL 1.1 (expressions, filters, bindings, and aggregations) to the purpose of the direct data analytics of vanilla RDF graphs. We realize this by designing a new instance of the N<A>F design pattern, i.e. new kinds of ASTs, along with their transformations, their formalization, and verbalization. Starting from the instance on simple graph patterns (see Sect. 2), this new instance introduces two new kinds of ASTs that cover the computation features of SPARQL, in addition to graph patterns: *tables* and *expressions*. The ASTs of analytical queries are *table* ASTs, and are composed of *graph pattern* ASTs and *expression* ASTs. A simple graph pattern AST P evaluates to a set of mappings $M(P)$, where each mapping $\mu \in M(P)$ is a partial function from variables of the graph pattern to RDF terms. An expression AST E evaluates to an RDF term, computed as $eval(E)$. A table AST T evaluates to a tabular structure with a set of *columns* $C(T)$, and a set of *rows* $R(T)$ where each row $r \in R(T)$ is a partial mapping from columns to RDF terms.

In the following subsections we progressively cover the computation features of SPARQL by defining new AST constructs. Each subsection presents one or two use cases to motivate the new feature, and then formally defines the new construct. Use cases are based on a concrete dataset, MONDIAL [12], that contains geographical knowledge (e.g., countries, cities, continents, bodies of water) with a lot of numerical data (e.g., population, area).

The constructs of expression ASTs are defined at once in Sect. 3.2. For each new construct of a table AST T, we define:

- $C(T)$: the set of columns,
- $R(T)$: the set of rows (defined with relational algebra),
- $sparql(T)$: the formalization in SPARQL,
- $nl(T)$: the verbalization in NL (here English),
- a set of transformations to build the construct.

An important note is that function $sparql()$ is not always applied to the table AST itself but sometimes to a variation of it that depends on the focus. Variations are explained below where needed. The global formalization of a table T is SELECT * WHERE $\{sparql(T')\}$ where T' is the focus-dependent variant of T.

3.1   Primitive Tables

All of our computation constructs define a table as a function of another table, and so we need primitive tables to start with. Possible candidates for a primitive table are a table of a relational database, an OLAP data cube or a spreadsheet. However, in order to allow direct analytics of vanilla RDF graphs, we propose to use SPARQL simple graph patterns (SGP) to extract arbitrary tables of facts. Indeed, the results of a SPARQL SELECT query are returned as a table. We can then reuse previous work on the N<A>F-based building of SGPs, implemented in the Sparklis tool [7], to help users build those primitive tables.

Definition 1. *Let P be a simple graph pattern AST, and $sparql(P)$ its translation to SPARQL. The table AST $T = $ **GetAnswers**(P) represents the primitive table whose columns are the variables of $sparql(P)$, and rows are the solutions.*

- $C(T) = Vars(sparql(P))$
- $R(T) = Sols(sparql(P))$
- $sparql(T) = sparql(P)$
- $nl(T) = $ 'give me $nl(P)$'

For example, if a user wants to build a primitive table of countries along with their population and area, four steps are enough to build the following AST:

$T0 := $ **GetAnswers**(**That**(**A**(:Country),

 And(**Has**(:population, **Something**), **Has**(:area, **Something**)))))

which translates to SPARQL: `?x1 a :Country. ?x1 :population ?x2. ?x1 :area ?x3.` and to English: 'give me every country that has a population and that has an area'.

3.2   Expressions in Bindings and Filters

Use case (E): *Give me the population density for each country, from population and area.* SPARQL expressions (e.g., `?pop / ?area`) are used in two kinds of contexts: *filterings* (`FILTER`) and *bindings* (`SELECT, BIND, GROUP BY`). Given a table, a filtering performs a selection on the set of rows based on a Boolean expression. Given a table, a binding adds a column and computes its value for each row with an expression. In both cases, the expression can only refer to the columns of the table. In data analytics, filterings are important to select subsets of data, and bindings are important to derive information that is not explicitly represented, e.g. *population density* in use case (E).

We first define expression ASTs as they are a component of filterings and bindings. We define them in a classical way, as a composition of constants, variables, and operators/functions.

Definition 2 (expression). *An expression AST E is composed of RDF terms (constants), table columns (variables), and SPARQL operators/functions. We add the undefined expression construct ?? to allow for the incremental building of expressions. An expression E is said defined when it does not contain ??. We note $C(E)$ the set of columns refered to in the expression.*

The evaluation of an expression AST E is denoted by $eval_r(E)$, where r is the row on which the evaluation is performed. $eval_r(E)$ and $sparql(E)$ are defined in the obvious way, but are only defined when E is defined itself. If the focus is on a subexpression E', then only that subexpression is evaluated and formalized in SPARQL in order to show the value at focus. The verbalization of expression ASTs results from the nesting of the verbalization of its functions and operators. It mixes mathematical notations and text depending on which is the clearer: '$E_1 + E_2$' is clear to everybody and less verbose than 'the addition of E_1 and E_2', while 'E_1 or E_2' is less obscure than 'E_1 || E_2' for non-IT people.

The verbalization of columns is derived from the names of classes and properties used in the graph pattern that introduce them as variables: e.g., in $sparql(T0)$, 'the population' for x_2, 'the area' for x_3. The parts of the expression that are not under focus are displayed in a different way (e.g., gray font) to show that they are not actually computed.

The transformations used to build expression ASTs are the following: (a) insert an RDF term at focus, (b) insert a column at focus, (c) apply an operator or a function at focus. When an operator/function is applied, the focus is automatically moved to the next undefined expression if any (e.g., other function arguments), and to the whole expression otherwise. For instance, the sequence of ASTs and transformations that builds the expression of use case (E), which computes population density from population and area, is the following (the focus is underlined):

$$
\begin{array}{lll}
\text{(0) inital expression} & : E = \underline{??} \\
\text{(1) insert column } p \text{ (population):} & E = \underline{p} \\
\text{(2) apply operator / (division)} & : E = p \; / \; \underline{??} \\
\text{(3) insert column } a \text{ (area)} & : E = p \; / \; \underline{a}
\end{array}
$$

There are constraints on which transformations are applicable so as to avoid misformed expressions. Only columns that are in scope can be inserted. That scope is defined by table AST constructs that contain expressions. Type constraints are also used to determine which operators and functions can be applied, and for which datatypes RDF terms can be inserted. In previous example, at step (2) only numeric operators/functions can be applied because p is an integer, and at step (3) only numeric columns and terms can be inserted.

We now define the two table constructs that contain an expression.

Definition 3 (filtering). *Let T_1 be a table AST, and E be a Boolean expression AST s.t. $C(E) \subseteq C(T_1)$. The table AST $T = \textbf{SelectRows}(T_1, E)$ represents a filtering of the rows of T_1 that verify E.*

- $C(T) = C(T_1)$
- $R(T) = \begin{cases} \{r \mid r \in R(T_1), eval_r(E) = true\} & \text{if } E \text{ is defined,} \\ R(T_1) & \text{otherwise} \end{cases}$
- $sparql(T) = \begin{cases} sparql(T_1) \text{ FILTER } (sparql(E)) & \text{if } E \text{ is defined} \\ sparql(T_1) & \text{otherwise} \end{cases}$
- $nl(T) = {}'nl(T_1) \text{ where } nl(E)'$

Definition 4 (binding). *Let T_1 be a table AST, x be a column s.t. $x \notin C(T_1)$, and E be an expression AST s.t. $C(E) \subseteq C(T_1)$. The table AST $T = \textbf{AddColumn}(T_1, x, E)$ represents the addition of a column x to T_1, and the binding of x to E.*

- $C(T) = C(T_1) \cup \{x\}$
- $R(T) = \begin{cases} \{r \cup \{x \mapsto eval_r(E)\} \mid r \in R(T_1)\} & \text{if } E \text{ is defined,} \\ R(T_1) & \text{otherwise } (x \text{ is unbound}) \end{cases}$

$$- sparql(T) = \begin{cases} sparql(T_1) \text{ BIND } (sparql(E) \text{ AS } ?x) & \text{if } E \text{ is defined,} \\ sparql(T_1) & \text{otherwise} \end{cases}$$

$$- nl(T) = \begin{cases} \text{'}nl(T_1) \text{ and give me } name(x) = nl(E)\text{ '} & \text{if } name(x) \text{ is defined,} \\ \text{'}nl(T_1) \text{ and give me } nl(E)\text{ '} & \text{otherwise} \end{cases}$$

In both constructs, the columns that are in scope of the expression are the columns $C(T_1)$. If the focus is on a subexpression E', then function $sparql()$ is applied respectively to $T' = \textbf{SelectRows}(T_1, E')$ and $T' = \textbf{AddColumn}(T_1, x, E')$, thus ignoring the rest of the expression in the computation. It suffices to move the focus upward in the AST in order to recover the complete computation.

Filterings and bindings are introduced in the AST by putting the focus on a column, and by applying a function or operator, this initiates the building of an expression. The choice between **SelectRows** and **AddColumn** is based on the type of the whole expression under the assumption that Boolean expressions are primarily used to select rows. However, another transformation allows to force the choice of **AddColumn** to allow a column of Boolean values. Finally, there is a transformation to give a user-defined name $name(x)$ to the new column, which can be used in the verbalization. For instance, starting from the primitive table $T0$ defined in Sect. 3.1, use case (E) can be built through the following sequence of transformations and ASTs:

(0-3) ...   : $T = T0$ (see Section 3.1)
   (4) focus on x_2 (population):
   (5) apply operator /   : $T = \textbf{AddColumn}(T0, x_4, x_2 \text{ / } \underline{??})$
   (6) insert column x_3 (area) : $T = \textbf{AddColumn}(T0, x_4, \underline{x_2 \text{ / } x_3})$
   (7) name column x_4 as 'population density':

The resulting table AST can be translated to SPARQL:
`?x1 a :Country. ?x1 :population ?x2. ?x1 :area ?x3. BIND (?x2/?x3 AS ?x4)`
and to English:
`'give me every country that has a population and that has an area, and give me the population density = the population/the area'.`

3.3 Aggregations

We call a *basic aggregation* the application of an aggregation operator on a set of entities or values, resulting in a single value. Use case (A1): *How many countries are there in Europe?*. A *simple aggregation* consists in making groups out of a set of values according to one or several criteria, and then applying an aggregation operator on each group of values. A *multiple aggregation* extends simple aggregation by having several aggregated values for each group. Use case (A2): *Give me the average population and the average area of countries, for each continent.* An aggregation corresponds to an OLAP view, where the grouping criteria are its *dimensions*, and where the aggregated values are its *measures*. In SPARQL, aggregations rely on the use of aggregation operators in the SELECT clause, and on GROUP BY clauses. We introduce a new construct for table ASTs that cover all those aggregations.

Definition 5 (aggregations). *Let T_1 be a table AST, $X \subseteq C(T_1)$ be a set of columns (possibly empty), and $G = \{(g_j, y_j, z_j)\}_{j\in 1..m}$ be a set of triples (aggregation operator, column, column) s.t. for all $j \in 1..m$, $y_j \in C(T_1) \setminus X$ and $z_j \notin C(T_1)$. The table AST $T = Aggregate(T_1, X, G)$ represents the table obtained by grouping rows in T_1 by columns X, and for each $(g_j, y_j, z_j) \in G$, by binding z_j to the application of g_j to the multiset of values of y_j in each group.*

- $C(T) = X \cup \{z_j\}_{j\in 1.m}$
- $R(T) = \{r_X \cup \{z_j \mapsto g_j(V_j)\}_{j\in 1..m} \mid r_X \in \pi_X R(T_1),$ for each $(g_j, y_j, z_j) \in G,$
$$V_j = \{\{r(y_j) \mid r \in R(T_1), \pi_X r = r_X\}\} \}$$
- $sparql(T) = \{$ SELECT $?x_1 \ldots ?x_n$ $(g_1(?y_1)$ AS $?z_1) \ldots (g_m(?y_m)$ AS $?z_m)$
            WHERE $\{$ $sparql(T_1)$ $\}$ GROUP BY $?x_1 \ldots ?x_n$ $\}$
- $nl(T) = $ '$nl(T_1)$ and [for ... each $nl(x_i), \ldots$] give me ... $nl(z_j) \ldots$'

In $C(T)$, the y-columns disappear and are replaced by the aggregated z-columns. In the definition of $R(T)$, the notation $\{\{...\}\}$ is for multisets (a.k.a. bags), and the distinction with sets is important for aggregators such as AVG or SUM. Because other table constructs generate a SPARQL graph pattern, we here use a subquery in the definition of $sparql(T)$ to allow the free combinations of different kinds of computations (see Sect. 3.4 for examples). If the focus is in T_1 then both $R()$ and $sparql()$ are applied to T_1 instead of T, hence ignoring the aggregation. In this way, the columns that are hidden by the aggregation ($C(T_1)\setminus X$) can be temporarily accessed by moving the focus in T_1. The verbalization of each aggregated column z_j is the verbalization of $g_j(y_j)$: e.g., 'the number of $nl(y_j)$', 'the average $nl(y_j)$'. The brackets around 'for each...' indicate an optional part, in the case where $X = \emptyset$.

Similarly to bindings and filters, an aggregation is introduced in the AST by moving the focus on a column, and by applying an aggregation operator. Then, other columns can be selected, either as grouping criteria or as an additional aggregated column. Type constraints are also used here to restrict which aggregator can be applied to which column. Here is the sequence of transformations that leads to use case (A2) from primitive table $T0$:

(0-4) ...   : $T = T0$ (see Section 3.1)
(5) property :continent   : $T = T1 = \mathbf{GetAnswers}(\ldots, \mathbf{Has}(:continent, \ldots))$
(6) move focus on x_2 (population)
(7) apply aggregation AVG : $T = \mathbf{Aggregate}(T1, \{\}, \{(AVG, x_2, x_5)\})$
(8) group by x_4 (continent): $T = \mathbf{Aggregate}(T1, \{x_4\}, \{(AVG, x_2, x_5)\})$
(9) apply AVG on x_3 (area) : $T = \mathbf{Aggregate}(T1, \{x_4\}, \{(AVG, x_2, x_5), (AVG, x_3, x_6)\})$

Different sequences are possible, elements can be introduced in almost any order, and it is also possible to remove query parts. For example, in (A2), it is possible to first build the query without column x_4 in $T1$ (continent), and without grouping by x_4. This computes the average population and area over all countries. Then the focus can be moved back in $T1$ on x_1 (country), insert property :continent to add column x_4 in $T1$, and finally move the focus back on the aggregation to group by continent. The resulting AST for (A2) can be translated to SPARQL:

```
{ SELECT ?x4 (AVG(?x2) AS ?x5) (AVG(?x3) AS ?x6)
    WHERE { ?x1 a :Country. ?x1 :population ?x2.
            ?x1 :area ?x3. ?x1 :continent ?x4. }
  GROUP BY ?x4 }
```

and to English:

```
'give me every country
    that has a population and that has an area and that has a continent
and for each continent,
    give me the average population and the average area'
```

3.4   Combinatorics of Table Constructs

The real power of our approach lies in the combinatorics of the above table constructs (**GetAnswers, SelectRows, AddColumn, Aggregate**), which can be chained arbitrarily to build more and more sophisticated tables. We illustrate this with three new use cases.

Aggregation of Bindings. Use case (C1): *What is the average GDP per capita, for each continent?*. This use case requires to retrieve information about countries, the GDP per capita as (total GDP $\times 10^6$/ population) for each country, and to average the GDP per capita over each continent. The query can be built in 11 steps, producing 3 nested table constructs.

Comparison of Aggregations. Use case (C2): *Which continents have an average agricultural GDP greater than their average service GDP?*. This use case requires to retrieve information about countries, to compute two aggregations for the same grouping (multiple aggregation), and then to express an inequality between the two aggregations (filtering). It can be built in 9 steps, and a nesting of 3 table constructs.

Nested Aggregations. Use case (C3): *Give me for every number of islands in an archipelago, the number of archipelagos having that number of islands*. This use case requires to retrieve islands and their archipelagos, to compute the number of islands per archipelago (simple aggregation), and then to compute for each number of islands, the respective number of archipelagos (simple aggregation). The query can be built in 6 steps, and 3 nested table constructs.

3.5   Implementation

We have fully implemented our approach into Sparklis. Its previous version covered all simple graph patterns, and therefore provided everything needed for the building of our primitive tables. Thanks to the genericity of N<A>F, no change was required in the user interface. The impact of our approach appears to users only through a richer query language, and additional suggestions. This makes it easy for users to transit to the new version. On the implementation side, however, a major refactoring of the intermediate language was necessary with the introduction of the new kinds of ASTs for tables and expressions in addition to simple graph patterns. Entirely new components were also introduced, e.g., type inference and type checking for computing some of the new suggestions.

4   Evaluation

We conducted two evaluations. The first evaluates expressivity and responsiveness from our participation to the QALD-6 challenge. The second evaluates usability with a user study comparing Sparklis to a SPARQL editor.

4.1   Evaluation on the QALD-6 Challenge

The QALD-6 challenge (Question Answering over Linked Data) introduced a new task on "Statistical question answering over RDF datacubes" [16]. The dataset contains about 4 million transactions on government spendings all over the world, organized into 50 datacubes. There are about 16M triples in total. Note that, although this dataset is represented as a set of datacubes, we answered the challenge questions by building primitive tables from graph patterns, like we would do for any other RDF dataset. We officially took part in the challenge and submitted the answers that we obtained from Sparklis by building queries.

Expressivity. We evaluated expressivity by measuring the coverage of QALD-6 questions. Out of 150 questions (training+test), 148 questions are basic or simple aggregations, and are therefore covered by our approach; and 2 questions (training Q23 and test Q23) are comparisons of two aggregations, and are not covered by our approach. The reason is that the two aggregations use disconnected graph patterns, whereas our approach is limited to a single connected graph pattern. In the challenge, we managed to answer 49/50 test questions, out of which 47 were correct, hence a success rate of 94% (official measure: $F_1 = 0.95$). The two errors come from an ambiguity in questions Q35 and Q42, which admit several equally plausible answers (URIs with the same label).

Responsiveness. We evaluated responsiveness by measuring the time needed to build queries in our implementation by a user mastering its user interface (the author of this paper). The measures include user interactions and are therefore an upper bound on the system runtime. The query building time ranged from 31 s to 6 min 20 s, and half of the queries were built in less than 1 min 30 s (median time). Most QALD-6 questions need 5–10 steps to build the query. It shows that our implementation is responsive enough to satisfy real information needs on large datasets.

4.2   Comparison with Writing SPARQL Queries in Yasgui

Methodology. The objective of this user study is to evaluate the benefits of our approach compared to writing SPARQL queries directly. The subjects were 12 pairs of post-graduate students in Computer Science applied to Business Management. They all recently attended a Semantic Web course with about 10 h of teaching and practice of SPARQL. Their task was to answer two similar series of 10 questions on the MONDIAL dataset, covering all kinds of SPARQL computations. The subjects had to use a different system for each series of questions: Yasgui [14], a SPARQL query editor improved with syntax highlighting, and our Sparklis-based implementation. The subjects had only a short presentation of Sparklis before, and no practice of it. Each subject was randomly assigned an order (Yasgui first vs Sparklis first) to avoid bias. For each system/series, they were given 10 min for setup, and 45 min for question answering. To help the writing of SPARQL queries, they were given the list of classes and properties used in MONDIAL. Finally, the subjects filled in a questionnaire to report their feelings and comments.

Objective Results. With Yasgui, only the first question was correctly answered by the majority, instead of 5 questions (out of 10) for Sparklis. On average, the number of subjects who correctly answered a question was 3.8 times higher for Sparklis compared to writing SPARQL queries. With Yasgui, the subjects managed to produce answers for 1–3 questions, 1.67 on average. The rate of correct answers is 71%. The best subject answered 3 questions, all correctly, and with an average of 15 min per question. In comparison, with Sparklis, the subjects managed to produce answers for 3–10 questions, 6.17 on average. This is 3.7 more questions, and the weakest result for Sparklis is equal to the strongest result for Yasgui. The rate of correct answers is also higher at 85%. Most errors (8/13) were done by only two subjects out of 12. The most common error is the omission of groupings in aggregations, suggesting to make them more visible in the user interface. The best subject answered 10 questions, 8 of which correct, and with an average of 4.5 min per question. The time spent per question is generally higher for the first 2 questions, and generally stays under 10 min for the other questions, although they are more complex, and can be as low as 2–3. Those results demonstrate that, even with practice of SPARQL query writing and no practice of Sparklis, subjects quickly learn to use Sparklis, and are much more effective with it. The weakest subject on Sparklis is still as good as the strongest subject on Yasgui. Moreover, all subjects had better results with Sparklis than with Yasgui.

Subjective Results. Over the 12 subjects, 9 *clearly prefer Sparklis* and 3 *would rather use Sparklis*, hence unanimous preference for Sparklis. On a 0–10 scale, Yasgui got marks between 2 and 8, 4.8 on average, and Sparklis got marks between 7 and 10, 8.3 on average (half of the subjects gave 9–10 marks).

5 Conclusion

We have shown how SPARQL 1.1 can be leveraged to offer rich data analytics on vanilla RDF graphs through a guided query builder user interface. We have implemented the approach in Sparklis, and validated its expressivity, responsiveness, and usability through the QALD-6 challenge and a user study. The extended Sparklis has been officially adopted as a query tool by Persée[2], a French organization that provides open access to more than 600,000 scientific publications to researchers in humanities and social sciences.

References

1. Atzori, M., Mazzeo, G., Zaniolo, C.: QA^3: a natural language approach to statistical question answering (2016). http://www.semantic-web-journal.net/system/files/swj1847.pdf. Submitted to the Semantic Web Journal
2. Chaudhuri, S., Dayal, U.: An overview of data warehousing and OLAP technology. ACM SIGMOD Rec. **26**(1), 65–74 (1997)
3. Colazzo, D., Goasdoué, F., Manolescu, I., Roatiş, A.: RDF analytics: lenses over semantic graphs. In: International Conference on World Wide Web, pp. 467–478. ACM (2014)
4. Cyganiak, R., Reynolds, D., Tennison, J.: The RDF data cube vocabulary (2013)
5. Ferré, S.: Bridging the gap between formal languages and natural languages with zippers. In: Sack, H., Blomqvist, E., d'Aquin, M., Ghidini, C., Ponzetto, S.P., Lange, C. (eds.) ESWC 2016. LNCS, vol. 9678, pp. 269–284. Springer, Cham (2016). https://doi.org/10.1007/978-3-319-34129-3_17
6. Ferré, S.: Semantic authoring of ontologies by exploration and elimination of possible worlds. In: Blomqvist, E., Ciancarini, P., Poggi, F., Vitali, F. (eds.) EKAW 2016. LNCS (LNAI), vol. 10024, pp. 180–195. Springer, Cham (2016). https://doi.org/10.1007/978-3-319-49004-5_12
7. Ferré, S.: Sparklis: an expressive query builder for SPARQL endpoints with guidance in natural language. Semant. Web Interoperability Usability Applicability **8**(3), 405–418 (2017). http://www.irisa.fr/LIS/ferre/sparklis/
8. Hermann, A., Ferré, S., Ducassé, M.: An interactive guidance process supporting consistent updates of RDFS graphs. In: ten Teije, A., et al. (eds.) EKAW 2012. LNCS (LNAI), vol. 7603, pp. 185–199. Springer, Heidelberg (2012). https://doi.org/10.1007/978-3-642-33876-2_18
9. Höffner, K., Lehmann, J., Usbeck, R.: CubeQA—question answering on RDF data cubes. In: Groth, P., et al. (eds.) ISWC 2016. LNCS, vol. 9981, pp. 325–340. Springer, Cham (2016). https://doi.org/10.1007/978-3-319-46523-4_20
10. Kaminski, M., Kostylev, E.V., Cuenca Grau, B.: Semantics and expressive power of subqueries and aggregates in SPARQL 1.1. In: International Conference World Wide Web, pp. 227–238. ACM (2016)
11. Kovacic, I., Schuetz, C.G., Schausberger, S., Sumereder, R., Schrefl, M.: Guided query composition with semantic OLAP patterns. In: EDBT/ICDT Workshops, pp. 67–74 (2018)
12. May, W.: Information extraction and integration with Florid: the Mondial case study. Technical report 131, Universität Freiburg, Institut für Informatik (1999). http://dbis.informatik.uni-goettingen.de/Mondial
13. Papadaki, M.-E., Tzitzikas, Y., Spyratos, N.: Analytics over RDF graphs. In: Flouris, G., Laurent, D., Plexousakis, D., Spyratos, N., Tanaka, Y. (eds.) ISIP 2019. CCIS, vol. 1197, pp. 37–52. Springer, Cham (2020). https://doi.org/10.1007/978-3-030-44900-1_3

---

14. Rietveld, L., Hoekstra, R.: YASGUI: not just another SPARQL client. In: Cimiano, P., Fernández, M., Lopez, V., Schlobach, S., Völker, J. (eds.) ESWC 2013. LNCS, vol. 7955, pp. 78–86. Springer, Heidelberg (2013). https://doi.org/10.1007/978-3-642-41242-4_7

15. Sherkhonov, E., Cuenca Grau, B., Kharlamov, E., Kostylev, E.V.: Semantic faceted search with aggregation and recursion. In: d'Amato, C., et al. (eds.) ISWC 2017. LNCS, vol. 10587, pp. 594–610. Springer, Cham (2017). https://doi.org/10.1007/978-3-319-68288-4_35

16. Unger, C., Ngomo, A.-C.N., Cabrio, E.: 6th open challenge on question answering over linked data (QALD-6). In: Sack, H., Dietze, S., Tordai, A., Lange, C. (eds.) SemWebEval 2016. CCIS, vol. 641, pp. 171–177. Springer, Cham (2016). https://doi.org/10.1007/978-3-319-46565-4_13

Realization of a Natural Logic
in a Database System

Troels Andreasen[1(✉)], Henrik Bulskov[1], and Jørgen Fischer Nilsson[2]

[1] Computer Science, Roskilde University, Roskilde, Denmark
{troels,bulskov}@ruc.dk
[2] Mathematics and Computer Science, Technical University of Denmark,
Lyngby, Denmark
jfni@dtu.dk

Abstract. Natural logics are formal logics whose sentences resemble simplified natural language. As such they are suitable for knowledge bases. The offered logical proof rules apply directly to the natural logic sentences, ensuring explainability of query inferences. We describe a natural logic, NATURALOG, suited for ontology-structured knowledge bases, and explain how it can be implemented in a database system for conducting deductive querying.

Keywords: Natural logics · Deductive querying · Explainability

1 Introduction

In a number of papers we have advanced a form of natural logic, termed NATURALOG, suited for qualitative domain modelling and deductive querying of logic-based knowledge bases. The key ideas of this natural logic are to provide a formal logic with knowledge bases coming close to formulations within a fragment of natural language. Furthermore, the natural logic enables versatile query facilities by means of computational deductive inference. These concerns are to facilitate, if not ensure, a high degree of explainability of computed results from a knowledge base.

The basic ideas of the considered form of natural logic was put forward in [9] and consolidated in [4]. The recent [5] offers a comprehensive account of the proposed syntax, the semantics of NATURALOG and the devised inference rules. In [6] we describe a proposal for realizing NATURALOG as a data base application. In a forthcoming paper we focus on the relation to natural language formulations. These various papers contain references to the literature concerning natural logic. Some important key references to natural logic are [8,11,13,14].

In this paper we aim at an easily accessible survey with discussion of the applied ideas and principles, while we refer to the above-mentioned papers for technicalities and further details. The proposed systems design exploits the sophisticated retrieval algorithms and mechanism for efficiently combining data

T. Andreasen et al. (Eds.): FQAS 2021, LNAI 12871, pp. 54–66, 2021.
https://doi.org/10.1007/978-3-030-86967-0_5

by bulk processing in equi-joins in contemporary relational database systems. Thereby we envisage realisation of large knowledge bases, e.g. in the life science domain, for provision of deductive query facilities on top of database systems.

2   The Natural Logic NATURALOG

A NATURALOG knowledge base simply consists of a unordered set of NATU-RALOG sentences. Let us begin considering a couple of sample NATURALOG sentences

> every betacell produce insulin
> insulin isa hormone

These sentences instantiate and display – simplified for the moment – the general form of NATURALOG sentences as being rather straightforwardly

> *Det Cterm Relation Det Cterm*

where *Det* is one of the determiners every and some. In case of every, the front determiner is optional, so we can write betacell produce insulin. The second determiner can also be omitted in case of some. So the full form of the second sample sentence is every insulin isa some hormone, which is to be understood as 'every amount of insulin is (also) some amount of hormone', thereby stating that the class of insulin is a subclass of the class of hormones. *Cterm* stands for class term and is in the simplest case a common noun. More generally it is a nominal phrase consisting of a common noun with restrictive attributions, for instance in the form of relative clauses or prepositional phrases. Therefore we also call *Cterm* a concept term. *Relation* is represented by a linguistically transitive verb, optionally attributed with adverbial restrictions.

This sentence form directly reflects the common and basic form of natural language declarative sentences as being *subject verb object*. Accordingly, in the two sample sentences the subject and object consists of a optional determiner followed by a common noun, and the relation is signified by a transitive verb.

The morphological flaw in the first sentence, witness 'produce/produces', and the use of 'isa' for 'is' in the second one remind that the sentences belong to a formal logic, although they look like and can be read as natural language sentences.

2.1   Data Base Representation

Since we are here heading for the realization in a database system, one may trivially propose the following tuple representations in a database relation:

> kb(every, betacell, produce, insulin)
> kb(every, insulin, isa, hormone)

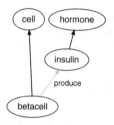

Fig. 1. Knowledge base with propositions given in Sect. 2.1

This representation affords simple computational querying as achievable by introduction of variables for the sentence components representing an interrogative sentence posited to the knowledge base, as in

X produce insulin

reminiscent of querying in logic programming. Now, suppose that we ask for types of cells that produce hormone with

X produce hormone

However, in the simplistic understanding with logic programming the answer is empty. By contrast, the common sense answer with the two sample sentences is obviously 'betacell' as instantiation of the variable X.

The desired effect calls for introduction of logical inference rules that would deduce the derived sentence kb(every, betacell, produce, hormone), from which the answer is then readily obtainable. This deduction applies a so-called monotonicity rule in natural logic. It is a key point here that the computational inference is taken place directly on the natural language sentences rather than on the predicate logical construal described in Sect. 2.3.

As another key point to mention, there is no notion of "back-ground information" in the knowledge base. All the available knowledge is to be represented as NATURALOG sentences on equal terms. One notices that we don't need any information about what 'betacell' and 'insulin' etc. "really is": The applied sample deduction is topic independent and purely logical. As a matter of fact, in order to make clear that 'betacell' is indeed a cell, we should add the sentence

betacell isa cell.

Let us forward the remark that in Sect. 2.7 we introduce more complex NATURALOG sentence forms possessing a recursive phrase structure.

2.2   Graph Representation

In our above-mentioned papers we devise a graph visualization for the NATURALOG sentences in a knowledge base such as Fig. 1 showing the concept graph for the three sample NATURALOG sentences above. Notice that in the graph notation unlabelled arrows represent isa by convention.

A knowledge base forms one, usually coherent, graph, where a given concept term is represented by a single node being shared by diverse sentences throughout the knowledge base, as in Fig. 3. Thus, the concept graph shows how the knowledge base sentences are interrelated. The directed edges representing the relations are equipped with quantifier symbols with the mentioned default conventions for omitting the symbols in the common cases.

Every directed edge comes with a dual directed edge in the opposite direction due to the mathematical existence of inverse relations, though often omitted in graph figures. For instance the sentence betacell isa cell comes with its dual some cell isa betacell. See further Sect. 2.6.

The graph form is also helpful for illustrating the functioning of the inference rule as demonstrated with many figures in [5,6].

These concept graphs appear as generalized ontologies, where the isa relationships make up the ontology proper, which is adorned with the remainder relationships recorded in the knowledge base.

2.3 Predicate-Logical Construal of NATURALOG

As explained in [5,6] NATURALOG can be reconstructed in predicate logic. As an example, the NATURALOG sentence every betacell produce some insulin in predicate logic becomes what we call a $\forall\exists$ form due to the order of the quantifiers, cf. [10]:

$$\forall x(\mathsf{betacell}(x) \rightarrow \exists y(\mathsf{insulin}(y) \wedge \mathsf{produce}(x,y)))$$

However, it is important to observe that we do not translate NATURALOG sentences to predicate logic in order to compute inferences. According to the doctrines of natural logic the computational reasoning is conducted directly at the surface forms, and in NATURALOG in particular by embedding in a metalogic. The metalogic is next realized as a database application.

2.4 Inference in NATURALOG

We have already exemplified the computational representation of NATURALOG sentences as logical facts with an auxiliary predicate kb reflecting the database tuple representation in Sect. 2.1. At the explanatory level for the database realization we use DATALOG as metalogic. The inferred NATURALOG sentences are kept in a predicate p:

$$p(Q, C, R, D) \leftarrow kb(Q, C, R, D)$$

We refer to [4–6] for a presentation of the applied inference rules. Here we just mention a monotonicity rule used in Sect. 2.1.

$$p(Q, C, R, Dsup) \leftarrow p(Q, C, R, D) \wedge p(\mathsf{every}, D, \mathsf{isa}, Dsup)$$

and a weakening rule

$$p(some, C, R, D) \leftarrow kb(every, C, R, D)$$

The latter rule relies throughout on the adopted principle of existential import according to which all concept terms appearing in some sentence in the knowledge base are assumed to denote a non-empty set of individuals, cf. e.g. [5, 9, 10].

In the present version of NATURALOG affirmative sentences, only, are admitted in the knowledge base, no negative ones. This is because we appeal to negation as non-provability with the closed world assumption (CWA) as known from logic programming and database query languages.

2.5   The Distinguished Class Inclusion Relation and Ontologies

As mentioned, there is the distinguished, well-known and important class-class relation, isa, with [every] C isa D, stating that C is a subclass of D.

In predicate logic this yields $\forall x(C(x) \to D(x))$ from the $\forall \exists$ form $\forall x(C(x) \to \exists y(D(y) \wedge x = y))$, cf. [5, 9]. The isa relation forms a partial order with accompanying inference rules used for building formal ontologies.

The sentence form some C isa D is omitted in NATURALOG for explicit inclusion in a knowledge base. However, it emerges as a derived sentence as explained in the next section. The declaration of a non-empty overlap of C and D intended by this sentence form we prefer to express by stating [every] CD isa C together with [every] CD isa D, introducing a freely named intersection class CD. This is because we subscribe to a doctrine that all introduced classes be named. The intention is to prevent introduction of unnamed overlapping concepts that would obscure query answering.

2.6   Inverse Relationships and Active-Passive Voice

One notices that from a sentence every C R D by the omnipresent existential import follows logically the sentence some D R^{inv} C. Here R^{inv} is the inverse relations of R, bound to exist and coming about by swapping of its two arguments.

In natural language this conforms with active to passive voice switching, so that the $\forall \exists$ form in every betacell produce insulin is accompanied by the NATURALOG $\exists \exists$ sentence some insulin is produced by betacell, endorsed by the NATURALOG syntax specification given in [5]. In the graph picture every $\forall \exists$ or $\exists \exists$ arc comes with a derived opposite directed $\exists \exists$ arc due to the inference rule

$$p(some, D, Rinv, C) \leftarrow p(Q, C, R, D) \wedge inverse(R, Rinv)$$

This infered dual proposition holds due to the principle of existential import, which assumes non-empty concepts as mentioned in Sect. 2.4.

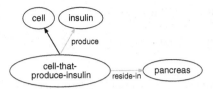

Fig. 2. Compound concept from [5]

2.7 Compound Concepts

So far the concept terms in NATURALOG sentences simply have been common nouns. However, NATURALOG further features recursively structured compound terms consisting of a core common noun with attributed restrictions in the form of restrictive relative clauses and prepositional phrases.

As an example, we have the compound concept cell that produce insulin in, say, cell that produce insulin reside in pancreas. The NATURALOG approach to compound terms is to decompose these internally into ∀∃ sentences that refer to an auxiliary new concept, cell-that-produce-insulin, representing the compound concept. The definition of the new auxiliary concept is introduced to the knowledge base by the pair of sentences

cell-that-produce-insulin isa cell
cell-that-produce-insulin produce insulin

with the original sentence being replaced by

cell-that-produce-insulin reside in pancreas.

The resulting graph is shown in Fig. 2. The introduced concept term is defined by the above pair of defining sentences. The defined compound concept cell-that-produce-insulin becomes a proxy, non-compound individual constant in DATA-LOG. There is a snag, though: This decomposition mechanism calls for a subsumption procedure that makes the newly generated proxy concept subsume all concepts in the entire knowledge base that are subsumed by the considered compound concept cf. [5,6]. This is in order to obtain definitional contributions functioning as "if-and-only-if". For the definition in the example in Fig. 2 the corresponding predicate logical expression would be:

$$\forall x (\text{cell-that-produce-insulin}(x) \leftrightarrow \text{cell}(x) \land \exists y (\text{produce}(x, y) \land \text{insulin}(y))).$$

The treatment of compound phrases such as noun-noun compounds and adjectival restrictions are projected along the same line, but calls for more elaborate semantical procedures as touched in Sect. 2.8.

The verb in a sentence may also be subjected to restrictive attributions: In [5] we devise a method for handling adverbial prepositional phrases by introduction of a metalogical predicate that relate verbs with their nominalized counterpart common noun.

2.8 Inference Rules and Deduction

We distinguish between logical rules and extra-logical rules. Let us first list the logical rules.

1. Ordinary logical inference rules enable computation of logical consequences. We have seen an example for active to passive voice conversion in Sect. 2.6.
2. Subsumption rules are motivated in Sect. 2.7.
3. Materialization rules generate new concept terms bound to be nonempty, and relate these properly to existing terms with appropriate sentences. They are to ensure that all concept terms that potentially candidate for participation in a query answer are made present, being "materialized" as it were, in knowledge base sentences as detailed in [5, 6], cf. also Sect. 3.

The following open-ended list of extra-logical rules is intended to be known and under control of the domain expert building and applying the knowledge base.

1. Common sense rules are for instance rules that endow selected relations expressed by linguistically transitive verbs with special properties. As an example one may choose to make the relation 'cause' logically transitive.
2. Application of specific rules introduce *ad hoc* properties. As an example one might posit that properties of cells expressed by the verb 'produce' are "exherited" upwards, as it were, to organs to which the cell belongs.
3. Linguistic rules are rules that serve to decode certain compound concept terms such as noun-noun compounds, which call for abduction of the unstated relation between the two nouns. Given the abduced relation, the restriction on the head noun then logically resembles restrictive relative clauses. For instance 'lung disease' by rule application thereby may be resolved as disease that is located in lung.

2.9 Deductive Querying of NATURALOG Knowledge Bases

As already hinted at in the introduction, query sentences are obtained by replacing a term in a NATURALOG sentence with a variable. Query answer terms are then computed as those term instantiations of the variables that make the instantiated sentence follow from the knowledge base using the inference rules. This is reminiscent of answer computation in logic programming, though algorithmically to be obtained in quite another way as explained in Sect. 3 below.

The deduced set of answer sentences diverge somewhat from those prescribed by the standard notion of logical consequence, since extra-logical rules of Sect. 2.8 beside the strict logical inference rules may be engaged.

The encoding of NATURALOG sentences into the database representation opens for establishment of versatile query- and constraint checking functionalities. In the following section we explain how these functionalities can be realized through database querying.

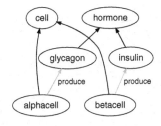

Fig. 3. Knowledge base with given propositions

3   Realization of NATURALOG in Databases

In Sect. 2.4 we explained how NATURALOG sentences can readily be represented as logical atomic facts by their encoding in DATALOG. Moreover, we explained how inference rules can be expressed as definite DATALOG clauses extended with negation-by-nonprovability.

It is well-known that DATALOG clauses in turn can be realized by the relational database operations of projection, selection, equi-join and difference, see for instance [1]. These operations are also indirectly available in contemporary database query languages. Therefore, the various NATURALOG inference rules, some of which shown above, can be implemented using standard database query expressions.

Rather than relying on a query evaluation involving reasoning through a top-down goal directed computation as suggested by DATALOG, in [6] we propose and describe an implementation model where the closure corresponding to the inference rules is calculated in a pre-processing stage. As exemplified below (see Figs. 3 and 4), the knowledge base is extended through iterative bottom-up processing with inferable tuples (nodes and edges). Thus in the trade-off between computation and memory we consume memory for re-computation.

3.1   Encoding of Natural Logic in Database Relations

The NATURALOG sentences are, as indicated above, to be represented in a database relation kb forming the knowledge base. The knowledge base shown in Fig. 3, adding a few concepts to that of Fig. 1, can be represented by the following tuples:

kb(every, alphacell, isa, cell),   kb(every, alphacell, produce, glucagon),
kb(every, betacell, isa, cell),   kb(every, betacell, produce, insulin),
kb(every, glucagon, isa, hormone), kb(every, insulin, isa, hormone)

The pre-processing of the knowledge base iteratively builds the closure regarding the inference rules. New tuples, that can be inferred by the rules taking the present tuples into consideration, are added. A first iteration of the knowledge base from Fig. 3 would add tuples such as:

kb(every, alphacell, isa, cell-that-produce-glucagon),
kb(every, alphacell, produce, hormone), ...

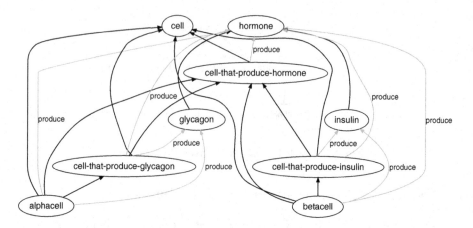

Fig. 4. Closure of the knowledge base shown in Fig. 3 (dual propositions omitted) from [6]

In Fig. 4 the closure of the graph from Fig. 3 is shown. In this simple example only the monotonicity, materialization and dual proposition rules contribute with new edges (the latter not shown). In this case three iterations was needed to provide the closure and the materialized node cell-that-produce-hormone subsuming the materialized compounds cell-that-produce-glucagon and cell-that-produce-insulin was introduced in the last iteration. The dual proposition rule would introduce inversions of all edges such as:

    kb(some, glucagon, produced_by, alphacell),
    kb(some, hormone, isa, insulin)

as also shown in Fig. 5.

3.2   Query Processing of a Sample Knowledge Base

Below we introduce different types of queries and describe how these can be evaluated by accessing the kb relation. The attributes of kb are QUANT, SUB, REL, OBJ representing the quantifier, subject, relation and object terms. The idea is that query computation then reduces to mere selection without appeal to rules.

Concept Querying

A basic query form is an open proposition with one or more free query variables. To pose a query as "what produce insulin" the following parameterized NATURALOG sentence can be used:

    X produce insulin

For the knowledge base shown in Fig. 4 this query would yield {betacell, cell-that-produce-insulin} as possible instantiations for the variable X. The query X produce hormone would lead to the answer {alphacell, cell-that-produce-glucagon, betacell, cell-that-produce-insulin, cell-that-produce-hormone}, while the query betacell produce Y would yield the answer {insulin, hormone}. Obviously also queries involving compound logical expressions are supported. An example of a conjunctive concept query is:

X produce glucagon AND X produce insulin

This query would yield {cell-that-produce-hormone} as the only possible instantiation for the variable X. Using a variable in the position of the relation provides similarily possible instantiations of the relation. For instance, the query betacell R hormone yields {produce}, while X R hormone leads to the answer {(glucagon, isa), (cell-that-produce-hormone, produce), (cell-that-produce-glucagon, produce), (cell-that-produce-insulin, produce), (insulin, isa), (alphacell, produce), (betacell, produce)}.

Expressions in SQL for such concept queries with one or more free variables are straightforwardly derived from the proposition form. The first and the last of the queries mentioned above can be expressed in SQL as follows.

```
SELECT sub FROM kb
 WHERE rel = 'produce' and obj = 'insulin';
```

```
SELECT sub, rel FROM kb
 WHERE obj = 'hormone';
```

In the query examples above we evaluate the default proposition form every $C\ R\ D$. As noticed, the indicated closures shown in Figs. 3 and 4 do not include propositions derived from the dual relationship rule that take the form some D $R^{-1}\ C$. This is to avoid cluttering and maintain readability, especially in the last of these figures. It should be emphasized that, due to the dual proposition rule, the relationships can always be read in two directions. The opposite of the given direction, however, should be read by the inverted relation, such as produce_by as dual to produce.

For instance the query X R insulin to the knowledge base in Fig. 4 would yield, explicating also the quantifier: {(every, betacell, produce), (some, hormone, isa)}. The SQL expression to retrieve this would simply be:

```
SELECT quant, sub, rel FROM kb
 WHERE obj = 'hormone';
```

In the same vein, consider the query X isa cell that produce insulin. The answer is to be obtained from the sentence betacell isa cell that produce insulin. However, this sentence is absent in the given knowledge base, but present in the closure, cf. Fig. 4, with the answer retrieved with:

```
SELECT sub FROM kb
 WHERE rel = 'isa' AND obj = 'cell-that-produce-insulin'
```

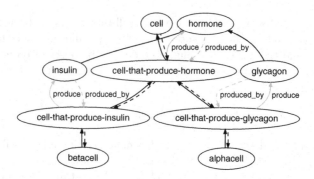

Fig. 5. A transitively reduced version of the knowledge base in Fig. 4 (dual propositions included)

Commonality Querying

With NATURALOG and especially with the graph view of the knowledge base comes various more sophisticated query forms that affords browsing at a conceptual level. One of these is commonality querying. The commonality for a pair of stated concepts C and D are the properties they have in common. Considering for instance alphacell and betacell in Fig. 4 the commonality would be {(produce, hormone), (isa, cell), (isa, cell-that-produce-hormone)}. This can be retrieved by the simple SQL expression:

```
SELECT rel, obj FROM kb
WHERE quant = 'every' AND sub = 'alphacell';
INTERSECT
SELECT obj FROM kb
WHERE quant = 'every' AND obj = 'betacell';
```

However, the most interesting contribution to the answer in this case would be the most specific part, that is, {(isa, cell-that-produce-hormone)}. This can also be expressed in SQL in a straightforward manner as shown in [6].

Pathway Querying

The entire knowledge base graph forms a road map between all the applied concepts. Background ontologies as well as introduction of a universal concept at the top of the ontology supports additional general and domain knowledge and ensure that all concepts are connected. This concept map can be queried by means of dedicated rules searching pathways in the graph between two stated concepts in the knowledge base. The pathway querying applies the given sentences supplemented with their duals, while other derived propositions can be ignored, if needed, to provide more intuitive answers. Obviously, the closure corresponding to the inference rules, as shown in Fig. 4, introduces transitive edges connecting concepts which do not contribute to interesting pathways. Accordingly, the pathway querying is to be done on a transitively reduced knowledge base with dual propositions included, as visualized in Fig. 5. Pathway querying is particularly relevant in life science applications with causal relations in connection, say, with partonomic- and inclusion relations.

As an example, consider pathway query for the concepts alphacell and hormone

path(alphacell, hormone)

and assume usage of some form of shortest path algorithm to find paths connecting these concepts in the knowledge base shown in Fig. 5. The pathways

(alphacell isa cell-that-produce-glucagon, cell-that-produce-glucagon produce glucagon, glucagon isa hormone),
(alphacell isa cell-that-produce-glucagon, cell-that-produce-glucagon isa cell-that-produce-hormone, cell-that-produce-hormone produce hormone)

would be in the result, while the query path(alphacell, betacell) would introduce dual propositions in order to find the pathways

(alphacell isa cell-that-produce-glucagon, cell-that-produce-glucagon isa cell-that-produce-hormone, some cell-that-produce-hormone isa cell-that-produce-insulin, some cell-that-produce-insulin isa betacell),
(alphacell isa cell-that-produce-glucagon, cell-that-produce-glucagon produce glucagon, glucagon isa hormone, some hormone isa insulin, some insulin produce_by cell-that-produce-insulin, some cell-that-produce-insulin isa betacell)

The small knowledge base in Fig. 5 only have the above pathways between alphacell and betacell, excluding cycles. But for larger graphs many paths will connect the concepts in question and simple shortest path would not be enough to select only interesting pathways. Further rules and heuristics can be taken into consideration, such as weighting of edges, depth in the graph, and path specificity, where the latter would be advanced least upper bounds differentiating between concepts and derived concepts.

4   Concluding Remarks

In our [5] we discuss the relationship to Sowa's conceptual graphs [12] and to description logics. A key difference to descriptions logics [7] is that we admit arbitrary transitive verbs pertaining to the application rather than just the subclass relationship between concepts. A theorem prover for a natural logic similar to NATURALOG is described in [2] and an online prototype is provided at [3]. In comparison, our NATURALOG setup is distinguished by offering deductive querying by means of parameterized sentences yielding concept terms as answers.

In conclusion we have outlined a natural logic system affording deductive querying of knowledge bases. The knowledge base sentences and query answers can be read and understood by the domain expert thereby promoting explainability. We have indicated how the natural logic system can be realized as database application, thereby taking advantage of the efficient retrieval and join algorithms of database systems. We are conducting experiments in order validate the viability of our proposed approach.

References

1. Abiteboul, S., Hull, R., Vianu, V.: Foundations of Databases: The Logical Level, 1st edn. Addison-Wesley Longman Publishing Co., Inc., New York (1995)
2. Abzianidze, L.: Langpro: natural language theorem prover. In: Conference on Empirical Methods in Natural Language Processing (2017)
3. Abzianidze, L.: LangPro: natural language theorem prover (2021). https://naturallogic.pro/LangPro/. Accessed 31 May 2021
4. Andreasen, T., Bulskov, H., Jensen, P.A., Nilsson, J.F.: Deductive querying of natural logic bases. In: Cuzzocrea, A., Greco, S., Larsen, H.L., Saccà, D., Andreasen, T., Christiansen, H. (eds.) FQAS 2019. LNCS (LNAI), vol. 11529, pp. 231–241. Springer, Cham (2019). https://doi.org/10.1007/978-3-030-27629-4_22
5. Andreasen, T., Bulskov, H., Jensen, P.A., Nilsson, J.F.: Natural logic knowledge bases and their graph form. Data Knowl. Eng. **129**, 101848 (2020)
6. Andreasen, T., Bulskov, H., Fischer Nilsson, J.: A natural logic system for large knowledge bases. In: Tropmann-Frick, M., Thalheim, B., Jaakkola, H., Kiyoki, Y., Yoshida, N. (eds.) Information Modelling and Knowledge Bases, vol. 333, pp. 119–133. IOS Press (2021). https://ebooks.iospress.nl/volumearticle/56439
7. Grosof, B.N., Horrocks, I., Volz, R., Decker, S.: Description logic programs: combining logic programs with description logic. In: Proceedings of the 12th International Conference on World Wide Web, WWW 2003, New York, NY, USA, pp. 48–57. ACM (2003)
8. Moss, L.S.: Syllogistic logics with verbs. J. Log. Comput. **20**(4), 947–967 (2010)
9. Nilsson, J.F.: In pursuit of natural logics for ontology-structured knowledge bases. In: The Seventh International Conference on Advanced Cognitive Technologies and Applications (2015)
10. Nilsson, J.F.: A cube of opposition for predicate logic. Logica Universalis **14**(1), 103–114 (2020)
11. Pratt-Hartmann, I., Moss, L.S.: Logics for the relational syllogistic. Rev. Symb. Logic **2**(4), 647–683 (2009)
12. Sowa, J.F.: Knowledge Representation: Logical, Philosophical and Computational Foundations. Brooks/Cole Publishing Co., Pacific Grove (2000)
13. van Benthem, J.: Natural logic, past and future. In: Workshop on Natural Logic, Proof Theory, and Computational Semantics (2011)
14. van Benthem, J.: Essays in logical semantics, Volume 29 of Studies in Linguistics and Philosophy. D. Reidel, Dordrecht (1986)

Generalized Weighted Repairs

Horacio Tellez Perez and Jef Wijsen[(✉)] [ID]

University of Mons, Mons, Belgium
{horacio.tellezperez,jef.wijsen}@umons.ac.be

Abstract. This paper deals with the problem of repairing inconsistent relational database instances in which facts are associated with nonnegative weights, representing their quality or trustfulness. Given a numeric aggregation function $\mathcal{G}$, weighted repairs (or $\mathcal{G}$-repairs) are defined as inclusion-maximal consistent subinstances with maximum aggregated value. The weighted repair notion extends existing repair notions, like subset- and cardinality-repairs. We study the complexity of repair-checking and some related problems, in a setting where database integrity constraints are represented by a hypergraph whose hyperedges correspond to constraint violations. In this setting, $\mathcal{G}$-repairs can be viewed as maximum-weight independent sets relative to the aggregation function $\mathcal{G}$.

Keywords: Conflict hypergraph · Consistent query answering · Database repairing · Maximum-weight independent set

1 Motivation

In today's era of "big data," database management systems have to cope more and more with dirty information that is inconsistent with respect to some integrity constraints. Such integrity constraints are commonly expressed in decidable fragments of some logic, for example, as dependencies [1] or ontologies in some Description Logic [4]. The term *repair* is commonly used to refer to a consistent database that is obtained from the inconsistent database by some minimal modifications. This notion was introduced twenty years ago in a seminal paper by Arenas et al. [3], and has been an active area of research ever since. In particular, the field of *Consistent Query Answering (CQA)* studies the question of how to answer database queries if multiple repairs are possible. Two surveys of this research are [6,18].

This paper's aim is to contribute to the research in *preferred repair semantics*, whose goal is to capture more of the meaning of the data into the repairing process. To this end, we introduce and study *weighted repairs*. We will assume that database tuples are associated with numerical weights such that tuples with higher weights are preferred over tuples with lower weights. Then, among all possible repairs, weighted repairs are those with a maximum aggregated value, according to some aggregation function. We will study the relationship between

© Springer Nature Switzerland AG 2021
T. Andreasen et al. (Eds.): FQAS 2021, LNAI 12871, pp. 67–81, 2021.
https://doi.org/10.1007/978-3-030-86967-0_6

the complexity of computing weighted repairs and certain properties of the aggregation function used.

The remainder of this section is an informal guided tour that introduces and motivates our research questions by means of a simple example. We start with a graph-theoretical view on database repairing.

A Graph-Theoretical Perspective on Database Repairing. Consider the following relational table $TEACHES$, in which a fact $TEACHES(p, c, s)$ means that professor p teaches the course c during semester s.

$TEACHES$	$Prof$	$Course$	Sem	
	Jeff	A	fall	(f_1)
	Jeff	B	fall	(f_2)
	Ed	C	spring	(s_1)
	Rob	C	spring	(s_2)
	Rob	D	spring	(s_3)

The integrity constraints are as follows: no professor teaches more than one course in a given semester, and no course is taught by more than one professor. In terms of functional dependencies, we have: $\{Prof, Sem\} \rightarrow \{Course\}$ and $\{Course\} \rightarrow \{Prof\}$. The relation $TEACHES$ violates these integrity constraints; its conflict graph is shown in Fig. 1. The vertices of the conflict graph are the facts in the relation $TEACHES$; two vertices are adjacent if together they violate some functional dependency.

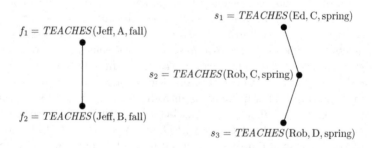

$s_1 = TEACHES(\text{Ed}, \text{C}, \text{spring})$

$f_1 = TEACHES(\text{Jeff}, \text{A}, \text{fall})$

$s_2 = TEACHES(\text{Rob}, \text{C}, \text{spring})$

$f_2 = TEACHES(\text{Jeff}, \text{B}, \text{fall})$

$s_3 = TEACHES(\text{Rob}, \text{D}, \text{spring})$

Fig. 1. Conflict graph for the running example.

Given a database instance, it is common to define a *subset-repair* as an inclusion-maximal subinstance that satisfies all integrity constraints. In terms of the conflict graph, every subset-repair is an *inclusion-maximal independent set (IMIS)*, and vice versa. Recall that in graph theory, a set of vertices is *independent* if no two vertices of it are adjacent. It can be verified that the graph of

Fig. 1 has four IMISs: every IMIS includes either $\{f_1\}$ or $\{f_2\}$, and includes either $\{s_1, s_3\}$ or $\{s_2\}$. The term *cardinality-repair* refers to independent sets of maximum cardinality. In our running example, the cardinality-repairs are $\{f_1, s_1, s_3\}$ and $\{f_2, s_1, s_3\}$.

Maximum-Weight Independent Set (MWIS). As in [16], we will assume from here on that every fact is associated with a nonnegative weight, where larger weights are better. In practice, such weights may occur in data integration, where facts coming from more authoritative data sources are tagged with higher weights. For example, in the next relational table, among the first two facts—which are conflicting—the second fact has a higher weight and is therefore considered better.

TEACHES	Prof	Course	Sem	w
	Jeff	A	fall	1
	Jeff	B	fall	2
	Ed	C	spring	1
	Rob	C	spring	2
	Rob	D	spring	1

It is now natural to take these weights into account, and define repairs as maximum-weight independent sets (MWIS) of the conflict graph. In graph theory, an MWIS is an independent set that maximizes the sum of the weights of its vertices. In our example, there are two MWISs, both having a total summed weight of 4:

T_1	Prof	Course	Sem	w
	Jeff	B	fall	2
	Rob	C	spring	2

and

T_2	Prof	Course	Sem	w
	Jeff	B	fall	2
	Ed	C	spring	1
	Rob	D	spring	1

.

Aggregation Functions Other Than SUM. The aggregation function SUM is cooked into the definition of MWIS: among all independent sets, an MWIS is one that maximizes the *summed* weight. From a conceptual perspective, it may be natural to use aggregation functions other than SUM. For example, among the two repairs T_1 and T_2 shown above, we may prefer T_1 because it maximizes the *average* weight. Indeed, the average weights for T_1 and T_2 are, respectively, $\frac{2+2}{2}$ and $\frac{2+1+1}{3}$. Alternatively, we may prefer T_1 because it maximizes the *minimum* weight. Therefore, to capture these alternatives, we will allow other functions than SUM in this paper, including AVG and MIN.

Computing Repairs. In data cleaning and database repairing, we are often interested in finding one or more repairs for a given database instance. Now that we have introduced weights and different aggregation functions, this boils down to the following task: given a database instance with weighted facts, return an inclusion-maximal consistent subinstance that maximizes the aggregated weight according to some fixed aggregation function. Alternatively, in graph-theoretical terms: given a vertex-weighted graph, return an inclusion-maximal independent set that maximizes the aggregated weight according to some fixed aggregation function. Since for aggregation functions other than SUM, maximality with respect to set inclusion and maximality with respect to aggregated weight may not go hand in hand, it should be made precise which criterion prevails:

- among all inclusion-maximal independent sets, return one that maximizes the aggregated weight; or
- among all independent sets that maximize the aggregated weight, return one that is inclusion-maximal.

To illustrate the difference, let $G = (V, E)$ with $V = \{a, b\}$ and $E = \emptyset$. Let $w(a) = 1$ and $w(b) = 2$, and let MIN be the aggregation function. The first task would return $\{a, b\}$, while the second task would return $\{b\}$. In this paper, we will study the latter task.

It is known that under standard complexity assumptions (in particular, $\mathbf{P} \neq \mathbf{NP}$), there is no polynomial-time algorithm that returns an MWIS for a given vertex-weighted graph. Therefore, when the aggregation function SUM is used, it is intractable to return a repair with a maximum summed weight. In this paper, we will ask whether this task can become tractable for other aggregation functions of practical interest. Contributions of this paper can be summarized as follows.

- We introduce $\mathcal{G}$-repairs, generalizing existing repair notions.
- By taking a conflict hypergraph perspective on database integrity, we show that $\mathcal{G}$-repairs are a generalization of maximum-weight independent sets.
- We adapt classical decision problems to our setting, and study their computational complexity. While these problems are intractable in general, we identify classes of aggregation functions that allow for polynomial-time algorithms.

The rest of this paper is organized as follows. Section 2 discusses related work. Section 3 introduces aggregation functions and defines the (conflict) hypergraph perspective for studying inconsistent databases. Section 4 defines the notion of $\mathcal{G}$-repair and the computational problems we are interested in. Section 5 shows computational complexity results for these problems, culminating in our main tractability theorem, Theorem 3. Section 6 shows that tractability is lost under a slight relaxation of the hypotheses of that theorem. Finally, Sect. 7 concludes the paper.

2   Related Work

In their seminal paper [3], Arenas et al. define repairs of an inconsistent database as those consistent databases that can be obtained by inserting and deleting minimal (with respect to set inclusion) sets of tuples. Since then, many variants of this earliest repair notion have been introduced, several of which are discussed in [5,9,18]. For any fixed repair notion, *repair checking* is the following problem: given an inconsistent database and a candidate repair, is the candidate a true repair (i.e., does it satisfy all constraints imposed by the repair notion under consideration)? Afrati and Kolaitis [2] made important contributions to our understanding of the complexity of repair checking. For databases containing numerical attributes, repairs have also been defined as solutions to numerical constraint problems [7,8,13].

The notion of *conflict hypergraph* was introduced in [10], and later extended in [17]. The relationship between repairs and inclusion-maximal independent sets was observed in [10, Proposition 3.1]. If database tuples are associated with nonnegative weights, then it is natural to generalize this relationship by viewing repairs as maximum-weight independent sets (MWIS). We cannot cite here the vast amount of literature studying the computational complexity and algorithms related to MWIS. In our approach, however, we do not primarily focus on the maximum *summed* weight, but also allow for aggregation functions other than SUM. The problems we study are specifically motivated by database applications in which several other aggregation functions are sensible. We will show that some problems that are **NP**-hard in general, become tractable for aggregation functions that have some desirable properties. Inspired by database theory, weight-based approaches to inconsistency have also been studied for knowledge bases in Description Logics [12].

3   Preliminaries

Aggregation Functions over Weighted Sets. Informally, aggregation functions take as input a set of elements, each associated with a weight, and return an aggregated weight for the entire set. Examples are SUM and MIN. In this work, all weights will be nonnegative rational numbers, which we interpret as quality scores where higher values are better. These notions are formalized next.

Definition 1 (Weighted set). *A* weighted set *is a pair (I, w) where I is a finite set and w is a total mapping from I to $\mathbb{Q}^+$ (i.e., the set of nonnegative rational numbers). We will often assume that the* weight *function w is implicitly understood. That is, whenever we say that I is a weighted set, we mean that (I, w) is a weighted set for a mapping w that is implicitly understood.*

Two weighted sets (I_1, w_1) and (I_2, w_2) are isomorphic *if there is a bijection $\pi : I_1 \to I_2$ such that for every $x \in I_1$, $w_1(x) = w_2(\pi(x))$. Informally, two weighted sets are isomorphic if the attained numeric values as well as their multiplicities coincide.*

Definition 2 (Aggregation function). *An* aggregation function $\mathcal{G}$ *is a function that maps every weighted set (I, w) to a nonnegative rational number, denoted $\mathcal{G}_{[w]}(I)$, such that:*

- $\mathcal{G}$ is closed under isomorphism, meaning that any two weighted sets that are isomorphic are mapped to the same value; and
- the empty weighted set is mapped to 0.

We write **AGG**^{poly} for the class of aggregation functions that are computable in polynomial time in $|I|$. Some well-known members of this class are denoted COUNT, SUM, MAX, MIN, and AVG, with their expected, natural semantics (not repeated here).

By measuring the complexity of an aggregation function $\mathcal{G}$ in terms of $|I|$, we do not take into account the size of the numeric values in the image of the mapping w. This complexity is appropriate for the applications we have in mind. The requirement that an aggregation function be closed under isomorphism is tantamount to saying that for a weighted set I, the value $\mathcal{G}_{[w]}(I)$ depends on, and only on, the multiset $\{\!\{w(x) \mid x \in I\}\!\}$. While it may be more common to define aggregation functions on multisets of numbers (see, e.g., [15, p. 159]), our Definition 2 is appropriate for the purposes we have in mind. Indeed, we will only apply aggregation on weighted sets formed by vertices of a vertex-weighted graph.

Conflict Hypergraphs. Conflict hypergraphs [10,11] generalize the conflict graphs introduced previously in Sect. 1. To detect violations of functional dependencies, it suffices to regard two tuples at a time. However, more involved constraints may consider three or more tuples at a time. For this reason, conflict graphs are generalized to conflict hypergraphs. Informally, a conflict hypergraph is a hypergraph whose vertices are the database facts; hyperedges are formed by grouping facts that together violate some integrity constraint.

Formally, a fact is an expression $R(c_1, \dots, c_n)$ where R is a relation name of arity n, and each c_i is a constant. A database is a finite set of facts. Let **db** be a database instance, and $\mathcal{C}$ be a set of integrity constraints. We will assume that $\mathcal{C}$ is satisfied by the empty database instance. The *(conflict) hypergraph* is defined as an hypergraph $H = (V, E)$ whose vertices are the facts of **db**; there is an hyperedge $e = \{R_1(\vec{c}_1), \dots, R_k(\vec{c}_k)\}$ if (and only if) the following properties hold:

1. the facts $R_1(\vec{c}_1), \dots, R_k(\vec{c}_k)$ taken together violate one or more integrity constraints of $\mathcal{C}$; and
2. every strict subset of e satisfies $\mathcal{C}$.

In other words, the hyperedges of H are the inclusion-minimal inconsistent subsets of **db**. Recall from graph theory that an *independent set* of a hypergraph $H = (V, E)$ is a set $I \subseteq V$ such that I includes no hyperedge of E. Then, by construction, the following expressions are equivalent for every database instance **db** and set $\mathcal{C}$ of integrity constraints:

- I is an independent set of the (conflict) hypergraph; and
- I is consistent, i.e., I satisfies $\mathcal{C}$.

It is this equivalence between independent sets and database consistency that motivates the hypergraph perspective on database repairing. For most database integrity constraints, minimal (with respect to $\subseteq$) inconsistent sets are bounded in size. For example, for functional dependencies or primary keys, this bound is 2. This will be mimicked in the hypergraph perspective by assuming a bound b (some positive integer) on the size of the hyperedges.

Finally, we will consider vertex-weighted hypergraphs, i.e., the vertex set will be a weighted set, as defined by Definition 1.

Definition 3. *A hypergraph is called* weighted *if its vertex set is a weighted set. Technically, such a hypergraph is a nested pair* $((V, w), E)$ *with* (V, w) *a weighted set of vertices, and* E *a set of hyperedges. However, as announced in Definition 1, we often omit the explicit mention of the weight function* w. *For simplicity, we will assume that no hyperedge is a singleton. For every integer* $b \geq 2$, *we define* **WH**$[b]$ *as the set of weighted hypergraphs containing no hyperedge of cardinality strictly greater than* b.

To conclude this section, we argue that for most common database integrity constraints, the hypergraph perspective is appropriate for our computational complexity studies, even if constraints are given as expressions in relational calculus. The reason is that **P** (i.e., polynomial time) is the smallest complexity class considered in our complexity analysis, while for most database constraints, conflict hypergraphs can be obtained by a query in relational calculus, which is strictly contained in **P**. For example, for a functional dependency $R : X \rightarrow Y$, the edges of the conflict hypergraph are all pairs of tuples in R that agree on all attributes of X but disagree on some attribute in Y.

4 Repair Checking and Related Problems

A repair of an inconsistent databases **db** is often defined as a maximal consistent subinstance of **db**, where maximality can be with respect to set inclusion or cardinality, yielding subset- and cardinality-repairs, respectively. These notions carry over to the hypergraph perspective defined in Sect. 3. For any aggregation function $\mathcal{G}$ and weighted hypergraph, we now define $\mathcal{G}$-repairs as a natural generalization of existing repair notions. Significantly, from a graph-theoretical viewpoint, $\mathcal{G}$-repairs generalize *maximum-weight independent sets*, which are independent sets of vertices whose weights sum to the maximum possible value. In $\mathcal{G}$-repairs, other functions than SUM can be used.

Definition 4 ($\mathcal{G}$-repair). *Let* $\mathcal{G}$ *be an aggregation function, and* $H = ((V, w), E)$ *a weighted hypergraph. A* $\mathcal{G}$-repair *of* H *is a subset* $I \subseteq V$ *with the following three properties:*

Independence: I *is an independent set of* H;
Maximality: *for every other independent set* $J \subseteq V$, *it holds that* $\mathcal{G}_{[w]}(I) \geq \mathcal{G}_{[w]}(J)$; *and*

Saturation: *for every other independent set* $J \subseteq V$, *if* $\mathcal{G}_{[w]}(I) = \mathcal{G}_{[w]}(J)$ *and* $I \subseteq J$, *then* $I = J$.

Informally, among all independent sets that maximize $\mathcal{G}_{[w]}$, a weighted repair is one that is inclusion-maximal. Subset-repairs and cardinality-repairs are special cases of $\mathcal{G}$-repairs. Indeed, if we let $\mathcal{G} = \mathsf{SUM}$ and $w(v) = 1$ for every vertex v, then $\mathcal{G}$-repairs coincide with cardinality-repairs. If we let $\mathcal{G} = \mathsf{MIN}$ and $w(v) = 1$ for every vertex v, then $\mathcal{G}$-repairs coincide with subset-repairs.

We now relax $\mathcal{G}$-repairs by replacing the *Maximality* requirement in Definition 4 by a lower bound on the aggregated value. This corresponds to real-life situations where we may already be happy with a guaranteed lower bound.

Definition 5 (q-suitable vertex set). *This definition is relative to some fixed aggregation function $\mathcal{G}$. Let $H = ((V, w), E)$ be a weighted hypergraph, and $q \in \mathbb{Q}^+$. A set $I \subseteq V$ is said to be a q-suitable set of H if the following three properties hold true:*

Independence: *I is an independent set of H;*
Suitability: $\mathcal{G}_{[w]}(I) \geq q$; *and*
Saturation: *for every other independent set $J \subseteq V$ such that $I \subseteq J$, if $\mathcal{G}_{[w]}(I) \leq \mathcal{G}_{[w]}(J)$, then $I = J$.*

Informally, an independent set I is q-suitable if its aggregated value is at least q and every strict extension of I is either not independent or has a strictly smaller aggregated value. The decision problems of our interest generalize repair checking, which is central in consistent query answering [18].

Definition 6. *The following problems are relative to an aggregation function $\mathcal{G}$ in $\mathbf{AGG}^{\mathsf{poly}}$ and a positive integer b.*

PROBLEM REPAIR-CHECKING($\mathcal{G}, b$)
Input: *A weighted hypergraph H in $\mathbf{WH}[b]$; a set I of vertices.*
Question: *Is I a $\mathcal{G}$-repair of H?*
PROBLEM REPAIR-EXISTENCE($\mathcal{G}, b$)
Input: *A weighted hypergraph H in $\mathbf{WH}[b]$; a rational number q.*
Question: *Does H have a $\mathcal{G}$-repair I such that $\mathcal{G}_{[w]}(I) \geq q$?*
PROBLEM SUITABILITY-CHECKING($\mathcal{G}, b$)
Input: *A weighted hypergraph H in $\mathbf{WH}[b]$; a set I of vertices; a rational number q.*
Question: *Is I a q-suitable set of H (with respect to $\mathcal{G}$)?*

These problems obviously have relationships among them. For example, if the answer to SUITABILITY-CHECKING($\mathcal{G}, b$) on input H, I, q is "yes," then the answer to REPAIR-EXISTENCE($\mathcal{G}, b$) on input H, q is also "yes." Also, for a weighted hypergraph H, if $q := \max\{\mathcal{G}_{[w]}(J) \mid J \text{ is an independent set of } H\}$, then every $\mathcal{G}$-repair is a q-suitable set, and vice versa. We now give some computational complexity results. The proof of the following result is straightforward.

Theorem 1 (Complexity upper bounds). *For every* $\mathcal{G} \in \mathbf{AGG}^{\mathsf{poly}}$ *and* $b \geq$ 2, REPAIR-CHECKING$(\mathcal{G}, b)$, *and* SUITABILITY-CHECKING$(\mathcal{G}, b)$ *are in* **coNP**, *and* REPAIR-EXISTENCE$(\mathcal{G}, b)$ *is in* **NP**.

The following result means that our problems are already intractable under the simplest parametrization.

Theorem 2 (Complexity lower bounds). REPAIR-CHECKING(COUNT, 2) *is* **coNP**-*hard and* REPAIR-EXISTENCE(COUNT, 2) *is* **NP**-*hard*.

Proof. The following is a well-known **NP**-complete problem [14]:

PROBLEM: INDEPENDENT SET
Input: A simple graph $G = (V, E)$; a positive integer $k \leq |V|$.
Question: Does G have an independent set I with cardinality $|I| \geq k$?

This problem is also referenced as MAX INDEPENDENT SET in the literature. There is a straightforward polynomial-time many-one reduction from the problem INDEPENDENT SET to REPAIR-EXISTENCE(COUNT, 2). We show next a polynomial-time many-one reduction from INDEPENDENT SET to the complement of REPAIR-CHECKING(COUNT, 2). Let $G = (V, E)$, k be an input to INDEPENDENT SET. Let I be a set of fresh vertices such that $|I| = k - 1$. Let F be the set of all edges $\{u, v\}$ such that $u \in I$ and $v \in V$. Clearly, I is an inclusion-maximal independent set of the graph $H := (V \cup I, E \cup F)$, and the pair H, I is a legal input to REPAIR-CHECKING(COUNT, 2). It is now easily verified that G has an independent set of cardinality $\geq k$ if and only if I is not a COUNT-repair of H. This concludes the proof. □

On the other hand, SUITABILITY-CHECKING(COUNT, 2) is tractable (i.e., in **P**). Indeed, tractability holds for a larger class of aggregation functions that contains COUNT and is defined next.

Definition 7 ($\subseteq$-monotone). *An aggregation function is called $\subseteq$-monotone if for every weighted set* (I, w), *for all* $J_1, J_2 \subseteq I$ *such that* $J_1 \subseteq J_2$, *it holds that* $\mathcal{G}_{[w]}(J_1) \leq \mathcal{G}_{[w]}(J_2).$[1]

It is easily verified that COUNT and MAX are $\subseteq$-monotone. SUM is also $\subseteq$-monotone, because we do not consider negative numbers. On the other hand, MIN and AVG are not $\subseteq$-monotone. We give the following claim without proof, because we will shortly prove a stronger result.

Claim (Complexity upper bound). For every $\mathcal{G} \in \mathbf{AGG}^{\mathsf{poly}}$ and $b \geq 2$, if $\mathcal{G}$ is $\subseteq$-monotone, then SUITABILITY-CHECKING$(\mathcal{G}, b)$ is in **P**.

---

[1] In the notation $\mathcal{G}_{[w]}(J_1)$, the weight function is understood to be the restriction of w to J_1.

5   Main Tractability Theorem

Theorem 2 shows that REPAIR-CHECKING($\mathcal{G}, b$) becomes already intractable for simple aggregation functions and conflict hypergraphs. The aim of the current section is to better understand the reason for this intractability, and to identify aggregation functions for which REPAIR-CHECKING($\mathcal{G}, b$) is tractable. In Sects. 5.1 and 5.2, we define two properties of aggregation functions that give rise to some first tractability results. Then, in Sect. 5.3, we combine these results in our main tractability theorem for REPAIR-CHECKING($\mathcal{G}, b$).

5.1   Monotone Under Priority

The converse of the claim at the end of Sect. 4 does not hold. Indeed, MIN is not $\subseteq$-monotone, but it is easily verified that SUITABILITY-CHECKING(MIN, b) is in **P**. We now aim at larger classes of aggregation functions $\mathcal{G}$ for which SUITABILITY-CHECKING($\mathcal{G}, b$) is in **P**. The computational complexity of this problem is mainly incurred by the saturation property in Definition 5, as there can be exponentially many sets including a given independent set. Therefore, we are looking for conditions that avoid such an exponential search. Such a condition is given in Definition 8.

Definition 8 (Monotone under priority). *We say that an aggregation function* $\mathcal{G}$ *is* monotone under priority *if for every weighted set* V, *for every* $I \subseteq V$, *it is possible to compute, in polynomial time in* $|V|$, *a set* $S \subseteq V \setminus I$ *whose powerset* 2^S *contains all and only those subsets of* $V \setminus I$ *that can be unioned with* I *without incurring a decrease of the aggregated value (i.e., for every* $J \subseteq V \setminus I$, *the following holds true:* $J \subseteq S$ *if and only if* $\mathcal{G}_{[w]}(I) \leq \mathcal{G}_{[w]}(I \cup J)$).

We write $\mathbf{AGG}_{\mathsf{mon}}^{\mathsf{poly}}$ *for the set of aggregation functions in* $\mathbf{AGG}^{\mathsf{poly}}$ *that are* monotone under priority.

To illustrate Definition 8, we show that MIN is monotone under priority. To this end, let V be a weighted set and $I \subseteq V$. Clearly, $\mathsf{MIN}_{[w]}(I) \leq \mathsf{MIN}_{[w]}(I \cup J)$ if (and only if) J contains no element with weight strictly smaller than $\mathsf{MIN}_{[w]}(I)$. Therefore, the set $S = \{v \in V \setminus I \mid w(v) \geq \mathsf{MIN}_{[w]}(I)\}$ shows that MIN is monotone under priority. It is even easier to show that every $\subseteq$-monotone aggregation function in $\mathbf{AGG}^{\mathsf{poly}}$ is monotone under priority, by letting $S = V \setminus I$. Therefore, the following lemma is more general than the claim at the end of Sect. 4.

Lemma 1. *For every* $\mathcal{G} \in \mathbf{AGG}_{\mathsf{mon}}^{\mathsf{poly}}$ *and* $b \geq 2$, SUITABILITY-CHECKING($\mathcal{G}, b$) *is in* **P**.

Proof. Let $\mathcal{G} \in \mathbf{AGG}^{\mathsf{poly}}$ be a function that is monotone under priority. Let H, I, q be an input to SUITABILITY-CHECKING($\mathcal{G}, b$). If $\mathcal{G}_{[w]}(I) < q$ or I is not an independent set, return "no"; otherwise the *saturation* condition in the definition of q-suitable sets remains to be verified. To this end, compute in polynomial time the set S mentioned in Definition 8. Then compute in polynomial time its subset $S' := \{v \in S \mid I \cup \{v\}$ is an independent set$\}$. By Definition 5, I is saturated (and hence q-suitable) if and only if there is no nonempty set $J \subseteq V \setminus I$ such that $I \cup J$ is independent and $\mathcal{G}_{[w]}(I) \leq \mathcal{G}_{[w]}(I \cup J)$. Consequently, by Definition 8, I is saturated if and only if $S' = \emptyset$, which can be tested in polynomial time. $\square$

Among the five common aggregation functions COUNT, SUM, MAX, MIN, and AVG, the latter one is the only one that is not in $\mathbf{AGG}_{\mathsf{mon}}^{\mathsf{poly}}$, as illustrated next.

Example 1. We show that the aggregation function AVG is not monotone under priority. Let $V = \{a, b, c, d\}$. Let $w : V \rightarrow \{1, 2\}$ such that $w(a) = w(b) = 1$ and $w(c) = w(d) = 2$. Let $I = \{a, c\}$. Then, $\mathsf{AVG}_{[w]}(I) = \frac{3}{2}$. The subsets of $V \setminus I = \{b, d\}$ that can be unioned with I without incurring a decrease of AVG are $\{\}, \{d\}$, and $\{b, d\}$. However, the set of the latter three sets is not the powerset of some other set.

5.2 k-Combinatorial

Lemma 1 tells us that SUITABILITY-CHECKING$(\mathcal{G}, b)$ is in $\mathbf{P}$ if $\mathcal{G} = \mathsf{MIN}$ or $\mathcal{G} = \mathsf{MAX}$. However, an easier explanation is that the aggregated values of MIN and MAX over a weighted set are determined by a single element in that set. This observation motivates the following definition.

Definition 9 (k-combinatorial). *Let k be a positive integer. We say that an aggregation function $\mathcal{G}$ is k-combinatorial if every weighted set I includes a subset J such that $|J| \leq k$ and $\mathcal{G}_{[w]}(J) = \mathcal{G}_{[w]}(I)$. If $\mathcal{G}$ is not k-combinatorial for any k, we say that $\mathcal{G}$ is* full-combinatorial.
We write $\mathbf{AGG}_{(k)}^{\mathsf{poly}}$ for the set of aggregation functions in $\mathbf{AGG}^{\mathsf{poly}}$ that are k-combinatorial.

Obviously, the aggregation functions MIN and MAX are 1-combinatorial. From this, we can easily obtain an aggregation function that is 2-combinatorial. For example, define SPREAD as the aggregation function such that for every weighted set I, $\mathsf{SPREAD}_{[w]}(I) := \mathsf{MAX}_{[w]}(I) - \mathsf{MIN}_{[w]}(I)$. The notion of k-combinatorial also naturally relates to the well-studied notion of top-k queries. For example, for a fixed k and an aggregation function $\mathcal{G}$, we can define a new aggregation function that, on input of any weighted set (I, w), returns $\max\{\mathcal{G}_{[w]}(J) \mid J \subseteq I, |J| = k\}$, i.e., the highest $\mathcal{G}$-value found in any subset of size exactly k (and returns 0 if $|I| < k$). This new aggregation function is k-combinatorial by construction.

Lemma 2. *Let k be a positive integer. For every $\mathcal{G} \in \mathbf{AGG}_{(k)}^{\mathsf{poly}}$ and $b \geq 2$, REPAIR-EXISTENCE$(\mathcal{G}, b)$ is in $\mathbf{P}$.*

Proof. Let H, q be an input to REPAIR-EXISTENCE$(\mathcal{G}, b)$. We can compute in polynomial time the value m defined as follows:

$$m := \max\{\mathcal{G}_{[w]}(J) \mid J \text{ is an independent set of } H \text{ with } |J| \leq k\}. \tag{1}$$

Since $\mathcal{G}$ is k-combinatorial, every repair I of H satisfies $\mathcal{G}_{[w]}(I) = m$. Thus, the answer to REPAIR-EXISTENCE$(\mathcal{G}, b)$ is "yes" if $q \leq m$, and "no" otherwise. $\square$

5.3   Main Tractability Theorem

By bringing together the results of the two preceding subsections, we obtain our main tractability result.

Theorem 3 (Main tractability theorem). *Let k be a positive integer. For every $\mathcal{G} \in \mathbf{AGG}_{(k)}^{\mathrm{poly}} \cap \mathbf{AGG}_{\mathrm{mon}}^{\mathrm{poly}}$, for every $b \geq 2$, REPAIR-CHECKING($\mathcal{G}, b$) is in $\mathbf{P}$.*

Proof. Let $\mathcal{G} \in \mathbf{AGG}_{(k)}^{\mathrm{poly}} \cap \mathbf{AGG}_{\mathrm{mon}}^{\mathrm{poly}}$. Let H, I be an input to the problem REPAIR-CHECKING($\mathcal{G}, b$). We can compute, in polynomial time, the value m defined by (1) in the proof of Lemma 2. If $\mathcal{G}_{[w]}(I) < m$, return "no"; otherwise we solve SUITABILITY-CHECKING($\mathcal{G}, b$) with input H, I, m, which is in $\mathbf{P}$ by Lemma 1. In particular, if H, I, m is a "no"-instance of the problem SUITABILITY-CHECKING($\mathcal{G}, b$), return "no". If we have not answered "no" so far, then $\mathcal{G}_{[w]}(I) = m$ and I is an m-suitable set of H; in this case, return "yes". It is clear that this decision procedure is correct and runs in polynomial time. □

6   On Full-Combinatorial Aggregation Functions

Lemma 2 stated that the problem REPAIR-EXISTENCE($\mathcal{G}, b$) is tractable if $\mathcal{G}$ is k-combinatorial for some fixed k. We will now show that dropping this condition quickly results in intractability. For a technical reason that will become apparent in the proof of Theorem 4, we need the following definition.

Definition 10 (Witnessable). *Let $\mathcal{G}$ be an aggregation function that is full-combinatorial. We say that $\mathcal{G}$ is* witnessable *if the following task is in polynomial time:*

Input: *A positive integer k in unary. That is, a string $111 \cdots 1$ of length k.*
Output: *Return a shortest sequence $(q_1, q_2, \ldots, q_n)$ of nonnegative rational numbers witnessing that $\mathcal{G}$ is not k-combinatorial ($n > k$). Formally, for the weight function w that maps each i to q_i ($1 \leq i \leq n$), it must hold that for every $N \subseteq \{1, 2, \ldots, n\}$ with $|N| \leq k$, we have $\mathcal{G}_{[w]}(N) \neq \mathcal{G}_{[w]}(\{1, 2, \ldots, n\})$.*

Clearly, if $\mathcal{G}$ is full-combinatorial, the output requested in Definition 10 exists for every k. Therefore, the crux is that the definition asks to return such an output in polynomial time, where it is to be noted that the input is encoded in unary, i.e., has length k (and not $\log k$). Since aggregation functions $\mathcal{G}$ are closed under isomorphism, any permutation of a valid output is still a valid output. An example of a witnessable aggregation function is SUM: on input k, a valid output is the sequence $(1, 1, \ldots, 1)$ of length $k + 1$. For full-combinatorial functions in $\mathbf{AGG}^{\mathrm{poly}}$, the requirement of being witnessable seems very mild, and is expected to be fulfilled by natural aggregation functions.

The following result generalizes a complexity lower bound previously established by Theorem 2, because COUNT obviously satisfies the conditions imposed on $\mathcal{G}$ in the following theorem statement.

Theorem 4. *Let* $\mathcal{G} \in \mathbf{AGG}^{\mathsf{poly}}$ *be a full-combinatorial aggregation function that is $\subseteq$-monotone and witnessable. Then* REPAIR-EXISTENCE$(\mathcal{G}, 2)$ *is* **NP-complete.**

Proof. Membership in **NP** follows from Theorem 1. The **NP**-hardness proof is a polynomial-time many-one reduction from 3SAT. To this end, let φ be an instance of 3SAT with k clauses. Let $(q_1, q_2, \ldots, q_n)$ with $n > k$ be the output of the task defined in Definition 10. Let w be the weight function that maps each i to q_i $(1 \leq i \leq n)$, and let $Q := \mathcal{G}_{[w]}(\{1, \ldots, n\})$. Assume for the sake of contradiction that for some strict subset N of $\{1, \ldots, n\}$, we have $\mathcal{G}_{[w]}(N) = Q$. By Definition 10, $|N| \geq k+1$. Then the sequence $(q_i)_{i \in N}$ of length $< n$ witnesses that $\mathcal{G}$ is not k-combinatorial, contradicting that Definition 10 requires a shortest witness. We conclude by contradiction that $N \subsetneq \{1, 2, \ldots, n\}$ implies $\mathcal{G}_{[w]}(N) \neq Q$. Since $\mathcal{G}$ is $\subseteq$-monotone, it follows that $N \subsetneq \{1, 2, \ldots, n\}$ implies $\mathcal{G}_{[w]}(N) < Q$.

The reduction constructs, in polynomial time in the length of φ, a weighted graph $H = ((V, w'), E)$ as follows. If the ith clause of φ is $\ell_1 \vee \ell_2 \vee \ell_3$, where ℓ_1, ℓ_2, ℓ_3 are positive or negative literals, then (i, ℓ_1), (i, ℓ_2), (i, ℓ_3) are vertices of V that form a triangle in E, and these three vertices are mapped to q_i by w'. For every propositional variable p, if (i, p) and $(j, \neg p)$ are vertices, then they are connected by an edge. Finally, we add isolated fresh vertices $v_{k+1}, v_{k+2}, \ldots, v_n$, and let $w'(v_j) = q_j$ for $k+1 \leq j \leq n$. We claim that the following are equivalent:

1. φ has a satisfying truth assignment; and
2. H has a $\mathcal{G}$-repair I such that $\mathcal{G}_{[w']}(I) \geq Q$.

For the direction $1 \implies 2$, let τ be a satisfying truth assignment for φ. Construct I as follows. First, I includes $\{v_{k+1}, v_{k+2}, \ldots, v_n\}$. Then, for i ranging from 1 to the number k of clauses, if the ith clause of φ is $\ell_1 \vee \ell_2 \vee \ell_3$, we pick $g \in \{1, 2, 3\}$ such that ℓ_g evaluates to true under τ, and add (i, ℓ_g) to I. In this way, I contains exactly one vertex from each triangle. Moreover, since τ is a truth assignment, we will never insert into I both (i, p) and $(j, \neg p)$ for a same propositional variable p. By construction, I is an independent set of H containing n elements, and $\mathcal{G}_{[w']}(I) = \mathcal{G}_{[w]}(\{1, \ldots, n\}) = Q$.

For the direction $2 \implies 1$, let I be a $\mathcal{G}$-repair such that $\mathcal{G}_{[w']}(I) \geq Q$. Then, from our construction of H and our previous result that Q can only be attained if all q_is are aggregated, it follows that for every $i \in \{1, \ldots, k\}$, there is a literal ℓ in the ith clause such that I contains the vertex (i, ℓ). Moreover, since I is an independent set, it cannot contain both (i, p) and $(j, \neg p)$ for a same propositional variable p. Then I obviously defines a satisfying truth assignment for φ. This concludes the proof. $\square$

7   Conclusion and Future Work

Our work combines and generalizes notions from databases and graph theory. From a database-theoretical viewpoint, $\mathcal{G}$-repairs extend subset- and cardinality-repairs by allowing arbitrary aggregation functions. From a graph-theoretical viewpoint, $\mathcal{G}$-repairs extend maximum weighted independent sets by allowing hypergraphs as well as aggregation functions other than SUM. With minor effort, complexity lower bounds for REPAIR-CHECKING($\mathcal{G}, b$) were obtained from known results about maximum (weighted) independent sets. Our main result is the computational tractability result of Theorem 3, which shows a polynomial upper time bound on this problem under some restrictions that are not unrealistic (and are actually met by several common aggregation functions).

Throughout this paper, aggregation functions and their properties were defined and treated in an abstract, semantic way. In the future, we want to study logical languages that allow expressing aggregation functions (e.g., first-order logic with aggregation), and in particular their syntactic restrictions that guarantee tractability.

Another question for future research is whether the intractability result of Theorem 4 can be overcome by approximating full-combinatorial aggregation functions with k-combinatorial ones.

References

1. Abiteboul, S., Hull, R., Vianu, V.: Foundations of Databases. Addison-Wesley, Boston (1995)
2. Afrati, F.N., Kolaitis, P.G.: Repair checking in inconsistent databases: algorithms and complexity. In: ICDT, volume 361 of ACM International Conference Proceeding Series, pp. 31–41. ACM (2009)
3. Arenas, M., Bertossi, L., Chomicki, J.: Consistent query answers in inconsistent databases. In: PODS, pp. 68–79. ACM Press (1999)
4. Baader, F., Horrocks, I., Lutz, C., Sattler, U.: An Introduction to Description Logic. Cambridge University Press, Cambridge (2017)
5. Bertossi, L.E.: Database Repairing and Consistent Query Answering. Synthesis Lectures on Data Management. Morgan & Claypool Publishers, San Rafael (2011)
6. Bertossi, L.E.: Database repairs and consistent query answering: origins and further developments. In: PODS, pp. 48–58. ACM (2019)
7. Bertossi, L.E., Bravo, L., Franconi, E., Lopatenko, A.: The complexity and approximation of fixing numerical attributes in databases under integrity constraints. Inf. Syst. **33**(4–5), 407–434 (2008)
8. Bohannon, P., Fan, W., Flaster, M., Rastogi, R.: A cost-based model and effective heuristic for repairing constraints by value modification. In: SIGMOD Conference, pp. 143–154. ACM (2005)
9. Chomicki, J.: Consistent query answering: five easy pieces. In: Schwentick, T., Suciu, D. (eds.) ICDT 2007. LNCS, vol. 4353, pp. 1–17. Springer, Heidelberg (2006). https://doi.org/10.1007/11965893_1
10. Chomicki, J., Marcinkowski, J.: Minimal-change integrity maintenance using tuple deletions. Inf. Comput. **197**(1–2), 90–121 (2005)
11. Chomicki, J., Marcinkowski, J., Staworko, S.: Computing consistent query answers using conflict hypergraphs. In: CIKM, pp. 417–426. ACM (2004)
12. Du, J., Qi, G., Shen, Y.: Weight-based consistent query answering over inconsistent $\mathcal{SHIQ}$ knowledge bases. Knowl. Inf. Syst. **34**(2), 335–371 (2013). https://doi.org/10.1007/s10115-012-0478-9

13. Flesca, S., Furfaro, F., Parisi, F.: Querying and repairing inconsistent numerical databases. ACM Trans. Database Syst. **35**(2):14:1–14:50 (2010)
14. Garey, M.R., Johnson, D.S.: Computers and Intractability: A Guide to the Theory of NP-Completeness. W. H. Freeman, New York (1979)
15. Libkin, L.: Elements of Finite Model Theory. Texts in Theoretical Computer Science. An EATCS Series, Springer, Heidelberg (2004). https://doi.org/10.1007/978-3-662-07003-1
16. Maslowski, D., Wijsen, J.: Uncertainty that counts. In: Christiansen, H., De Tré, G., Yazici, A., Zadrozny, S., Andreasen, T., Larsen, H.L. (eds.) FQAS 2011. LNCS (LNAI), vol. 7022, pp. 25–36. Springer, Heidelberg (2011). https://doi.org/10.1007/978-3-642-24764-4_3
17. Staworko, S., Chomicki, J.: Consistent query answers in the presence of universal constraints. Inf. Syst. **35**(1), 1–22 (2010)
18. Wijsen, J.: Foundations of query answering on inconsistent databases. SIGMOD Rec. **48**(3), 6–16 (2019)

Dealing with Data Veracity in Multiple Criteria Handling: An LSP-Based Sibling Approach

Guy De Tré[1]([envelope]) [ORCID] and Jozo J. Dujmović[2] [ORCID]

[1] Department of Telecommunications and Information Processing,
Ghent University, St.-Pietersnieuwstraat 41, B9000 Ghent, Belgium
`Guy.DeTre@UGent.be`
[2] Department of Computer Science, San Francisco State University,
San Francisco, CA 94132, USA
`jozo@sfsu.edu`

Abstract. In a big data context, data often originate from various unreliable sources and cannot be considered perfect. Data veracity denotes the overall confidence we have in the data and clearly has an impact on the results of querying and decision making processes. In this paper, we study the impact of data veracity on criterion handling and propose a novel, LSP-based sibling evaluation approach that explicitly copes with data veracity. Logic Scoring of Preference (LSP) is a computational intelligence method that is based on logic criteria selection, evaluation and aggregation. In our proposal, LSP techniques are independently used for scoring preferences on data and preferences on data confidence. This results for each preference on data in an elementary sibling pair, consisting of a satisfaction score and its associated confidence score. Sibling pairs are aggregated using a novel sibling aggregation structure. The resulting sibling pairs, being indicators of both suitability and confidence, provide better interpretable and explainable evaluation results.

Keywords: Big data · Veracity · Querying · Decision support · Interpretable computational intelligence · LSP

1 Introduction

1.1 Scope

Nowadays, data are often characterized by huge volumes, originating from different sources, and being diverse in variety [16]. Along with such characteristics one can often observe a decrease in data quality and trust in the data themselves. This is described in literature as the data veracity problem [2,19]. Data veracity propagates through data processing and hence will finally be reflected in the computational outputs: if there is no confidence in the input data, there will be no confidence in outputs of data processing and data analysis [24]. Hence, the

T. Andreasen et al. (Eds.): FQAS 2021, LNAI 12871, pp. 82–96, 2021.
https://doi.org/10.1007/978-3-030-86967-0_7

importance and relevance of research on data veracity and the proper handling of partially confident data.

In this work we study the impact of data veracity on criteria evaluation and aggregation. Criteria handling is an important component of, among others, flexible query answering systems and decision support systems. Confidence in data is herewith considered as a characteristic of these data, and will hence be treated as metadata. In view of criteria handling we will make an explicit distinction between (regular) *criteria* on data and criteria on the metadata that are used to denote the confidence in these data, further called *confidence criteria*.

As an example, let us consider a mean hospital access time (HAT) as an input attribute in the evaluation of suitability of a home location. A sample HAT criterion is shown in Fig. 1(a). This criterion expresses a user's preferences with respect to the time it takes to reach a hospital and is modelled by a so-called *attribute criterion function*

$$g^{HAT} : dom_{HAT} \rightarrow [0, 1],$$

which returns for each possible HAT domain value $t \in dom_{HAT}$ its corresponding satisfaction (or suitability) degree $s_t = g^{HAT}(t)$. A satisfaction degree 1 herewith denotes full satisfaction, whereas 0 means no satisfaction at all. If for a given home location the HAT to hospital A is 20min, this corresponds in the example to a satisfaction degree $s_t^A = 0.83$.

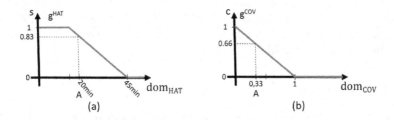

Fig. 1. An illustrative example.

For the sake of illustration, in this simplified example we consider random variation in the data acquisition process as being the only factor that impacts data veracity. As will be described further on, in realistic cases data veracity will usually be more complex. The approach presented in this work aims to address these complex cases as well.

When data are subject to random variation, a data value is typically interpreted as a mean value of a corresponding (known or unknown) distribution. Unsurprisingly, the confidence in the use of the mean value decreases if the coefficient of variation of the analysed data increases. Therefore, we can define the confidence degree as a function of the coefficient of variation. Reconsidering the HAT criterion, the road conditions between a home location and a hospital can significantly vary from location to location. If the coefficient of variation of access time is very low, then we can have a high confidence in the resulting location suitability. However, if the coefficient of variation is high, we must consider that the resulting location suitability indicator has a lower confidence. Therefore, we suggest the coefficient of variation function $\max(0, 1 - \sigma/t)$ (with σ being the standard deviation of all time distance measurements used to compute the HAT t), to estimate the confidence we have in HAT t. So, a coefficient of variation (COV) confidence criterion as depicted in Fig. 1(b), expressing a user's confidence in HAT measurement is introduced. This confidence criterion is modelled by a *confidence criterion function*

$$g^{COV} : dom_{COV} \to [0,1],$$

which returns for each possible value $c = \max(0, 1 - \sigma/t) \in dom_{COV}$ (with $t \in dom_{HAT}$), its corresponding confidence degree $c_t = g^{COV}(c)$. A confidence degree 1 herewith denotes full confidence, whereas 0 means no confidence. If $c = 0.33$ for a given HAT to hospital A, this corresponds in the example with a confidence degree $c_t^A = 0.66$.

Attribute and confidence criterion functions have similar characteristics as membership functions in fuzzy set theory [31]. The way how confidence is approximated in the illustrative example is compatible with Zadeh's PRUF representation [32].

Taken together, the overall satisfaction degree and the corresponding degree of confidence provide more information to the user than the satisfaction degree alone. For example, consider two locations: A and B. The location A has $s_t^A = 0.83$ and $c_t^A = 0.66$, and the location B has $s_t^B = 0.83$ and $c_t^B = 0.95$. Then, although locations A and B are both suitable to the same extent, selecting B is preferable because of the higher confidence.

1.2   Related Work

Associating a confidence degree with each satisfaction degree is one way to handle confidence criterion evaluation. Other approaches are possible, for example exploiting the facilities of interval methods [17], type-2 fuzzy logic systems [3], or R-sets [25]. These methods approximate a membership grade by specifying a kind of upper and lower bound and could be used to model uncertainty on satisfaction degrees. Yager studied the issue of determining an alternative's satisfaction to a criterion when the alternative's associated attribute value is imprecise and introduced two approaches: one based on containment and one based on possibility [29]. The handling of skyline queries in the context of databases that may contain data of bad quality has been studied in [15]. Herewith it is assumed that each tuple or attribute in a relational database has an associated (known) quality level. Skyline queries are extended to take data quality into account when checking tuple domination in skyline query answer set construction.

In this work, we opt to use pairs of satisfaction and confidence grades instead, because our focus is to track down the origin of veracity problems, i.e., to find the criteria in the querying or decision making process that caused the veracity issue in an easy and interpretable way. The approach of working with a pair of values is in line with Zadeh's concept of Z-numbers [33], which has been further developed in, among others, [9].

Other frameworks for data quality handling exist [7]. Some are focussing on data integration strategies in case of multiple data sources containing data of different quality [4,22], others focus on data quality monitoring and notification of changes [1,20], or on data quality aware query plan construction [21]. In [30] a query answering framework is presented that considers user data quality preferences over a collaborative information systems architecture that measures data quality, models user's data quality preferences, and answers queries by maximizing the data quality of the query results considering the user's preferences on data quality.

The framework we propose focuses on reflecting data quality propagation during query evaluation in order to provide the user with adequate information on the estimated confidence in the evaluation results and hence come to better explainable query answers.

A general framework for the automatic generation of an explanation of the results of a multi-attribute preference model has been studied in [18]. That framework is based on decision theory and built on three models: an expected utility model, a qualitative pessimistic minmax model and a concordance model, all three being constructed from a weight vector.

1.3   Approach

The framework we propose is based on a multiple criteria evaluation model. As stated above we opted for working with pairs of satisfaction and confidence grades. Prior work, initiating the basic ideas of this approach, has been presented in [8,12]. In this paper the generation and handling of pairs of satisfaction and confidence grades is studied in more detail. More specifically, the scientific contributions of this work are:

- A sibling approach for integrating satisfaction and confidence in a general criteria evaluation framework, which is based on the Logic Scoring of Preferences (LSP) technique [10].
- A study on how the aggregation of satisfaction grades impacts the aggregation of associated confidence grades in so-called sibling aggregation.
- A novel configurable LSP-based sibling aggregation structure for associated satisfaction and confidence grades.

The structure of the paper is as follows. In Sect. 2 we give some preliminaries on data veracity and criteria handling in LSP. In Sect. 3, we present how veracity handling can be integrated in a general explainable LSP-based sibling framework. First, we focus on explainable single criterion evaluation. Second, we study aggregation and present a novel explainable sibling aggregation structure. Some illustrative examples are given in Sect. 4. Finally, in Sect. 5 our conclusions with some proposals for future work are presented.

2   Preliminaries

2.1   Data Veracity

In a context of big data, criteria handling is often complicated by a lack of confidence in the available data. Discarding data veracity is commonly not an option because trusted data are in short supply and because trust is subjective: depending on the context and use, the same piece of information might be considered as being adequate or not. Hence, evaluating data veracity and providing the user with extra information regarding the confidence in criteria handling outcomes is important [6].

In literature, it is generally recognized that *veracity* is one of the main characteristic of big data [2,19]. Data veracity is a complex concept which has multiple dimensions including *consistency, accuracy, completeness, validity* and *timeliness* [7,23,26]. As illustrated in the introduction, data veracity (truthfulness or reliability) is in general not a binary indicator, but rather a matter of degree. Computational intelligence techniques are believed to be an important aspect of veracity handling [5].

To give an impression of what data veracity dimensions entail, we briefly describe the ones mentioned above. More details and an overview of generally consolidated dimensions of data veracity are given in [7,26]. Being able to adequately cope with the dimensions of data veracity that are relevant for a given querying or decision making context is one of the main objectives of the framework that we propose in this work.

Consistency. Data inconsistency refers to situations where data delivered by different data sources do not match. Inconsistent data cannot be trusted because usually some of the data sources are to some extent wrong. Detecting, assessing and, if possible, resolving data inconsistencies improves data veracity.

In the HAT example, time measurement recordings for a given route might differ significantly in different data sources (e.g., those sources available over the Internet). Consequently, such data are inconsistent.

Accuracy. Accuracy refers to 'the proximity of a given value to a value that is considered as being correct in both content and form' [23]. A distinction has been made between syntactic proximity and semantic proximity. Accuracy assessment focusses on quantifying accuracy.

In the HAT example, time measurements might be accurate to the minute while others might be given with an accuracy of a five minute frame.

It is useful to differentiate the accuracy of objectively measurable attributes (e.g. the area of a home) and the accuracy of human percepts (e.g. the attractiveness of a home location). In the case of measurable attributes the true value does exist and can be measured with various degrees of precision (e.g. square meters vs. square feet). In the case of human percepts, the 'accurate value' refers to the inherently unknown value that could be generated by the population of all existing qualified evaluators [11].

Completeness. Completeness refers to 'the extent to which data are of sufficient breadth, depth and scope for the task at hand' [26]. A distinction has been made between schema completeness (a measure for the missing properties, e.g., attributes, of data), column completeness (a measure for the missing values of a specific property) and population completeness (a measure for the missing data entries with respect to a reference population).

In the HAT example, some time measurement data sets might not include a timestamp attribute for their recordings, while others do. Some recordings might lack data for their timestamp attribute, or HAT data of some hospitals might not be included in the data sets.

Validity. Validity denotes whether the data are what these are intended to be, and as such indicates to what extent the data are conform to specific formats or business rules. In the case of measurement data, validity expresses how good a method measures what it is intended to measure.

In the HAT example, time measurement could be derived from GPS tracking or be manually measured using a stopwatch. The used measurement method impacts the validity of the data.

Timeliness. Timeliness has been defined as 'the extent to which the age of the data is appropriate for the task at hand' [26]. Research on timeliness, among others, focusses on defining metrics that are based on probabilistic considerations like the conditional probability that a considered data value is still up-to-date at the instant of use [14].

In the HAT example, older time measurements might become obsolete because of recent changes in traffic loads.

2.2 LSP

Logic Scoring of Preference (LSP) is a computational intelligence method for object evaluation that has been successfully applied in multiple criteria decision making (MCDM) [10,11]. Computational intelligence is used to adequately reflect human expert knowledge in the modelling and processing of the data.

A detailed presentation of the LSP method can be found in [11]. The main steps of the LSP method are:

1. Development of an attribute tree with attributes as leaves.
2. Specification of evaluation criteria for all attributes.
3. Logic aggregation of suitability degrees, generating the overall suitability.

The attribute tree must create (as leaves) a complete set of attributes that affect the suitability. Each attribute is separately evaluated using an appropriate attribute criterion that for each value of the attribute domain provides a corresponding suitability degree. Suitability degrees are aggregated using logic aggregators. The logic aggregators are selected from a spectrum of logic operators that are models of hyperconjunction, pure conjunction, hard partial conjunction, soft partial conjunction, neutrality, soft partial disjunction, hard partial disjunction, pure disjunction, and hyperdisjunction. The results of logic aggregation is an overall suitability degree. Overall suitability degrees of evaluated objects can finally be compared for selecting the best object given the decision making problem under consideration. Besides being applicable in decision making, LSP can also be used for database record evaluation during flexible query processing in which case suitability degrees are called satisfaction degrees.

Attribute Tree Construction. In this first step the relevant characteristics of objects with respect to evaluation are identified. Such characteristics are called *attributes*. Due to the human way of analysing and reasoning, attributes are organized in a hierarchic way, resulting in a so-called *attribute tree*. Attributes in child nodes, herewith further detail the attribute of their parent node. For example, for describing availability of medical support, time distance to hospital might be an attribute, which might be further detailed into time distance by car, time distance by public transportation and time distance by medical transport service.

Attributes in leaf nodes are called *elementary attributes*. The result of attribute tree construction is a tree structure of attributes with a finite set of elementary attributes

$$\{A_1, \ldots, A_n\}, \ n \in \mathbb{N}. \tag{1}$$

The structure of the attribute tree will be used as guideline for the construction of the aggregation structure in step three.

Criterion Specification and Evaluation. For each elementary attribute A_i, $i = 1, \ldots, n$ resulting from the previous step, an associated *elementary criterion*

$$g^{A_i} : dom_{A_i} \to [0,1] : x \mapsto g^{A_i}(x) \tag{2}$$

is specified. Herewith, dom_{A_i} denotes the domain of allowed values for A_i. An elementary criterion g^{A_i} expresses which domain values of the attribute A_i are preferred by the user and which are not. By specifying all user preferences by attribute criterion functions, as exemplified in Fig. 1(a), all criteria are specified and evaluated in a uniform way.

By evaluating each elementary criterion g^{A_i}, $i = 1, \ldots, n$, for a given object o, n *elementary satisfaction degrees*

$$s^o_{A_i} = g^{A_i}(A_i[o]) \in [0,1] \tag{3}$$

are obtained. Herewith, $A_i[o]$ denotes the value of attribute A_i of object o.

Aggregation of Evaluation Results. The n elementary satisfaction degrees $s^o_{A_i}$ have to be aggregated to an *overall satisfaction degree* s^o for the object o. Aggregation is done using an LSP aggregation structure. Such a structure is constructed using LSP aggregators, herewith reflecting the structure of the attribute tree. Different forms of LSP aggregators exists [11]. The basic form is the Generalized Conjunction Disjunction (GCD) aggregator, which takes q elementary satisfaction degrees s_i, $i = 1; \ldots, q$ as input and is parameterized by (i) q weights $w_i \in [0,1]$, $i = 1, \ldots, q$, denoting the relative importance of each s_i among all the inputs of the aggregator, $\sum_{i=1}^{q} w_i = 1$ and (ii) a global andness α, $0 \leq \alpha \leq 1$ determining the logical behaviour of the aggregator. If $\alpha = 1$, then the aggregator behaves like a full conjunction ('and'), whereas for $\alpha = 0$ a full disjunction ('or') is obtained. With the intermediate parameter values, a continuous transition from full conjunction to full disjunction is modelled.

A GCD aggregator can be defined in a variety of ways. A survey and comparison of alternative forms of aggregators can be found in [13]. The most general GCD form is the andness-directed interpolative GCD form (ADIGCD) that covers all aggregators along the path from drastic conjunction to drastic disjunction [11,13]. In a simple special case the GCD aggregator can be implemented as a weighted power mean (WPM), where the exponent r is a function of the desired andness α:

$$a_{(w_1,\ldots,w_q;r)}^{gcd} : [0,1]^q \to [0,1]$$

$$(s_1,\ldots,s_q) \mapsto \begin{cases} (w_1 s_1^r + \cdots + w_q s_q^r)^{(1/r)}, & \text{if } 0 < |r| < +\infty \\ \min(s_1,\ldots,s_q), & \text{if } r = -\infty \\ \max(s_1,\ldots,s_q), & \text{if } r = +\infty. \end{cases} \qquad (4)$$

GCD aggregation is related to Ordered Weighted Average (OWA) aggregation [27,28]. ADIGCD can model the following logic conditions: hyperconjunction, pure conjunction, hard partial conjunction, soft partial conjunction, neutrality, soft partial disjunction, hard partial disjunction, pure disjunction, and hyperdisjunction [11]. All these aggregators can be used for evaluation purposes. Classic additive OWA can model only pure conjunction, soft partial conjunction, neutrality, soft partial disjunction, and pure disjunction. Therefore, it supports only five out of nine necessary aggregator types and the absence of four frequently needed hard aggregators is the reason for using ADIGCD instead of OWA.

For simplicity and illustration the WPM implementation of GCD, as defined by Eq. (4)), will be used in the remainder of this paper.

3   An Explainable Sibling LSP Framework

Considering the work done in data quality framework development [7], we observe that multidimensional properties of data veracity are being studied intensively. Hence, it makes sense to consider so-called *confidence criteria* expressing the user's preferences with respect to such properties. In this section, we propose to extend the LSP framework to an explainable framework including as well criteria for elementary attributes as confidence criteria for the relevant data quality aspects of these attributes. Herewith, we opt for a general approach that makes it possible to take into account any data quality aspect of any dimension that is considered to be relevant for the data under consideration.

The outline of the proposed explainable sibling LSP framework is presented in Fig. 2 and is further detailed in the subsequent subsections.

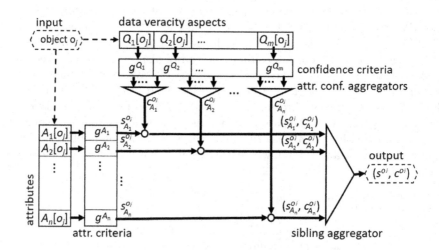

Fig. 2. An explainable sibling LSP framework.

3.1   Explainable Single Criterion Evaluation

Consider an LSP attribute tree and an object o that has to be evaluated. For each elementary attribute A_i, $i = 1, \ldots, n$ of the attribute tree, the confidence in its data value $A_i[o]$ has to be determined. In general, multiple data veracity aspects like those introduced in Sect. 2 can be relevant for determining the confidence in the values of an elementary attribute A_i. The relevant data veracity aspects for a given attribute A_i can be hierarchically structured. Hence, each attribute will have zero or more *elementary veracity aspects*. In this work we assume that all of these can be (approximately) assessed. Considering all elementary attributes together, this results in a finite set of elementary, assessable veracity aspects

$$\{Q_1, \ldots, Q_m\}, \ m \in \mathbb{N}. \tag{5}$$

For each elementary veracity aspect Q_i, $i = 1, \ldots, m$, an associated *elementary confidence criterion*

$$g^{Q_i} : dom_{Q_i} \to [0,1] : x \mapsto g^{Q_i}(x) \tag{6}$$

is specified. Here, dom_{Q_i} denotes the set of possible assessment values for Q_i. As can be seen in Fig. 1(b), assessment values can depend on the value of the attribute of which Q_i is a veracity aspect. The elementary confidence criterion

g^{Q_i} expresses the user's confidence in the result stemming from the assessment of veracity aspect Q_i. For example, w.r.t. the time-distance-to-hospital attribute t presented in Sect. 1 Q_i is the coefficient of variation σ/t and the confidence criterion g^{Q_i} is specified as shown in Fig. 1(b). In the example, full confidence is assigned to coefficients for which $\max(0, 1 - \sigma/t) = 0$, there is no confidence in a coefficient for which $\max(0, 1 - \sigma/t) = 1$, and there is a linear decrease in confidence for coefficients for which $0 < \max(0, 1 - \sigma/t) < 1$.

By evaluating each elementary confidence criterion g^{Q_i}, $i = 1, \ldots, m$, for a given object o, m *elementary confidence degrees*

$$c^o_{Q_i} = g^{Q_i}(Q_i[o]) \in [0, 1] \tag{7}$$

are obtained. Herewith, $Q_i[o]$ denotes the assessment value of veracity aspect Q_i, considering the attribute value in o to which Q_i relates.

In the next step, for each attribute A_i, $i = 1, \ldots, n$, an overall confidence degree $c^o_{A_i}$ is computed. This confidence degree reflects the confidence we have in the single criterion evaluation result $s^o_{A_i} = g^{A_i}(A_i[o])$ (cf. Eq. (3)). Three cases are distinguished:

1. None of the veracity aspects Q_i, $i = 1, \ldots, m$ is associated with A_i. In this case $c^o_{A_i} = c_u$ with c_u being a user assigned value. If the user fully trusts the values of A_i, then $c_u = 1$ else a value lower than 1 can be chosen.
2. Only one of the veracity aspects, say Q_j, $1 \le j \le m$, is associated with A_i. In this case $c^o_{A_i} = c^o_{Q_j}$.
3. More than one veracity aspect, say $\{Q^i_1, \ldots, Q^i_k\} \subseteq \{Q_1, \ldots, Q_m\}$, is associated with A_i. Then an LSP aggregation structure, called an *attribute confidence aggregator*, is used to compute $c^o_{A_i}$. This aggregator takes $c^o_{Q^i_j}$, $j = 1, \ldots, k$, as inputs and is configured as described in Sect. 2.2.

The pair $(s^o_{A_i}, c^o_{A_i})$ denotes the confidence $c^o_{A_i}$ in the result $s^o_{A_i}$ of evaluating criterion g^{A_i} using the actual value $A_i[o]$ of attribute A_i in object o. Tracking the origin of the value $c^o_{A_i}$, herewith eventually exploring the attribute confidence aggregation structure, allows to explain why and to what extent the satisfaction degree $s^o_{A_i}$ can be trusted (or not).

3.2   Explainable Sibling Aggregation

A *sibling LSP aggregation structure*, taking n pairs $(s^o_{A_i}, c^o_{A_i})$, $i = 1, \ldots, n$ as input, is used to compute the pair (s^o, d^o) that reflects the *overall satisfaction* $s^o \in [0, 1]$ of the evaluation of o and the *overall confidence* $c^o \in [0, 1]$ in this evaluation result.

The sibling aggregation structure is constructed using so-called *sibling LSP aggregators* and reflects the attribute tree, as it is the case in the LSP method. For sibling aggregation the following assumptions have been taken into account:

– The satisfaction degrees $s^o_{A_i}$, $i = 1, \ldots, n$ are aggregated in exactly the same way as in the LSP method.

- The confidence degrees $c^o_{A_i}$, $i = 1, \ldots, n$ are aggregated in such a way that each confidence degree has a similar impact in the computation of the overall confidence degree, as its corresponding 'sibling' satisfaction degree has in the computation of the overall satisfaction degree.

In a general case of LSP evaluation criteria, each input has a different impact on the overall satisfaction. Our approach is based on the concept that those inputs that have high impact should be provided with higher confidence than those inputs that produce low impact. In cases where the confidence is associated with cost, such an approach is justified by producing the overall confidence with minimum cost.

In this paper, we focus on the weighted power mean definition of a sibling GCD aggregator (cf. Eq. (4)), which is proposed as follows.

$$ga^{gcd}_{(w_1,\ldots,w_q;r)} : [0,1]^q \times [0,1]^q \to [0,1] \times [0,1]$$

$$[(s_1, c_1), \ldots, (s_q, c_q)] \mapsto (s, c) \tag{8}$$

where s is obtained by applying Eq. (4), i.e.

$$s = a^{gcd}_{(w_1,\ldots,w_q;r)}(s_1, \ldots, s_q) \tag{9}$$

and c is computed from $c_1, \ldots, c_q$ in such a way that the impact of each c_i, $i = 1, \ldots, q$ in the computation of c is similar to the impact that its corresponding value s_i has on the computation of s. For obtaining this we propose the following novel approach, where c is a weighted mean of $c_1, \ldots, c_q$, i.e.

$$c = \begin{cases} \dfrac{\sum_{i=1}^{q} \rho_i c_i}{\sum_{i=1}^{q} \rho_i}, & \text{iff } \sum_{i=1}^{q} \rho_i > 0, \\ 1, & \text{otherwise.} \end{cases} \tag{10}$$

The weights $\rho_1, \ldots, \rho_q$ are computed normalized indicators of impact. Various indicators of impact exist [11]. In this work we approximate impact by the 'total range'

$$\rho_i = a^{gcd}_{(w_1,\ldots,w_q;r)}(s_1, \ldots, s_{i-1}, 1, s_{i+1}, \ldots, s_q) - \tag{11}$$

$$a^{gcd}_{(w_1,\ldots,w_q;r)}(s_1, \ldots, s_{i-1}, 0, s_{i+1}, \ldots, s_q), \ i = 1, \ldots, q.$$

Hence, the 'total range' impact indicator for a pair (s_i, c_i) is defined by the difference between the overall satisfaction degree that is obtained when input s_i is replaced by the maximal satisfaction 1 and the overall satisfaction degree that is obtained when input s_i is replaced by the minimal satisfaction 0.

Applying the sibling LSP aggregation structure leads to a better interpretable overall criteria aggregation. Beside an overall satisfaction degree s^o, an overall confidence degree c^o is obtained. This overall confidence degree denotes how confident we can be about the criteria evaluation result for object o and backtracking through the aggregation structure allows to find out what attributes contribute to the resulting satisfaction score and what confidence aspects of those attributes influence the confidence in that score. This makes that the user will be better informed when having to make decisions on the basis of the criteria evaluation results.

4 Illustrative Examples

For the sake of illustration, we present in Table 1 the aggregation of ten (s, c)-pairs resulting from the evaluation of three attributes 1, 2, 3 (with relative importance weights $w_1 = 0.5$ and $w_2 = w_3 = 0.25$) for ten objects $o_1, \ldots, o_{10}$, using the sibling aggregators based on resp. the minimum (min), maximum (max), weighted average (avg), harmonic mean (harm) and quadratic mean (quad) operators, all obtained by applying Eq. (8) with resp. values $r = -\infty, r = +\infty, r = 1$, $r = -1$ and $r = 2$.

Table 1. Applying $ga^{gcd}_{(w_1, \ldots, w_q; r)}$ with $w_1 = 0.5$ and $w_2 = w_3 = 0.25$.

o_j	$(s_1^{o_j}, c_1^{o_j})$	$(s_2^{o_j}, c_2^{o_j})$	$(s_3^{o_j}, c_3^{o_j})$	min	max	avg	harm	quad
o_1	$(1, 1)$	$(0.5, 1)$	$(0.1, 1)$	$(0.1, 1)$	$(1, 1)$	$(0.67, 1)$	$(0.32, 1)$	$(0.76, 1)$
o_2	$(1, 0.5)$	$(0.5, 1)$	$(0.1, 1)$	$(0.1, 0.93)$	$(1, 0.5)$	$(0.67, 0.75)$	$(0.32, 0.89)$	$(0.76, 0.7)$
o_3	$(1, 0.1)$	$(0.5, 1)$	$(0.1, 1)$	$(0.1, 0.87)$	$(1, 0.1)$	$(0.67, 0.55)$	$(0.32, 0.8)$	$(0.76, 0.45)$
o_4	$(1, 0.5)$	$(0.5, 0.5)$	$(0.1, 0.5)$	$(0.1, 0.5)$	$(1, 0.5)$	$(0.67, 0.5)$	$(0.32, 0.5)$	$(0.76, 0.5)$
o_5	$(1, 1)$	$(0.5, 0.1)$	$(0.1, 1)$	$(0.1, 0.87)$	$(1, 1)$	$(0.67, 0.73)$	$(0.32, 0.78)$	$(0.76, 0.79)$
o_6	$(1, 1)$	$(0.5, 1)$	$(0.1, 0.5)$	$(0.1, 0.64)$	$(1, 1)$	$(0.67, 0.9)$	$(0.32, 0.73)$	$(0.76, 0.92)$
o_7	$(1, 1)$	$(0.5, 1)$	$(0.1, 0.1)$	$(0.1, 0.36)$	$(1, 1)$	$(0.67, 0.82)$	$(0.32, 0.52)$	$(0.76, 0.86)$
o_8	$(1, 1)$	$(1, 1)$	$(1, 1)$	$(1, 1)$	$(1, 1)$	$(1, 1)$	$(1, 1)$	$(1, 1)$
o_9	$(0, 1)$	$(0, 1)$	$(0, 1)$	$(0, 1)$	$(0, 1)$	$(0, 1)$	$(0, 1)$	$(0, 1)$
o_{10}	$(1, 0.5)$	$(1, 0.5)$	$(1, 0.5)$	$(1, 0.5)$	$(1, 0.5)$	$(1, 0.5)$	$(1, 0.5)$	$(1, 0.5)$

As the main purpose is to illustrate the aggregation of confidence degrees, the same elementary satisfaction degrees, resp. 1, 0.5 and 0.1 are assumed for objects $o_1, \ldots, o_7$. For object o_1, full confidence is assumed for all satisfaction degrees, resulting in a full overall confidence for all aggregators. For objects $o_2, \ldots, o_7$, confidences are decreased to 0.5 and 0.1 for consecutively $s_1^{o_j}$, $s_2^{o_j}$ and $s_3^{o_j}$. By observing the results of the min and max aggregators, we can see that confidence is impacted by the confidence in the input satisfaction degrees that impact the computation of the overall satisfaction. E.g., for o_2 the confidence in case of the min aggregator is mainly determined by the full confidence in $s_3^{o_j}$, but is also to a much lesser extent influenced by the lack of confidence in $s_3^{o_j}$. Confidence in case of the max aggregator is only influenced by the lower confidence in $s_1^{o_j}$, because there is full confidence in $s_2^{o_j}$ and $s_3^{o_j}$, which both have no impact on the result. Similar observations can be made for $o_3, \ldots, o_7$. With objects o_8, o_9 and o_{10} some special cases are verified. For object o_8 it is assumed that all satisfaction degrees are 1 with full confidence, for object o_9 all satisfaction degrees are 0 with full confidence, whereas for object o_{10} all satisfaction degrees are 1, but the confidence for each satisfaction degree is only 0.5.

5   Conclusions and Future Work

Our investigation of confidence in the context of LSP criteria and the LSP evaluation method suggest that evaluation results should be presented as suitability-confidence pairs, where each degree of suitability is associated with a corresponding confidence degree. We promoted the concept of idempotent logic aggregation of confidence and proposed a novel basic sibling aggregation technique, based on 'total range' impact indicators for quantifying the confidence of evaluation results. This is particularly important in big data applications where inputs obtained from unreliable sources must be used for querying and decision making.

Future work should be directed towards the further development of sibling aggregation techniques, their experimental validation and their comparison, refinement, and support with appropriate software tools.

Funding Statement. This research received funding from the Flemish Government under the 'Onderzoeksprogramma Artificiële Intelligentie (AI) Vlaanderen' programme.

References

1. Batini, C., Scannapieco, M.: Data Quality: Concepts, Methodologies and Techniques. (Data-Centric Systems and Applications). Springer-Verlag Inc, New York, New Jersey, USA (2006)
2. Berti-Equille, L., Lamine Ba, M.: Veracity of big data: challenges of cross-modal truth discovery. ACM J. Data Inf. Qual. **7**(3), 12:1–12:3 (2016)
3. Biglarbegian, M., Melek, W.W., Mendel, J.M.: On the robustness of type-1 and interval type-2 fuzzy logic systems in modeling. Inf. Sci. **181**(7), 1325–1347 (2011)
4. Bressan, S., et al.: The context interchange mediator prototype. ACM SIGMOD Rec. **26**(2), 525–527 (1997)
5. Bronselaer, A., De Mol, R., De Tré, G.: A measure-theoretic foundation for data quality. IEEE Trans. Fuzzy Syst. **26**(2), 627–639 (2018)
6. Chengalur-Smith, I.N., Ballou, D.P., Pazer, H.L.: Data quality information on decision making: an exploratory analysis. IEEE Trans. Knowl. Data Eng. **11**(6), 853–864 (1999)
7. Cichy, C., Rass, S.: An overview of data quality frameworks. IEEE Access **7**, 24634–24648 (2019)
8. De Tré, G., De Mol, R., Bronselaer, A.: Handling veracity in multi-criteria decision-making: a multi-dimensional approach. Inf. Sci. **460–461**, 541–554 (2018)
9. Dubois, D., Prade, H.: A fresh look at z-numbers - relationships with belief functions and p-boxes. Fuzzy Inf. Eng. **10**(1), 1–14 (2018)
10. Dujmović, J.J.: Preference logic for system evaluation. IEEE Trans. Fuzzy Syst. **15**(6), 1082–1099 (2007)

11. Dujmović, J.J.: Soft Computing Evaluation Logic: The LSP Decision Method and Its Applications. Wiley, Hoboken (2018)
12. Dujmović, J.J.: Interpretability and explainability of lsp evaluation criteria. In: Proceedings of the 2020 IEEE International Conference on Fuzzy Systems (FUZZ-IEEE), pp. 1–8, Glasgow, UK (2020)
13. Dujmović, J.J., Torra, V.: Properties and comparison of andness-characterized aggregators. Int. J. Intell. Syst. **36**(3), 1366–1385 (2021)
14. Heinrich, B., Klier, M.: A novel data quality metric for timeliness considering supplemental data. In: Proceedings of the 17th European Conference on Information Systems, ECIS 2009, pp. 2701–2713. Verona, Italy (2009)
15. Jaudoin, H., Pivert, O., Smits, G., Thion, V.: Data-quality-aware skyline queries. In: Andreasen, T., Christiansen, H., Cubero, J.-C., Raś, Z.W. (eds.) ISMIS 2014. LNCS (LNAI), vol. 8502, pp. 530–535. Springer, Cham (2014). https://doi.org/10. 1007/978-3-319-08326-1_56
16. Kitchin, R.: Big data, new epistemologies and paradigm shifts. Big Data Soc. **1**(1), 1–12 (2014)
17. Kreinovich, V., Ouncharoen, R.: Fuzzy (and interval) techniques in the age of big data: an overview with applications to environmental science, geosciences, engineering, and medicine. Int. J. Uncertain. Fuzziness Knowl.-Based Syst. **23**(suppl. 1), 75–89 (2015)
18. Labreuche, C.: A general framework for explaining. Artif. Intell. **175**(7–8), 1410–1448 (2011)
19. Lukoianova, T., Rubin, V.L.: Veracity roadmap: is big data objective, truthful and credible? Adv. Classif. Res. Online **24**(1), 4–15 (2014)
20. Mecella, M., Scannapieco, M., Virgillito, A., Baldoni, R., Catarci, T., Batini, C.: Managing data quality in cooperative information systems. In: Proceedings of the Move to Meaningful Internet Systems, 2002-DOA/CoopIS/ODBASE 2002 Confederated International Conferences DOA, CoopIS and ODBASE 2002, Springer-Verlag, pp. 486–502. London, UK (2002)
21. Mihaila, G.A., Raschid, L., Vidal, M.E.: Using quality of data metadata for source selection and ranking. In: Proceedings of the Third International Workshop on the Web and Databases, WebDB 2000, pp. 93–98. Dallas, USA (2000)
22. Naumann, F.: Quality-Driven Query Answering for Integrated Information Systems. Springer-Verlag, Berlin, Germany (2002)
23. Redman, T.: Data Quality for the Information Age. Artech-House, Massachusetts, USA (1996)
24. Saha, B., Srivastava, D.: Data quality: the other face of big data. In: Proceedings of the 2014 IEEE 30th International Conference on Data Engineering, pp. 1294–1297. Chicago, USA (2014)
25. Seiti, H., Hafezalkotob, A., Martinez, L.: R-sets, comprehensive fuzzy sets risk modeling for risk-based information fusion and decision-making. IEEE Trans. Fuzzy Syst. **29**(2), 385–399 (2021)
26. Wang, R.Y., Ziad, M., Lee, Y.W.: Data Quality. Kluwer Academic Publishers, New York, USA (2002)
27. Yager, R.R.: On ordered weighted averaging aggregation operators in multi-criteria decision making. IEEE Trans. Syst. Man Cybern. **18**, 183–190 (1988)
28. Yager, R.R., Kacprzyk, J.: The Ordered Weighted Averaging Operators: Theory and Applications. Kluwer, Massachusetts, USA (1997)
29. Yager, R.R.: Validating criteria with imprecise data in the case of trapezoidal representations. Soft. Comput. **15**, 601–612 (2011)

30. Yeganeh, N.K., Sadiq, S., Sharaf, M.A.: A framework for data quality aware query systems. Inf. Syst. **46**, 24–44 (2014)
31. Zadeh, L.A.: Fuzzy sets. Inf. Control **8**(3), 338–353 (1965)
32. Zadeh, L.A.: PRUF - a meaning representation language for natural languages. Int. J. Man Mach. Stud. **10**(4), 395–460 (1978)
33. Zadeh, L.A.: A note on z-numbers. Inf. Sci. **8**(3), 2923–2932 (2011)

On Controlling Skyline Query Results: What Does Soft Computing Bring?

Allel Hadjali$^{(\boxtimes)}$

LIAS/ENSMA, Poitiers, France
`allel.hadjali@ensma.fr`

Abstract. Querying databases to search for the best objects matching
user's preferences is a fundamental problem in multi-criteria databases.
The skyline queries are an important tool for solving such problems.
Based on the concept of Pareto dominance, the skyline process extracts
the most interesting (not dominated in Pareto sense) objects from a set
of data. However, this process may often lead to the two scenarios: (i) a
small number of skyline objects are retrieved which could be insufficient
to serve the decision makers'needs ; (ii) a huge number of skyline objects
are returned which are less informative for the decision makers. In this
paper, we discuss and show how Soft Computing, and more particularly
fuzzy set theory, can contribute to solve the two above problems. First, a
relaxation mechanism to enlarge the skyline set is presented. It relies on
a particular fuzzy preference relation, called "much preferred". Second,
an efficient approach to refine huge skyline and reduce its size, using
some advanced techniques borrowed from fuzzy formal concepts analysis, is provided. The approaches proposed are user-dependent and allow
controlling the skyline results in a flexible and rational way.

Keywords: Skyline queries · Fuzzy formal concepts analysis · Fuzzy
dominance · Relaxation · Refinement

1 Introduction

Multi-criteria decision-making methods have been widely studied in the literature and used in several real-life fields. Skyline queries are one of these methods
that have gained a considerable interest in the scientific community in the last
two decades. They are introduced by Borzsönyi in [1] to formulate multi-criteria
searches. Since the end of 2000's, this paradigm has particularly been the subject of numerous studies in the database community. It has been integrated in
many database applications that require decision making (decision support [2],
personalized recommendation like hotel recommender [2], restaurant finder [3].

Skyline process aims at identifying the most interesting (not dominated in
sense of Pareto) objects from a set of data. They are then based on Pareto
dominance relationship. This means that, given a set D of d-dimensional points
(objects), a skyline query returns, the skyline S, set of points of D that are
not dominated by any other point of D. A point p dominates (in Pareto sense)

© Springer Nature Switzerland AG 2021
T. Andreasen et al. (Eds.): FQAS 2021, LNAI 12871, pp. 97–108, 2021.
https://doi.org/10.1007/978-3-030-86967-0_8

another point q iff p is better than or equal to q in all dimensions and strictly better than q in at least one dimension.

A great research effort has been devoted to develop efficient algorithms to skyline computation in both complete and incomplete databases [2–9]. It is worth noticing that when computing the skyline, two scenarios often occur: either (i) a huge number of skyline objects are returned which are less informative for the decision makers or (ii) a small number of skyline objects are retrieved which could be insufficient for the decision making purpose. In order to solve these two problems, several approaches have been developed, on the one hand, to relax the skyline and thus increasing its size [10–13] in the case of the problem (ii) and, on the other hand, to refine the skyline and thus reducing its size [11,14–21] in the context of the problem (i).

In this paper, we discuss the issue of controlling the skyline results when querying large-scale datasets, i.e., how to deal with the huge and small skylines problems. In particular, we show how ideas borrowed from fuzzy logic theory allow for controlling the results returned by the skyline queries in a flexible way and where the user is put in the loop.

First, we describe a solution to the problem of skyline refinement that relies on the fuzzy Formal Concept Analysis (FCA) field [22–24]. A formal concept is formed by an extent that contains a set of objects and an intent that contains the properties describing these objects. In our context, the objects correspond to the tuples of the target database and the properties represent the attributes of the database tuples. The idea of the solution advocated is to build a particular formal concept, called Ideal Formal Concept (IFC), and its fuzzy counterpart. IFC is defined such that its extent satisfies at best the skyline attributes. The refined skyline is then given either by the objects of this extent (in the crisp case) or by the $top - k$ objects (where k is a user-defined parameter) of this extent (in the fuzzy case).

Second, we present a solution to the problem of skyline relaxation that makes use of a particular fuzzy preference relation, called "much preferred". Based on this relation, a novel fuzzy dominance relationship is defined which makes more demanding the dominance between the points of interest. So, much points would be considered as incomparable and then as elements of the new relaxed skyline.

The rest of this paper is structured as follows. In Sect. 2, we define some basic notions and concepts necessary for reading the paper. In Sect. 3, we present our vision to refine the skyline and thus reduce its size by leveraging some techniques borrowed from fuzzy FCA. Section 4 describes our approach for relaxing the skyline and then enlarging its size. The approach makes use of a particular fuzzy dominance relationship. In Sect. 5, we conclude the paper and provide some discussion about our proposal.

2   Background

2.1   Skyline Queries

Skyline queries [1] are example of preference queries that can help users to make intelligent decisions in the presence of multidimensional data where different and often conflicting criteria must be taken. They rely on Pareto dominance principle which can be defined as follows:

Definition 1. *Let D be a set of d-dimensional data points (objects) and u_i and u_j two points (objects) of D. u_i is said to dominate, in Pareto sense, u_j (denoted $u_i \succ u_j$) iff u_i is better than or equal to u_j in all dimensions (property) and strictly better than u_j in at least one dimension(property) .*

Formally, we write:

$$u_i \succ u_j \Leftrightarrow (\forall k \in \{1,..,d\}, u_i[k] \geq u_j[k]) \wedge (\exists l \in \{1,..,d\}, u_i[l] > u_j[l]) \qquad (1)$$

where each tuple (object) $u_i = (u_i[1], u_i[2], \cdots, u_i[d])$ with $u_i[k]$ stands for the value of the tuple u_i for the attribute A_k.

In Eq. (1), without loss of generality, we assume that the largest value, the better.

Definition 2. *The skyline of D, denoted by S, is the set of objects which are not dominated by any other object.*

$$u \in S \Leftrightarrow \nexists u' \in D, u' \succ u \qquad (2)$$

Example 1. To illustrate the concept of the skyline, let us consider a database containing information on candidates as shown in Table 1. The list of candidates includes the following information: code, the marks of mathematics (MM), the marks of physics (MP) and the age of candidate. Ideally, we look for a candidate having a good (large) marks in mathematics (MM) and physics (MP) ignoring the other pieces of information. Applying the traditional skyline on the candidates list, shown in Table 1, returns the following skyline candidates: $S = \{M_1, M_2, M_4, M_7\}$, see Fig. 1.

Table 1. List of candidates

Code	Mathematics (MM)	Physics (MP)	Age
M_1	17	10	25
M_2	18	6	24
M_3	10	7.5	32
M_4	15	15	23
M_5	5	10	27
M_6	4	4	28
M_7	20	5	22

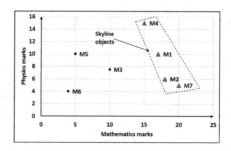

Fig. 1. Skyline of candidates

2.2   Formal Concept Analysis with Fuzzy Attributes

Formal Concept analysis (FCA) was introduced by Rudolf Wille in 1982 [22], it provides means to analyze data that describe objects, attributes, and their relationship. The data can be represented by a triplet $\mathcal{K} = (O, P, R)$ which is called formal context, where O is a set of objects, P is a set of properties (attributes) and R is a binary relation in the basic setting introduced by Wille [22]. The correspondences between O and P are called a Galois derivation operator denoted by $\triangle$.

As in many real-life applications, attributes are fuzzy rather than crisp, and in order to take into account relations allowing a gradual satisfaction of a property by an object, a fuzzy FCA was proposed by belohlávek and al. in [23]. In this case, the notion of satisfaction can be expressed by a degree in $[0, 1]$. A fuzzy formal context is a tuple (L, O, P, R), where $R : O \times P \longrightarrow L$ is a fuzzy relation. It assigns for each object $o \in O$ and each property $p \in P$, the degree $R(o, p)$ for which the object o has the property p. In general $L = [0, 1]$. Belohlávek et al. [23] generalize the Galois derivation operator to the fuzzy settings a follows. For a set $A \in L^O$ and a set $B \in L^P$, $A^\triangle$ and $B^\triangle$ are defined by

$$A^\triangle(p) = \bigwedge_{o \in O} (A(o) \rightarrow R(o, p)) \tag{3}$$

$$B^\triangle(o) = \bigwedge_{p \in P} (B(p) \rightarrow R(o, p)) \tag{4}$$

where $\bigwedge$ is the min conjunction operator and $\rightarrow$ is a fuzzy implication. In [23], three implications (Lukasiewicz, Goguen and Gödel) have been studied.

As in [25], we denote the fuzzy formal concept by $\langle A, B \rangle$ where $A \in L^O$, $B \in L^P$, $A = \{o_1^{\alpha_1}, o_2^{\alpha_2}, \cdots, o_n^{\alpha_n}\}$ and $B = \{p_1^{\beta_1}, p_2^{\beta_2}, \cdots, p_w^{\beta_w}\}$ where $\alpha_i \in [0, 1]$, $\beta_j \in [0, 1]$ and when we use a formal concept with crisp extent $\alpha_i \in \{0, 1\}$, $(1 \leq i \leq n, 1 \leq j \leq w)$. Since $\langle A, B \rangle$ is a fuzzy formal concept, we have $A^\triangle = B$ and $B^\triangle = A$. The following interpretations are then used [24, 25]:

- $B^\triangle(o_i) = A(o_i) = \alpha_i$ is the truth degree of "the object o_i has all the properties from B".

– $A^{\triangle}(p_j) = B(p_j) = \beta_j$ is the truth degree of "p_j is shared by all objects from A".

Note that in our approach, we make use of the implication of Gödel defined by Eq. (5).

$$p \longrightarrow q = \begin{cases} 1 & \text{if } p \le q \\ q & \text{else} \end{cases} \tag{5}$$

3 Skyline Refinement Based on Fuzzy FCA

In this section, we discuss our approach, named Attribute Satisfaction-Based Approach (ASBA), for refining the skyline. It relies on fuzzy FCA. See [26] for more details about ASBA approach and about two other approaches FSCBA (Fuzzy Satisfaction Concept-Based Approach) and DCBA (Distance Concept-Based Approach) introduced to address the same problem.

Let us first define the notations used in the rest of the paper:

– $O = \{o_1, o_2, \cdots, o_n\}$: a database formed by a set of n objects.
– $P = \{p_1, p_2, \cdots, p_d\}$: a set of d properties (dimensions or attributes) that describe each object o_i of O, i.e., each object o_i from the set O is evaluated w.r.t every property p_j.
– $R(o_i, p_j)$: relation that gives the value of the object o_i w.r.t property p_j.
– $S = \{o_1, o_2, \cdots, o_t\}$: the skyline of O where t is its size and $t \le n$.
– $degree(o_i, p_j)$: the truth degree for which the skyline object o_i has (satisfies) the property p_j.

As shown in [26], the solutions for skyline refinement advocated by DCBA and FSCBA approaches include a lattice structure building and scanning step. This can result in a highly time-consuming procedure. Moreover, the refined skyline S_{ref} returned by these two approaches is a flat set, so one cannot discriminate between its elements. ASBA approach allows for avoiding such drawbacks as explained below.

The idea of this approach is to compute the fuzzy formal concept whose intent maximizes the degrees of the skyline attributes (called the ideal fuzzy formal concept denoted IFFC). To do this, we start by computing, for each skyline object o_i, the degree $degree(o_i, p_j)$ expressing the extent to which the object o_i of the skyline S satisfies the property p_j. The refined skyline S_{ref} is then given by the $top - k$ elements of the fuzzy set $\tilde{A}^T$ sorted in a descending way:

– where $\tilde{A}^T$ stands for the fuzzy extent of the fuzzy concept IFFC $\langle \tilde{A}^T, \tilde{B}^T \rangle$, and
– the fuzzy intent $\tilde{B}^T$ is equal to $Intent\_max = \{p_1^{d_1^{max}}, \cdots, p_d^{d_d^{max}}\}$ where $d_j^{max} = max_{i=1,t} degree(o_i, p_j)$ for $j = 1, d$.

In summary, this approach involves the following steps.

Algorithm 1: ASASR

Input: A Skyline $S = \{o_1, o_2, \cdots, o_t\}$, k: the number of objects chosen by the user
Output: The refined skyline S_{ref}

1 $S_{ref} \leftarrow \emptyset$; $t \leftarrow S.size()$;
2 $M1 \leftarrow Max\_value(S)$; /*$Max\_value(S)$ return a vector that contains the maximum value of each skyline dimension.*/
3 **for** $i \leftarrow 1$ **to** d **do**
4   /* d is the number of skyline dimensions */
5     $Intent\_max(i) \leftarrow 1$;
6   **for** $j \leftarrow 1$ **to** t **do**
7         $degree(o_i, p_j) \leftarrow (R(o_i, p_j)/M1(i))$; /*If the skyline attribute is to maximize*/
8   **end**
9 **end**
10 $extent \leftarrow Compute\_Extent(Intent\_max, degrees)$;
11 $A \leftarrow Sorted(extent)$;
12 /*sorts the objects of the extent in a descending way according to their degrees and save it in A*/
13 $nbre \leftarrow 1$;
14 **while** $nbre <= k$ **do**
15     $S_{ref} \leftarrow S_{ref} \cup \{o_{nbre}\}$;
16     $nbre \leftarrow nbre + 1$;
17 **end**
18 **return** S_{ref};

---

1. **Skyline computation:** First, we compute the skyline S using $IBNL$ algorithm (an improved version of the Basic Nested Loop Algorithm), see [26].
2. **Computing the degrees of skyline objects:** For each object o_i of S, we compute the degree $degree(o_i, p_j)$ using Algorithm 1. Algorithm 1 calls the function **Max_value(S)** to compute the maximum value of each skyline property.
3. **IFFC concept building:** In this step, we compute the IFFC concept $\langle \tilde{A}^T, \tilde{B}^T \rangle$ using Algorithm 1 and the function **Compute_Extent()** that computes the fuzzy extent of a given fuzzy intent.
4. **Fuzzy extent sorting:** ASASR algorithm sorts the elements of $\tilde{A}^T$ in a descending way.
5. **Top-k Selection:** S_{ref} is given by the top-k of the above fuzzy extent $\tilde{A}^T$.

Example 2. Let us consider a database containing information on players of NBA as shown in Table 2. The list of players includes the following information: name of player, the number of games played, the number of shots marked and the number of decisive passes (denoted respectively $Name$, GP, SM, DP). Ideally, we look for a player having a large number of decisive passes (DP) and having scored a large number of points (SM), ignoring the other pieces of information.

Table 2. List of players.

Name	Games played (*GP*)	Shots marked (*SM*)	Decisive passes (*DP*)
N_1	19	137	70
N_2	19	138	61
N_3	20	89	68
N_4	20	105	125
N_5	19	55	126
N_6	18	140	48
N_7	20	43	31
N_8	15	39	16
N_9	15	39	05
N_{10}	14	12	05

Applying the traditional skyline on the players list shown in Table 2, we obtain $S = \{N_1, N_2, N_4, N_5, N_6\}$. Let us now apply our ASBA approach to refine S. First, the different degrees of the skyline objects are computed and illustrated by Table 3 (see [26] for more details).

Table 3. A short list of players and their degrees.

Name	Games played (*GP*)	Shots marked (*SM*)	Decisive passes (*DP*)	$degree(N_i, SM)$	$degree(N_i, DP)$
N_1	19	137	70	0.97	0.55
N_2	19	138	61	0.98	0.48
N_4	20	105	125	0.75	0.99
N_5	19	55	126	0.39	1
N_6	18	140	48	1	0.38

As for the IFFC concept $\langle \tilde{A}^T, \tilde{B}^T \rangle$, one can check that $d^{max} = (d_{SM}^{max}, d_{DP}^{max})$ $= (1,1)$ then $\tilde{B}^T = \{SM^1, DP^1\}$. Now, by Algorithm 1 and Table 3, $\tilde{A}^T$ can be computed as follows:

- The degrees w.r.t. the properties SM and DP of each skyline elements are: $N_1 = (0.97, 0.55); N_2 = (0.98, 0.48); N_4 = (0.75, 0.99); N_5 = (0.39, 1); N_6 = (1, 0.38)$.
- For each skyline element, we compute the extent to which this element belongs to $\tilde{A}^T$ (using Eq. (4)): $\{SM^1, DP^1\}^\triangle(N_1) = \bigwedge(1 \rightarrow 0.97, 1 \rightarrow 0.55) = \min(0.97, 0.55) = 0.55$
  $\{SM^1, DP^1\}^\triangle(N_2) = \bigwedge(1 \rightarrow 0.98, 1 \rightarrow 0.48) = \min(0.98, 0.48) = 0.48$
  $\{SM^1, DP^1\}^\triangle(N_4) = \bigwedge(1 \rightarrow 0.75, 1 \rightarrow 0.99) = \min(0.75, 0.99) = 0.75$
  $\{SM^1, DP^1\}^\triangle(N_5) = \bigwedge(1 \rightarrow 0.39, 1 \rightarrow 1) = \min(0.39, 1) = 0.39$
  $\{SM^1, DP^1\}^\triangle(N_6) = \bigwedge(1 \rightarrow 1, 1 \rightarrow 0.38) = \min(1, 0.38) = 0.38$

Then,

$$\tilde{A}^T = \{N_1^{0.55}, N_2^{0.48}, N_4^{0.75}, N_5^{0.39}, N_6^{0.38}\}.$$

In a descending way, $\tilde{A}^T$ writes

$$\{N_4^{0.75}, N_1^{0.55}, N_2^{0.48}, N_5^{0.39}, N_6^{0.38}\}$$

Now, the $top - 3$ of the sorted $\tilde{A}^T$ are $\{(N_4, 0.75), (N_1, 0.55), (N_2, 0.48)\}$ which represents the refined skyline S_{ref}. For instance, the player N_4 belongs to the S_{ref} with a degree 0.75

4   Fuzzy Dominance-Based Skyline Relaxation

Let $R(A_1, A_2, ..., A_d)$ be a relation defined in a d-dimensional space $D = (D_1, D_2, ..., D_d)$, where D_i is the domain attribute of A_i. We assume the existence of a total order relationship on each domain D_i. U is a set of n tuples belonging to the relationship R, $U = (u_1, u_2, ..., u_n)$. Let S be the skyline of U and S_{relax} the relaxed version S.

The main idea of this relaxation approach, called $\mathcal{MP2R}$[1], consists of computing the extent to which a point, discarded by the (classical) Pareto-dominance relationship, may belong to the relaxed skyline. To this end, and as it will be illustrated further, we associate with each skyline attribute A_i ($i \in \{1, \cdots, d\}$) a pair of parameters $(\gamma_{i1}, \gamma_{i2})$ where γ_{i1} and γ_{i2} respectively denote the bounds of the relaxation zone allowed to the attribute A_i.

$\mathcal{MP2R}$ approach relies on a new fuzzy dominance relationship that allows enlarging the skyline with the most interesting points among those ruled out when computing the initial skyline S. This fuzzy dominance relationship makes use of the relation *"Much Preferred (MP)"* to compare two tuples u and u'. So, u is an element of S_{relax} if there is no tuple $u' \in U$ such that u' is *much preferred* to u (denoted $MP(u', u)$) in all skyline attributes. Formally, we write:

$$u \in S_{relax} \Leftrightarrow \nexists u' \in U, \forall i \in \{1, ..., d\}, MP_i(u'_i, u_i) \tag{6}$$

where, MP_i is a fuzzy preference relation defined on the domain D_i of the attribute A_i and $MP_i(u'_i, u_i)$ expresses the extent to which the value u'_i is *much preferred* to the value u_i. Since MP relation is of a gradual nature, each element u of S_{relax} is associated with a degree ($\in [0, 1]$) expressing the extent to which u belongs to S_{relax}.
In fuzzy set terms, one can write:

$$\mu_{S_{relax}}(u) = 1 - \max_{u' \in U} \min_i \mu_{MP_i}(u'_i, u_i) = \min_{u' \in U} \max_i (1 - \mu_{MP_i}(u'_i, u_i)) \tag{7}$$

As for MP_i relation on D_i, its semantics can be provided by the formulae (8). In terms of trapezoidal membership function, MP_i writes $(\gamma_{i1}, \gamma_{i2}, \infty, \infty)$, and is denoted as $MP_i^{(\gamma_{i1}, \gamma_{i2})}$. It is easy to check that $MP_i^{(0,0)}$ corresponds to the

---

[1] $\mathcal{M}$uch $\mathcal{P}$referred $\mathcal{R}$elation for $\mathcal{R}$elaxation.

regular preference relation expressed by means of the crisp relation *"greater than"*.

$$\mu_{MP_i^{(\gamma_{i1},\gamma_{i2})}}(u_i', u_i) = \begin{cases} 0 & \text{if } u_i' - u_i \leq \gamma_{i1} \\ 1 & \text{if } u_i' - u_i \geq \gamma_{i2} \\ \frac{(u_i'-u_i)-\gamma_{i1}}{\gamma_{i2}-\gamma_{i1}} & \text{else} \end{cases} \quad (8)$$

Let $\gamma = ((\gamma_{11}, \gamma_{12}), \cdots, (\gamma_{d1}, \gamma_{d2}))$ be a vector of pairs of parameters where $MP_i^{(\gamma_{i1},\gamma_{i2})}$ denotes the MP_i relation defined on the attribute A_i and $S_{relax}^{(\gamma)}$ denotes the relaxed skyline computed on the basis of the vector γ. One can easily check that the classical Skyline S is equal to $S_{relax}^{(0)}$, where $\mathbf{0} = ((0,0), \cdots, (0,0))$. We say that $MP_i^{(\gamma_{i1},\gamma_{i2})}$ is more constrained than $MP_i^{(\gamma_{i1}',\gamma_{i2}')}$ if and only if $(\gamma_{i1}, \gamma_{i2}) \geq (\gamma_{i1}', \gamma_{i2}')$ (i.e., $\gamma_{i1} \geq \gamma_{i1}' \wedge \gamma_{i2} \geq \gamma_{i2}'$).

Definition 3. *Let γ and γ' be two vectors of parameters. We say that $\gamma \geq \gamma'$ if and only if $\forall i \in \{1, \cdots, d\}$, $(\gamma_{i1}, \gamma_{i2}) \geq (\gamma_{i1}', \gamma_{i2}')$.*

Proposition 1. *[10] Let γ and γ' be two vectors of parameters. The following property holds: $\gamma' \leq \gamma \Rightarrow S_{relax}^{(\gamma')} \subseteq S_{relax}^{(\gamma)}$.*

Lemma 1. *Let $\gamma = ((0, \gamma_{12}), \cdots, (0, \gamma_{d2}))$ and $\gamma' = ((\gamma_{11}', \gamma_{12}'), \cdots, (\gamma_{d1}', \gamma_{d2}'))$, the following holds: $S_{relax}^{(0)} \subseteq S_{relax}^{(\gamma)} \subseteq S_{relax}^{(\gamma')}$*

Example 3. Let us consider a database containing information on candidates as shown in Table 4. The list of candidates includes the following information: Code, Age, Management experience (man_exp in years), Technical experience (tec_exp in years) and distance work to Home (dist_wh in Km). Ideally, personnel manager is looking for a candidate with the largest management and technical experience (Max man_exp and Max tec_exp), ignoring the other pieces of information. Applying the traditional skyline on the candidate list shown in Table 4 returns the following candidates: $S = \{M_5, M_8\}$.

Assume that the *"much preferred"* relations corresponding to the skyline attributes (man_exp and tec_exp) are respectively given by:

$$\mu_{MP_{man\_exp}^{(1/2,2)}}(u', u) = \begin{cases} 0 & \text{if } u' - u \leq 1/2 \\ 1 & \text{if } u' - u \geq 2 \\ 2/3(u' - u) - 1/3 & \text{else} \end{cases} \quad (9)$$

$$\mu_{MP_{tec\_exp}^{(1/2,4)}}(u', u) = \begin{cases} 0 & \text{if } u' - u \leq 1/2 \\ 1 & \text{if } u' - u \geq 4 \\ 2/7(u' - u) - 1/8 & \text{else} \end{cases} \quad (10)$$

Now, applying the $\mathcal{MP2R}$ approach, to relax the skyline $S = \{M_5, M_8\}$ found in this example, leads to the following relaxed skyline $S_{relax} = \{(M_5, 1), (M_8, 1), (M_3, 0.85), (M_{10}, 0.85), (M_1, 0.66), (M_2, 0.66), (M_4, 0.57)\}$. For instance, the candidate M_3 belongs to the S_{relax} with a degree 0.85.

One can note that some candidates that were not in S are now elements of S_{relax} (such M_{10} and M_4). As can be seen, S_{relax} is larger than S. Let us now take

Table 4. List of candidates.

Code	Age	man_exp	tec_exp	dist_wh
M1	32	5	10	35
M2	41	7	5	19
M3	37	5	12	45
M4	36	4	11	39
M5	40	8	10	18
M6	30	4	6	27
M7	31	3	4	56
M8	36	6	13	12
M9	33	6	6	95
M10	40	7	9	20

a glance at the content of S_{relax}, one can observe that (i) the skyline elements of S are still elements of S_{relax} with a degree equal to 1 ; (ii) Appearance of new elements recovered by our approach whose degrees are less than 1 (such as M_3). Interestingly, the user can select from S_{relax}:

- the Top-k elements (k is a user-defined parameter) : elements of S_{relax} with highest degrees, or
- the subset of elements , denoted $(S_{relax})_\sigma$, with a degrees higher than a threshold σ provided by the user.

In the context of this example, it is easy to check that $Top-6 = \{(M_5, 1), (M_8, 1),$ $(M_3, 0.85),$ $(M_{10}, 0.85),$ $(M_1, 0.66),$ $(M_2, 0.66)\}$ and $(S_{relax})_{0.7} = \{(M_5, 1),$ $(M_8, 1), (M_3, 0.85), (M_{10}, 0.85)\}$.

5   Discussion and Conclusion

Improving database usability constitutes a modern and hot research topic in the presence of multidimensional data where different and often conflicting criteria must be used. This paper contributes to this research effort by addressing the problem of controlling the skyline size in the case of huge skyline (i.e., a large number of skyline objects are returned) and small skyline (i.e., a small number of skyline objects are retrieved). By this step, the decision making process becomes easier. The ideas discussed draw their theoretical foundations from fuzzy set theory field.

As it can be seen, the benefits of using fuzzy set theory can be summarized as follows: (i) the approaches, by construction, always guaranty the success of the refinement/relaxation process ; (ii) they are user-dependent and provide the user with a discriminated refined/relaxed skyline ; (iii) thanks to the various parameters of the approaches, one can control the size and the quality of the refined/relaxed skyline to meet the decision makers' needs and expectations in real-world applications ; (iv) as shown in [10,26], the refinement/relaxation skyline discussed presents good rate of refinement/relaxation and their execution time remains acceptable and reasonable even in large-scale datasets.

As for future work, we plan to apply the proposed approaches in the context of group skyline [27,28] to control its size for combinatorial decision making.

References

1. Börzsönyi, S., Kossmann, D., Stocker, K.: The skyline operator. In: Proceedings of the 17th International Conference on Data Engineering, Heidelberg, Germany, pp. 421–430 (2001)
2. Yiu, M.L., Mamoulis, N.: Efficient processing of top-k dominating queries on multidimensional data. In: Proceedings of the 33rd International Conference on Very Large Data Bases (VLDB), pp. 483–494. Austria, 23–27 September 2007
3. Khalefa, M.E., Mokbel, M.F., Levandoski, J.J.: Skyline query processing for incomplete data. In: Proceedings of the 24th International Conference on Data Engineering, ICDE 2008, pp. 556–565 (2008)
4. Siddique, M.A., Tian, H., Qaosar, M., Morimoto, Y.: MapReduce algorithm for variants of skyline queries: skyband and dominating queries. Algorithms 12(8), 166–186 (2019)
5. Hadjali, A., Pivert, O., Prade, H.: Possibilistic contextual skylines with incomplete preferences. In: Second International Conference of Soft Computing and Pattern Recognition, (SoCPaR), pp. 57–62. Paris, France, 7–10 December 2010
6. Pei, J., Jiang, B., Lin, X., Yuan, Y.: Probabilistic skylines on uncertain data. In: Proceedings of the 33rd International Conference on Very Large Data Bases, pp. 15–26. Austria, 23–27 September 2007
7. Lee, J., Hwang, S.: Scalable skyline computation using a balanced pivot selection technique. Inf. Syst. 39, 1–21 (2014)
8. Gulzar, Y., Alwan, A.A., Abdullah, R.M., Xin, Q., Swidan, M.B.: SCSA: evaluating skyline queries in incomplete data. Appl. Intell. 49(5), 1636–1657 (2018). https://doi.org/10.1007/s10489-018-1356-2
9. Ghosh, P., Sen, S., Cortesi, A.: Skyline computation over multiple points and dimensions. Innov. Syst. Softw. Eng. 17(2), 141–156 (2021). https://doi.org/10.1007/s11334-020-00376-1
10. Belkasmi, D., Hadjali, A., Azzoune, H.: On fuzzy approaches for enlarging skyline query results. Appl. Soft Comput. 74, 51–65 (2019)
11. Hadjali, A., Pivert, O., Prade, H.: On different types of fuzzy skylines. In: Kryszkiewicz, M., Rybinski, H., Skowron, A., Raś, Z.W. (eds.) ISMIS 2011. LNCS (LNAI), vol. 6804, pp. 581–591. Springer, Heidelberg (2011). https://doi.org/10.1007/978-3-642-21916-0_62
12. Goncalves, M., Tineo, L.: Fuzzy dominance skyline queries. In: Wagner, R., Revell, N., Pernul, G. (eds.) DEXA 2007. LNCS, vol. 4653, pp. 469–478. Springer, Heidelberg (2007). https://doi.org/10.1007/978-3-540-74469-6_46
13. Jin, W., Han, J., Ester, M.: Mining thick skylines over large databases. In: Boulicaut, J.-F., Esposito, F., Giannotti, F., Pedreschi, D. (eds.) PKDD 2004. LNCS (LNAI), vol. 3202, pp. 255–266. Springer, Heidelberg (2004). https://doi.org/10.1007/978-3-540-30116-5_25

14. Papadias, D., Tao, Y., Fu, G., Seeger, B.: An optimal and progressive algorithm for skyline queries. In: Proceedings of the International Conference on Management of Data (ACM SIGMOD), pp. 467–478. San Diego, California, USA, 9–12 June 2003

15. Chan, C.-Y., Jagadish, H.V., Tan, K.-L., Tung, A.K.H., Zhang, Z.: On high dimensional skylines. In: Ioannidis, Y., Scholl, M.H., Schmidt, J.W., Matthes, F., Hatzopoulos, M., Boehm, K., Kemper, A., Grust, T., Boehm, C. (eds.) EDBT 2006. LNCS, vol. 3896, pp. 478–495. Springer, Heidelberg (2006). https://doi.org/10.1007/11687238_30

16. Koltun, V., Papadimitriou, C.H.: Approximately dominating representatives. In: Proceedings of the 10th International Conference on Database Theory (ICDT), pp. 204–214. Edinburgh, UK, 5–7 January 2005

17. Chan, C.Y., Jagadish, H.V., Tan, K.L., Tung, A.K., Zhang, Z.: Finding k-dominant skylines in high dimensional space. In: Proceedings of the International Conference on Management of Data (ACM SIGMOD), pp. 503–514. Illinois, USA, 27–29 June 2006

18. Balke, W., Güntzer, U., Lofi, C.: User interaction support for incremental refinement of preference-based queries. In: Proceedings of the First International Conference on Research Challenges in Information Science (RCIS), pp. 209–220. Ouarzazate, Morocco, 23–26 April 2007

19. Lee, J., You, G., Hwang, S.: Telescope: zooming to interesting skylines. In: Kotagiri, R., Krishna, P.R., Mohania, M., Nantajeewarawat, E. (eds.) DASFAA 2007. LNCS, vol. 4443, pp. 539–550. Springer, Heidelberg (2007). https://doi.org/10.1007/978-3-540-71703-4_46

20. Sarma, A.D., Lall, A., Nanongkai, D., Lipton, R.J., Xu, J.: Representative skylines using threshold-based preference distributions. In: Proceedings of the 27th International Conference on Data Engineering, (ICDE), pp. 387–398. Hannover, Germany, 11–16 April 2011

21. Haddache, M., Belkasmi, D., Hadjali, A., Azzoune, H.: An outranking-based approach for skyline refinement. In 8th IEEE International Conference on Intelligent Systems, IS 2016, pp. 333–344. Sofia, Bulgaria, 4–6 September 2016

22. Wille, R.: Restructuring lattice theory: an approach based on hierarchies of concepts. In: Ferré, S., Rudolph, S. (eds.) ICFCA 2009. LNCS (LNAI), vol. 5548, pp. 314–339. Springer, Heidelberg (2009). https://doi.org/10.1007/978-3-642-01815-2_23

23. Belohlávek, R.: Fuzzy galois connections. Math. Log. Q. **45**, 497–504 (1999)

24. Belohlávek, R., De Baets, B., Outrata, J., Vychodil, V.: Computing the lattice of all fixpoints of a fuzzy closure operator. IEEE Trans. Fuzzy Syst. **18**(3), 546–557 (2010)

25. Djouadi, Y., Prade, H.: Possibility-theoretic extension of derivation operators in formal concept analysis over fuzzy lattices. FO DM **10**(4), 287–309 (2011)

26. Haddache, M., Hadjali, A., Azzoune, H.: Skyline refinement exploiting fuzzy formal concept analysis. Int. J. Intell. Comput. Cybern. **14**(3), 333–362 (2021)

27. Zhang, N., Li, C., Hassan, N., Rajasekaran, S., Das, G.: On skyline groups. IEEE Trans. Knowl. Data Eng. **26**, 942–956 (2014)

28. Nadouri, S., Hadjali, A., Sahnoun, Z.: Group skyline computation: an overview. In: Proceedings of the 36th Computer Workshop of Organizations and Information Systems and Business Intelligence Decision Making, Big Data and Data Science, INFORSID, Nantes, France, 28–31 May 2018

Management of Complex and Fuzzy Queries Using a Fuzzy SOLAP-Based Framework

Sinan Keskin[1] and Adnan Yazıcı[1,2]([✉])

[1] Department of Computer Engineering, Middle East Technical University,
Ankara, Turkey
keskin.sinan@metu.edu.tr
[2] Department of Computer Science, School of Engineering and Digital Sciences,
Nazarbayev University, Nur Sultan, Republic of Kazakhstan
adnan.yazici@nu.edu.kz

Abstract. With the use of data warehouses, the need for faster access and analysis to historical and multidimensional data has arisen. Online analytical processing (OLAP), developed for this purpose, has provided suitable data structures that overcome some of the limitations of relational databases by providing rapid data analysis. OLAP can display and collect large amounts of data while providing searchable access to any data point and handle a wide variety of complex queries that match user interests. While OLAP enables querying and analysis of multidimensional numeric and alphanumeric data, there is still a need to support flexible queries and analyses on uncertain and fuzzy data due to the nature of the data existing the complex applications such as multimedia and spatiotemporal applications. This study presents how to handle various types of fuzzy spatiotemporal queries using our fuzzy SOLAP (spatial OLAP) based framework on meteorological databases, which inherently contain spatiotemporal data in addition to uncertainty and fuzziness. In this context, we describe the support for non-spatial and fuzzy spatial queries as well as fuzzy spatiotemporal query types. In addition, while OLAP mainly includes historical data and associated queries and analyzes, we describe how to handle predictive fuzzy spatiotemporal queries, which may require an inference mechanism. We also show that various complex queries, including predictive fuzzy spatiotemporal queries, are effectively and efficiently handled using our fuzzy SOLAP framework.

Keywords: OLAP · Fuzzy spatial-temporal query · Predictive fuzzy spatial-temporal query

This study is supported in part by NU Faculty Development Competitive Research Grants Program, Nazarbayev University, Republic of Kazakhstan, under Grant Number 110119FD4543.

T. Andreasen et al. (Eds.): FQAS 2021, LNAI 12871, pp. 109–126, 2021.
https://doi.org/10.1007/978-3-030-86967-0_9

1   Introduction

Nowadays, the amount and variety of data used for analysis purposes have increased a lot. The improvement in data to be analyzed makes it necessary to use the expertise and suitable application for processing and interpreting this data. For this purpose, various methods and applications have been developed to analyze large amounts of data. One of the most common of these applications developed is Online Analytical Processing (OLAP) [1]. OLAP enables data analysis and query processes to help decision-making on the data source. It is a computing method that allows users to quickly and selectively extract and query data to analyze it from different perspectives. OLAP has emerged because classical databases cannot be functional in decision-making and require expertise in accessing data. While classical databases are concerned with retaining data more efficiently, OLAP is concerned with making better inferences.

We use challenging 40-year meteorological data from the General Directorate of Meteorology of Turkey to leverage significant knowledge. This meteorological data is massive with spatial and temporal information. Space and time are concepts in meteorological applications, and therefore data mining systems are needed to deal with spatial and temporal phenomena. At this point, we can use spatial OLAP (SOLAP) as an OLAP type that supports spatial analysis and queries. Since SOLAP has a multi-dimensional and hierarchical structure, it provides a suitable environment for querying and analyzing meteorological data. In other words, due to the hierarchical structure of the location and time information in the meteorology data and the multi-dimensional measurement results, it is an appropriate approach to consider them in the SOLAP structure.

In addition, SOLAP provides querying and analysis of numeric and alphanumeric multi-dimensional data. However, there is still a need to support flexible queries on uncertain and fuzzy data due to the nature of the complex applications such as meteorological and spatiotemporal applications. Here, uncertainty and fuzziness are inherent features of most meteorological applications [2]. That is, spatial and temporal information and various relationships in these applications frequently involve uncertainty and fuzziness. For example, in describing a rainy region, the region's boundary is a fuzzy concept. Likewise, in estimating a weather event, the need to determine its position at a particular time, or its time of occurrence at a specific location, gives rise to fuzzy estimations.

In this study, we show that using a fuzzy approach is suitable for handling meteorological data. This is so because meteorological databases inherently contain spatiotemporality, uncertainty, and fuzziness. Therefore, we present our approach to deal with different types of fuzzy spatiotemporal queries on this database. In this context, we explain how to support fuzzy non-spatial, fuzzy spatial, and fuzzy spatiotemporal query types on SOLAP. We have developed a fuzzy SOLAP-based framework that supports these complex and fuzzy query types. In general, our fuzzy SOLAP framework includes SOLAP, Fuzzy Module, Fuzzy Knowledge Base, and Fuzzy Inference System (FIS), as shown in Fig. 2. This framework allows us to make efficient and flexible fuzzy queries and analyses on meteorological data.

Usage of OLAP is mainly related to querying and analyzing historical data, but we have to make predictions based on meteorological data. In this study, we describe how to handle predictive fuzzy spatiotemporal queries that require an inference mechanism. We also show that various complex queries, including predictive fuzzy spatiotemporal queries, are effectively and efficiently handled using our fuzzy spatial OLAP framework. We do this with the support of the association rules and FIS components of the fuzzy SOLAP-based framework. In other words, the FIS component included in the framework supports predictive fuzzy query types.

The organization of this paper is as follows: previous work on the subject is discussed in Sect. 2. Information on the structure and characteristics of the meteorological data set is given in Sect. 3. The components of the proposed architecture are explained in Sect. 4, and then the details of fuzzy spatiotemporal query types are provided in Sect. 5. Finally, in Sect. 6, the conclusion and future works are presented.

2 Background and Related Works

The increase in spatial data and human limitations in analyzing spatial data in detail make querying spatial databases crucial in spatiotemporal applications. Supporting spatial queries is one of the key features in the spatial database management system due to its broad range of applications. Providing these types of queries involves introducing spatial components such as fuzzy topological relations in relational and object-relational databases. Fuzzy topological relations between fuzzy regions are explained in [25] and shown in Fig. 1b. The formal definitions of the fuzzy topological relations can be explained as follows:

Let A be a set of attributes under consideration and let a region be a fuzzy subset defined in two-dimensional space R^2 over A. We can define the membership function of the region as $\mu : X \times Y \times A \to [0,1]$, where X and Y are the sets of coordinates defining the region. Each point (x,y) within the region is assigned a membership value for an attribute $a \in A$. We can show a fuzzy region in Fig. 1a, which has the core, the indeterminate boundary, exterior, and $\alpha - cut$ levels.

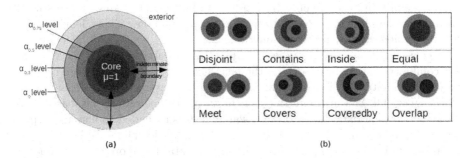

(a)   (b)

Fig. 1. (a) Visualisation of a simple fuzzy region. (b) Examples of topological relations between fuzzy regions.

The concept of $\alpha - cut$ level region is used to approximate the indeterminate boundaries of a fuzzy region and defined as follows:

$$R_\alpha = \{(x, y, a)|\mu_R(x, y, a) \geq \alpha\}(0 < \alpha < 1) \tag{1}$$

The degree of the fuzzy relation is measured by aggregating the $\alpha - cut$ level of fuzzy regions. The basic probability assignment $m(R_{\alpha i})$, which can be interpreted as the probability that $R_{\alpha i}$ is the true representative of R, is defined as in [26,27]:

$$m(R_{\alpha i}) = \alpha_i - \alpha_{i+1}, 1 \leq i \leq n, n \in N, 1 = \alpha_1 > \alpha_2 > ... > \alpha_n > \alpha_{n+1} = 0 \tag{2}$$

Assume that $\tau(R, S)$ be the value representing the topological relation between two fuzzy regions R and S, and $\tau(R_{\alpha i}, R_{\alpha j})$ be the value representing the topological relation between two $\alpha - cut$ level regions $R_{\alpha i}$ and $S_{\alpha j}$. Then the general relation between two fuzzy regions can be determined by

$$\tau(R, S) = \sum_{i=1}^{n} \sum_{j=1}^{m} m(R_{\alpha i})m(S_{\alpha j})\tau(R_{\alpha i}, S_{\alpha j}) \tag{3}$$

For example, the overlap relation between two fuzzy regions can be approximated by using the formula above as follows:

$$\tau(R, S) = \sum_{i=1}^{n} \sum_{j=1}^{m} m(R_{\alpha i})m(S_{\alpha j})\tau_{overlap}(R_{\alpha i}, S_{\alpha j}) \tag{4}$$

Since the spatial OLAP querying deals with some concepts expressed by verbal language, the fuzziness in spatial OLAP is frequently involved. Hence, the ability to query spatial data under fuzziness is an essential characteristic of any spatial database. The studies in [3,4] discuss the directional and topological relationships in fuzzy concepts. Some earlier works [5,12] provide a basis for fuzzy querying capabilities based on a binary model to support queries of this nature. Another study [13] is about unary operators on querying fuzzy multidimensional databases. The study discusses the properties of unary operators on fuzzy cubes and investigates the combination of several queries to explore the possibility for the definition of an algebra to manipulate fuzzy cubes. All of these studies mainly focus on modeling basic fuzzy object types and operations, leaving aside the processing of more advanced queries.

In existing fuzzy OLAP studies [14–16], OLAP mining and fuzzy data mining are combined to take advantage of the fact that fuzzy set theory treats numeric values more naturally, increases understanding, and extracts more generalizable rules. Fuzzy OLAPs are performed on fuzzy multidimensional databases. The multidimensional data model of data warehouses is extended to manage imperfect and imprecise data (i.e., rainy days) of the real world. These studies typically focus on finding knowledge about fuzzy spatial data, but more complex queries (i.e., select rainy regions) are unavailable.

In addition, there are studies [17,18] on nearest neighbor and range type queries in the field of fuzzy spatial queries. These studies work on the range and nearest neighbor queries in the context of fuzzy objects with indeterminate boundaries. They show that processing these types of queries in spatial OLAP is essential, but the query types are too limited. Support for complex spatial query types is still required.

Special structures are developed for efficient and effective queries on fuzzy spatiotemporal data [19,20]. In these studies, novel indexes such as R* tree [21], X-tree [22] for efficient and effective queries have been used, but the benefits of spatial OLAP lack for queries.

3 Meteorological Database

In this study, we utilize a spatiotemporal database including real meteorological measurements, which have been observed and collected in Turkey for many years. The spatial extent of Turkey is 36 N to 42 N in latitudes and from 26 E to 45 E in longitudes. The meteorological data measurement interval of the study is 1970 to 2017. There are seven geographical regions in Turkey. These geographic regions are separated according to their climate, location, flora and fauna, human habitat, agricultural diversities, transportation, topography, etc. The regions' names are; Mediterranean, Black Sea, Marmara, Aegean, Central Anatolia, Eastern Anatolian, Southeastern Anatolia. We have meteorological measurement data in our meteorological database from 1161 meteorological observation stations. These stations are selected from different geographic regions. The sample data of different meteorological stations are given in Table 1.

Table 1. Meteorological station samples from station database table

Station no	Station name	City	Town	Latitude	Longitude	Altitude
17038	Trabzon Havaalanı	Trabzon	Ortahisar	409.950	397.830	39
17040	Rize	Rize	Merkez	410.400	405.013	3
17050	Edirne	Edirne	Merkez	416.767	265.508	51
17064	İstanbul	İstanbul	Kartal	409.113	291.558	18

3.1 Tables in the Meteorological Database

In this study, we use database tables containing ten types of meteorological measurements for our different queries. The types of meteorological measurements are daily vapor pressure, daily hours of sunshine, daily max speed, and direction of the wind, daily average actual pressure, daily average cloudiness, daily average relative humidity, the daily average speed of the wind, daily average temperature, daily total rainfall - manual and daily total rainfall - omgi. The database table names of the measurement types and the details of each measurement are described in Table 2.

Table 2. Database tables and descriptions

Table name	Description	Units
station	Station code, names, city, and coordinates	latitude, longitude, and altitude
vapor-pressure	Daily vapor pressure	hectopascal (1 hPa = 100 Pa)
sunshine-hour	Daily hours of sunshine hours in a day	hours
speed-direction-wind	Daily max speed and direction of the wind	meter/second and direction
average-pressure	The daily average actual pressure	hectopascal (1 hPa = 100 Pa)
cloudiness	Daily average cloudiness	8 octa
average-humidity	Daily average relative humidity	percentage
average-speed-wind	The daily average speed of the wind	meter per second
average-temperature	Daily average temperature	celsius
total-rainfall-manual	Daily total rainfall - manual	kg per meter square
total-rainfall-omgi	Daily total rainfall - omgi	kg per meter square

These tables contain daily measurements from 01.01.1970 to 01.01.2017. Each table's records consist of station number, measurement type, measurement date, and measurement value. In addition, the sample data of the wind's daily average speed is given in Table 3.

Table 3. Sample data of daily average in the wind speed table

Station no	Station name	Year	Month	Day	The daily average speed of wind (m/s)
8541	HASSA	1977	1	1	1.3
8541	HASSA	1977	1	2	1.1
8541	HASSA	1977	1	3	3.1
8541	HASSA	1977	1	4	3.4

4   Fuzzy SOLAP-Based Framework

This section describes the architecture and provided query types that support fuzzy spatiotemporal queries on spatial OLAP-based structures. The proposed architecture basically includes the SOLAP server, Fuzzy Module (FM), Fuzzy Knowledge Base (FKB), Fuzzy Inference System (FIS), and Query Module (QM) components, as shown in Fig. 2.

Query Module (QM) is the component which handles query operations. It includes subcomponents such as Query Interface (QIn), Query Parser (QPr), and Query Processor (QPc). User queries are entered into the system via the query interface. QIn component gets user inquires and sends these queries to the QPr. After the query is evaluated, the query results are displayed to the user.

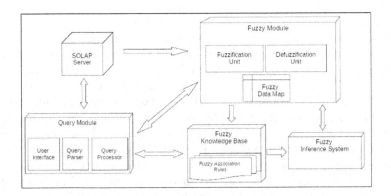

Fig. 2. Proposed fuzzy SOLAP based framework.

The QPr component parses and interprets the user query and determines which elements will process the query. The QPc works as a subcomponent responsible for running the query on the related systems and displaying the results by collecting them. In other words, the QPc component plays a coordinating role in query processing. The QPc performs the communication and interaction between the SOLAP, FIS, and the Fuzzy Module. It gets user queries, analyzes them, sends requests to the SOLAP and/or to the FKB/FM, retrieves the results, and sends them up to the query interface.

Fuzzy Module is the component that provides crisp to fuzzy or fuzzy to crisp transformations with fuzzification and defuzzification operations. In this module, by using the Fuzzy C-Means (FCM) algorithm [7,8], fuzzy clustering is done to generate membership classes and determine membership values. FCM needs the number of clusters as a parameter. Therefore, we use X-means clustering [6] to determine the appropriate number of clusters, and we cross-check the cluster with elbow [10] and silhouette [11] methods. In addition, the definitions of uncertain types, similarity relations, and membership functions are stored in the fuzzy data map.

Fuzzy Knowledge Base produces and stores fuzzy association rules. After fuzzifying the meteorological data on SOLAP, we generate fuzzy association rules with the FP-Growth algorithm [9] and keep them in the FKB. We optimize the resulting extensive list of rules using the confidence measure-based pruning method [28] for performance improvement. The rules in FKB are used in case of inference. Therefore, we use these rules as input for the FIS.

We use the FIS to support prediction-type queries. We apply the fuzzy association rules required for the criteria explored in the inquiry process in the FIS by taking their place in the FKB. In addition, we provide the fuzzy membership classes and membership values required for the values in the query as input to the FIS.

SOLAP server acts as a database server for objects and provides an application that stores meteorological measurement results, including spatial-temporal hierarchies, and supports Multi-Dimensional Extension (MDX) query types. We use GeoMondrian SOLAP Server [23] in our system. After the Extract Transform Load (ETL) process, we insert the meteorological data on the spatial OLAP server. We save this data on spatial OLAP as spatial, temporal, and measurement value hierarchies. The spatial hierarchy has region, city, and station breakdowns. We can do spatial hierarchy with a foreign key as in classical relational databases, or we can provide it with a minimum bounded rectangle (MBR) structure with the support of the spatial structure. The temporal hierarchy is organized according to year, month, and day divisions. Also, each measurement result is kept in a hierarchical structure in OLAP. The algorithm for implementing queries is given in Algorithm 1 and some sample queries are defined in the next section.

5   Supported Query Types

After we illustrate the architecture of the proposed environment for fuzzy spatiotemporal querying, we apply the following procedures to handle the various query types employing the given components.

5.1   Fuzzy Non-Spatial Query

This query type is about asking for fuzzy data, not dealing with spatial attributes. The QM, the FM, and the SOLAP server components are working in the execution step:

1. The QM retrieves the user query, parses it, and sends it to the FM for defuzzification.
2. The QM asks the SOLAP server for data using the defuzzified query. The objects retrieved by the QM are sent to the FM component to fuzzify the result.
3. Fuzzified query results are displayed in the QM component.

Algorithm 1. The generic query evaluation algorithm

Input: The user *query* with set of column members CLN and predicates PR
Output: Set of retrieved/predicted objects RSL

    Initialization :

    $FT_p \leftarrow \{\}$ //*fuzzy membership terms*
    $FAR \leftarrow \{\}$ //*fuzzy association rules*
    $SP_t \leftarrow \{\}$ //*spatial terms*
    $NSP_t \leftarrow \{\}$ //*non-spatial terms, measurement*
    $D_s \leftarrow \{\}$ //*SOLAP data cube query result holder*
    $S_O \leftarrow \{\}$ //*satisfying-objects*

1: Retrieve and Parse(*query*)
2: **if** query includes prediction predicate(PR) **then**
3:    Send query to FKB with (CLN,PR)
4:    Transfer to FIS with (CLN,PR)
5:    $FAR \leftarrow$ Retrieve fuzzy association rules from FKB with (CLN,PR)
6:    $FT_p \leftarrow$ Retrieve fuzzy memberships from FM with (CLN,PR)
7:    $SP_t \leftarrow$ Defuzzify spatial predicates with (CLN)
8:    $NSP_t \leftarrow$ Defuzzify non-spatial predicates with (PR)
9:    $D_s \leftarrow$ Query spatial temporal data from SOLAP with (SP_t,NSP_t)
10:    $S_O \leftarrow$ Make prediction with (FAR, FT_p,D_s)
11:    **return** S_O
12: **else**
13:    **if** query is spatial **then**
14:        $SP_t \leftarrow$ Defuzzify spatial predicates with (CLN)
15:        $NSP_t \leftarrow$ Defuzzify non-spatial predicates with (PR)
16:        $D_s \leftarrow$ Query spatial temporal data from SOLAP with (SP_t,NSP_t)
17:        $S_O \leftarrow$ Fuzzify satisfying objects with (D_s)
18:        **return** S_O
19:    **else**
20:        $NSP_t \leftarrow$ Defuzzify non-spatial predicates with (PR)
21:        $D_s \leftarrow$ Query spatial temporal data from SOLAP with (NSP_t)
22:        $S_O \leftarrow$ Fuzzify satisfying objects with (D_s)
23:        **return** S_O
24:    **end if**
25: **end if**

Query1: *Find all the cities at risk of flooding*

The query is expressed in MDX, which is an OLAP query language. This language provides a specialized syntax for querying and manipulating the multidimensional data stored in OLAP cubes [24]. While it is possible to translate some of these into traditional SQL, it would frequently require the synthesis of clumsy SQL expressions, even for elementary MDX expressions. Nevertheless, many OLAP vendors have used MDX, and it has become the standard for OLAP systems. While it is not an open standard, it is embraced by a wide range of OLAP vendors. Therefore, we extend MDX with fuzzy operators and write the query specified above in MDX form as follows:

```
SELECT {
    FILTER(
    {
        fuzzify_measure([Measures].[Rainfall])
    },
    fuzzify_measure([Measures].currentmember.rainfall)= "heavy"
    )
} ON COLUMNS,
{
    [Station.StationHierarchy].[Station City].members
} ON ROWS
FROM [MeteorologicalCube]
WHERE ([DateDimension1.Date Hierarchy 0].[All Dates])
```

To query the database, we first need to defuzzfy the fuzzy expression part of the query. The QM requests the FM to defuzzify the fuzzy expression in the query. The fuzzy term is defuzzified according to the fuzzy membership function, as shown in Fig. 3. The *heavy* class in the query has a triangular-shaped membership function defined by the triple (7.5, 8.5, 9.5) that overlaps the membership function of the *overmuch* class in the range [7.5, 8.5]. In this case, the *heavy* class includes measurements between 8.0 and 9.5. The QM rearranges the MDX query with the crisp values after defuzzification and sends it to the SOLAP server. As a result of the query on SOLAP, the results matching the searched criteria contain crisp data. We again fuzzify the crisp values in the result data with the help of the FM. Here, the Fuzzification subcomponent in FM includes a triangular or trapezoidal membership function for each measurement result. It generates fuzzy class and membership values as output using the crisp value of input from the relevant membership function. Finally, we display them to the user in a way that includes fuzzy terms. For our example, we show the R1 and R4 records in Table 4 as the query result that meets the criteria.

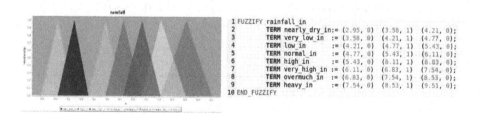

Fig. 3. Rainfall membership classes.

Suppose we execute this query in a relational database. In that case, we need to thoroughly scan all records because it is necessary to calculate the rainfall value and find the queried value by grouping based on the city within the station measurement records. The cost of scanning all the data and grouping them is critical; the query execution time is related to the number of records in the database. In the SOLAP environment, it is not necessary to access all records for the objects that satisfy the query criteria with the help of the hierarchical structure. The calculation of the measurements of the cities, which the stations are connected, does not imply such a cost. Therefore, the cost of searching rainy stations is limited to the number of stations registered in the database, and the query execution time is less than the relational database query execution time.

Table 4. Sample data of rainfall in database

ID	Date	City	Crisp val.	Fuzzy val.
R1	19.08.2016	Ankara	8.6	Heavy(0.7)
R2	19.08.2016	Konya	4.9	Low(0.7)
R3	19.08.2016	Adana	4.1	Very-low(0.6)
R4	19.08.2016	Rize	8.8	Heavy(0.8)

5.2   Fuzzy Spatial Query

Fuzzy spatial queries allow to interrogate fuzzy spatial objects and their relationships. The QM, the FM, and the SOLAP server components are employed to fetch query results. The user asks for the objects that have topological relations with the entities under inquiry.

Query2: *Retrieve the appropriate cities for the installation of a solar power plant*
A fuzzy rule definition uses linguistic values as follows in FKB regarding suitable places for solar power plants.

```
if city.sunshine_hour is high and city.position is south
                        then city.solar_power is high
```

We can define the query syntax's implementation in MDX as follows:

```
SELECT {
  FILTER(
  {
    fuzzify_measure([Measures].[Sunshine_hour])
  },
  fuzzify_measure(AVG([Measures].currentmember.sunshine_hour)) ="HIGH"
  )} ON COLUMNS,
  FILTER(
  {
    [Station].[Station City].members
  },
  fuzzify_geo([Station].currentmember.PROPERTIES("geom"),
              [Station].[Station Region].PROPERTIES("geom"))="SOUTH"
  ) ON ROWS
FROM [MeteorologicalCube]
WHERE ([DateDimension1.Date Hierarchy 0].[All Dates])
```

In this query, the regions in the south of Turkey with a very high sunshine duration are considered. The intersection of areas that are a positionally high sunshine hour and south fields are taken into account. We explained the operational structure of the *FUZZIFY_MEASURE* method in the previous query. New here is the *FUZZIFY_GEO* method. This method is run on the FM and determines the overlap relation between two geometric objects given as parameters. There are as many accesses in the query process as the number of stations in the database. On the other hand, the execution time for the relational database query, given in the following, can be longer because of averaging sunshine hour measurement and joining with the stations.

```
SELECT c.name_1, r.month, r.day, AVG(sunshine_hour)
FROM met_data_rainfall r, tr_city c,
     meteorological_station3 s, tr_region rg
WHERE s.id=r.station_id AND s.city_id=c.gid
  AND rg.id=c.region_id AND c.region_id in(5,7)
GROUP BY c.name_1, r.month, r.day HAVING AVG(sunshine_hour)>7
```

In this query, it has been taken into account that cities with an average daily sunshine duration of more than seven hours have a high sunshine duration. Also, these cities are in the Mediterranean and Southeastern Anatolia regions in the south.

5.3   Fuzzy Spatiotemporal Query

In this type of query, the user asks for the fuzzy spatial objects that meet the conditions of the predefined rules within a specified time interval. The rules can be evaluated by an examination of topological relations between fuzzy regions and fuzzy objects.

Query3: *Retrieve locations around Ankara that were at high risk of freezing between January 7, 2012 and January 14, 2012.*
FKB contains the following fuzzy rule definition that uses linguistic values regarding freezing events.

```
if city.temperature is cold and city.cloudiness is clear
                         then city.freeze_risk is high
```

The query syntax's implementation in MDX is represented as follows:

```
WITH MEMBER
 [Station.StationHierarchy].[Station Region]
                    .[IC ANADOLU REGION].[Around Somewhere in Ankara]
                      AS
AGGREGATE(
 FILTER(
   [Station.StationHierarchy].[Station Region].members,
   fuzzify_geo(st_transform([Station].currentmember.PROPERTIES("geom
         "), 4326, 2991), st_transform(st_geomfromtext("POINT(-120.215
         _44.998)"), 4326, 2991))= "AROUND")
 ), geom=st_transform(st_geomfromtext("POINT(-120.215_44.998)"),
     4326, 2991)
SELECT {
   FILTER({fuzzify_measure([Measures].[Temperature])},
          fuzzify_measure([Measures].currentmember.temperature)="
          COLD"
   ),
   FILTER({fuzzify_measure([Measures].[Cloudiness])},
```

```
           fuzzify_measure ([Measures].currentmember.cloudiness)="
              CLEAR"
   )
} ON COLUMNS,
{
  [Station.StationHierarchy].[Station Region].[IC ANADOLU REGION].
     children ,
     [Station.StationHierarchy].[All Stations]
              .[IC ANADOLU REGION].[Around Somewhere in Ankara]
} ON ROWS
FROM [MeteorologicalCube]
WHERE (
        [DateDimension1.Date Hierarchy 0].[All Dates].[2012].[1].[7]:
        [DateDimension1.Date Hierarchy 0].[All Dates].[2012].[1].[14]
   )
```

In addition to the previous query, we can make more specific queries using conditions on date attribute. The handling of the fuzzy predicates in the query operation is the same as that of the fuzzy spatial query. For the distance attribute, the membership classes in Fuzzy Data Map are NEAR, CLOSE, and AROUND. We create these fuzzy classes by calculating the paired distances of the geometric data of the stations and applying fuzzy clustering of these values. However, the date predicate greatly reduces the amount of data to be retrieved from the database. As we mentioned earlier, this situation, which requires a full scan of an indexless relational database, is easily handled with the temporal hierarchy in the SOLAP environment. The execution time of the query depends on the number of stations in the database. Relational database systems must fully search for temperature and cloudiness between the given dates. In this case, the query execution time is proportional to the number of records and the number of stations in the database.

5.4   Fuzzy Spatiotemporal Predictive Query

This type of query is about asking for fuzzy spatial relations and specified time with inference. The QM, the FM, FIS, the FKB, and the SOLAP server components are employed to fetch query results. The QM retrieves the user query, parses it, and sends it to the FM for defuzzification. If the QM detects the inference operand in the query, it sends the conditions to the FKB for inference. When the FKB receives the request from the QM, it determines and sends the fuzzy association rules to the FIS, and the FIS gets membership classes/functions from the Fuzzy Data Map subcomponent. The FIS makes predictions with the given parameters and the collected knowledge, and then it sends back the inference to the QM.

Query4: *Is there a possibility of a windstorm around Izmir during the last week of December?*
FKB contains the following rules for meteorological events that occur depending on wind speed.

```
if station.windspeed is high then city.storm_occurrence is
   possible
if station.windspeed is high and actual_pressure is low
                  then city.storm_occurrence is high—
                        possible
```

The MDX form of the query is given as follows:

```
WITH MEMBER
    [Station.StationHierarchy].[Station Region]
                    .[EGE REGION].[Around Somewhere in Izmir]
                        AS
AGGREGATE(
    FILTER(
        [Station.StationHierarchy].[Station Region].members,
        fuzzify_geo(st_transform([Station].currentmember.PROPERTIES("
           geom"),3145,3371), st_transform(st_geomfromtext("POINT_
           (−112.526_52.263)"), 3145,3371))="AROUND"
    )
), geom=st_transform(st_geomfromtext("POINT_(−112.526_52.263)"),
      3145, 3371)
SELECT {
    FILTER({fuzzify_measure([Measures].[Windspeed])},
            fuzzify_measure([Measures].currentmember.windspeed)="
           HIGH"
    )
} ON COLUMNS,

{ [Station.StationHierarchy].[Station Region].[EGE REGION].
    children,
    [Station.StationHierarchy].[All Stations].[EGE REGION]
                        .[Around Somewhere in Izmir]
} ON ROWS
FROM [MeteorologicalCube]
WHERE {
    PREDICT(
        [DateDimension1.Date Hierarchy 0].[All Dates].[12].[23]:
        [DateDimension1.Date Hierarchy 0].[All Dates].[12].[31]
    )
}
```

Unlike other query types, this query type supports predictions by using the FKB and the FIS. When QM detects the *PREDICT* expression in the query, it recognizes that the query is requiring our inference mechanism. As in other spatial queries, the QM organizes spatial data with fuzzify/defuzzify operations on the FM side and retrieves the data from stations around Izmir between December 23 and 31 on SOLAP.

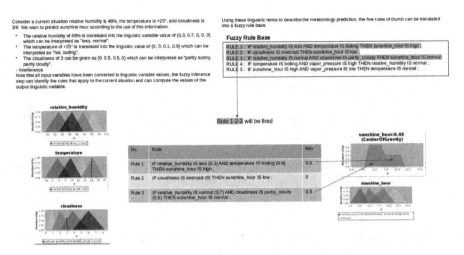

Fig. 4. A sample inference.

The FIS uses the measurement values in these obtained records as parameters when firing fuzzy association rules. After the QM gets SOLAP data, it fuzzifies them on the FM. It then sends the fuzzified data to the FKB, allowing it to determine which FIS will use fuzzy association rules. The FKB transfers the selected fuzzy association rules to the FIS. The FIS makes predictions by using these rules and the fuzzy membership classes obtained by the FM. Since there are 40 measurement results for the same month and day in 40 years of data, the FIS fires a different rule for each measurement input and stores the inference value. Finally, it determines the output with the maximum membership value and shows it to the user as the final prediction.

A sample inference is given in Fig. 4. In this example, consider a current situation in which the relative humidity is 48%, the temperature is +25°, and cloudiness is 3/8. We want to predict sunshine hour according to the use of this information. The relative humidity of 48% is translated into the linguistic variable value of $\{0.3, 0.7, 0, 0, 0\}$ which can be interpreted as "less, normal". Similarly, linguistic translation can be done in "hot, boiling" for temperature and "partly sunny, partly cloudy" for cloudiness. After all input variables have been converted to linguistic variable values, the fuzzy inference step can identify the rules that apply to the current situation and can compute the values of the output linguistic variable. We can translate the five rules of thumb into a fuzzy rule base by using these linguistic terms to describe the meteorology prediction, as seen in the figure. We select the rules according to the consequent part. There are three proper rules which have sunshine hour consequent to be fired for inference. After rules are executed, we apply the center of gravity method to find the final predicted value.

We have achieved the performance of the prototype application in the following environment with the specified specifications, technology, and tools below.

- *Application development environment*: Eclipse IDE 2021-03
- *System*: Windows 10 x64, Intel i5-7200U CPU, 16 GB RAM
- *Java*:1.8.0-281, Java HotSpot Client 64-bit Server VM 25.281-b09
- *SOLAP*: GeoMondrian 1.0 Server
- *DBMS*: PostgreSQL 13.3 64-bit
- *FIS*: jFuzzyLogic.jar
- *Data Size*: Approximately 10GB data consists of 1161 stations and 15M records for each measurements (15M × 10 types measurement)

We measure the query execution times by running each query type in both the fuzzy SOLAP-based framework and PostgreSQL database. Query execution time comparisons for all query types are shown in Table 5.

Table 5. Comparision of query execution time between Fuzzy SOLAP Based Framework query and Relational Database SQL query

	Fuzzy SOLAP based framework query execution time (ms)	Relational database SQL query execution time (ms)
Query1	596480	1630362
Query2	257054	643642
Query3	18314	172303
Query4	183717	Not Supported

6   Conclusion

The aim of this study is to carry out a generic fuzzy querying approach to process complex and fuzzy queries using our fuzzy SOLAP-based framework. We also aim to manage uncertainty in spatiotemporal database applications while querying the database. We used a real-life database involving meteorological objects with certain spatial and temporal attributes as a case study. The proposed mechanism has been implemented, and we have discussed several implementation issues that arise when querying the database.

In this study, meteorological aspects and geographic data are used as spatiotemporal objects. Furthermore, the inference system in the fuzzy SOLAP environment integrates the model with a fuzzy inference system for allowing prediction over spatiotemporal data. As a result, we can handle fuzzy spatiotemporal predictive query types.

For future study, modeling and querying spatiotemporal data requires further research. The model and method presented in this study can be adjusted and/or extended to other application fields, such as agriculture, environment, etc. We have implemented some fuzzy methods needed during this study, but the set of fuzzy methods should be further worked on and extended to different areas.

References

1. Codd, E.F., Codd, S.B., Salley, C.T.: Providing OLAP (On-Line Analytical Processing) to User-Analysts: An IT Mandate. Arbor Software Corporation (1993)
2. Kaya, M., Alhajj, R.: Fuzzy OLAP association rules mining-based modular reinforcement learning approach for multiagent systems. IEEE Trans. Syst. Man Cybern. Part B **35**(2), 326–338 (2005)
3. Taldmhi, E., Shima, N., Kishino, F.: An image retrieval method using inquires on spatial relationships. J. lnf. Process. **15**(3), 441–449 (1992)
4. Winter, S.: Topological relations between discrete regions. In: Egenhofer, M.J., Herring, J.R. (eds.) SSD 1995. LNCS, vol. 951, pp. 310–327. Springer, Heidelberg (1995). https://doi.org/10.1007/3-540-60159-7_19
5. Cobb, M.A.: Modeling spatial relationships within a fuzzy framework. J. Am. Soc. Inf. Sci. **49**(3), 253–266 (1998)
6. Pelleg, D., Moore, A.: X-means: extending K-means with efficient estimation of the number of clusters. In: Proceedings of 17th International Conference on Machine Learning, pp. 727–734 (2000)
7. Dunn, J.C.: A fuzzy relative of the ISODATA process and its use in detecting compact well-separated clusters. J. Cybern. **3**(3), 32–57 (1973)
8. Bezdek, J.: A convergence theorem for the fuzzy ISODATA clustering algorithms. IEEE Trans. Pattern Anal. Machine Intell. **PAMI-2**, 1–8 (1980)
9. Soni, H.K., et al.: Frequent pattern generation algorithms for association rule mining: strength and challenges. In: 2016 International Conference on Electrical, Electronics, and Optimization Techniques (ICEEOT) (2016)
10. Marutho, D., et al.: The determination of cluster number at K-mean using elbow method and purity evaluation on headline news. In: 2018 International Seminar on Application for Technology of Information and Communication (2018)
11. Rousseeuw, P.J.: Silhouettes: a graphical aid to the interpretation and validation of cluster analysis. J. Comput. Appl. Math. **20**, 53–65 (1987)
12. Yang, H., Cobb, M., Shaw, K.: A clips-based implementation for querying binary spatial relationships. In: Proceedings of Joint 9 U? IFSA World Congress and 20' NAFIPS International Conference, Vancouver, Canada (2001)
13. Laurent, A.: Querying fuzzy multidimensional databases: unary operators and their properties. Int. J. Uncertainty Fuzziness Knowl.-Based Syst. **11**(1), 31–45 (2003)
14. Duračiová, R., Faixová Chalachanová, J.: Fuzzy spatio-temporal querying the PostgreSQL/PostGIS database for multiple criteria decision making. In: Ivan, I., Horák, J., Inspektor, T. (eds.) GIS OSTRAVA 2017. LNGC, pp. 81–97. Springer, Cham (2018). https://doi.org/10.1007/978-3-319-61297-3_7
15. Kumar, K.P., et al.: Fuzzy OLAP cube for qualitative analysis. In: Proceedings of 2005 International Conference on Intelligent Sensing and Information Processing (2005). https://doi.org/10.1109/icisip.2005.1529464
16. Ladner, R., et al.: Fuzzy set approaches to spatial data mining of association rules. Trans. GIS **7**(1), 123–138 (2003)
17. Zheng, K., et al.: Spatial query processing for fuzzy objects. VLDB J. **21**(5), 729–751 (2012)
18. Nurain, N., et al.: Group nearest neighbor queries for fuzzy geo-spatial objects. In: Second International ACM Workshop on Managing and Mining Enriched Geo-Spatial Data (2015). https://doi.org/10.1145/2786006.2786011
19. Sözer, A., et al.: Querying fuzzy spatiotemporal databases: implementation issues. In: Uncertainty Approaches for Spatial Data Modeling and Processing Studies in Computational Intelligence, pp. 97–116 (2010)

126   S. Keskin and A. Yazıcı

20. Keskin, S., Yazıcı, A., Oğuztüzün, H.: Implementation of X-tree with 3D spatial index and fuzzy secondary index. In: Christiansen, H., De Tré, G., Yazici, A., Zadrozny, S., Andreasen, T., Larsen, H.L. (eds.) FQAS 2011. LNCS (LNAI), vol. 7022, pp. 72–83. Springer, Heidelberg (2011). https://doi.org/10.1007/978-3-642-24764-4_7
21. Beckmann, N., et al.: The R*-Tree: an efficient and robust access method for points and rectangles. In: Proceedings of the 1990 ACM SIGMOD International Conference on Management of Data - SIGMOD 1990 (1990)
22. Berchtold, S., et al.: The X-tree: an index structure for high-dimensional data. In: 22th International Conference on Very Large Data Bases (VLDB 1996), pp. 28–39. Morgan Kaufmann Publishers Inc., San Francisco (1996)
23. GeoMondrian SOLAP Server. http://www.spatialytics.org/blog/geomondrian-1-0-is-available-for-download. Accessed Dec 2020
24. Spofford, G., et al.: MDX-Solutions. Wiley, Hoboken (2006)
25. Schneider, M.: A design of topological predicates for complex crisp and fuzzy regions. In: S.Kunii, H., Jajodia, S., Sølvberg, A. (eds.) ER 2001. LNCS, vol. 2224, pp. 103–116. Springer, Heidelberg (2001). https://doi.org/10.1007/3-540-45581-7_10
26. Tang, X., Fang, Yu., Kainz, W.: Fuzzy topological relations between fuzzy spatial objects. In: Wang, L., Jiao, L., Shi, G., Li, X., Liu, J. (eds.) FSKD 2006. LNCS (LNAI), vol. 4223, pp. 324–333. Springer, Heidelberg (2006). https://doi.org/10.1007/11881599_37
27. Zhan, F.B., Lin, H.: Overlay of two simple polygons with indeterminate boundaries. Trans. GIS 7(1), 67–81 (2003). https://doi.org/10.1111/1467-9671.00130
28. Pach, F.P., et al.: Fuzzy association rule mining for the analysis of historical process data. Acta Agraria Kaposváriensis 10(3), 89–107 (2006)

Data Quality Management: An Overview of Methods and Challenges

Antoon Bronselaer$^{(\boxtimes)}$ (iD)

DDCM Lab, Department of Telecommunications and Information Processing,
Ghent University, Ghent, Belgium
`antoon.bronselaer@ugent.be`

Abstract. Data quality is a problem studied in many different research disciplines like computer science, statistics and economics. More often than not, these different disciplines come with different perspectives and emphasis. This paper provides a state-of-the-art of data quality management across these disciplines and organizes techniques on two levels: the macro-level and the micro-level. At the macro-level, emphasis lies on the assessment and improvement of processes that affect data quality. Opposed to that, the micro-level has a strong focus of the current database and aims at detection and repair of specific artefacts or errors. We sketch the general methodology for both of these views on the management of data quality and list common methodologies. Finally, we provide a number of open problems and challenges that provide interesting research paths for the future.

Keyword: Data quality management

1 Introduction

Over the past twenty-five years, the importance of data quality management has silently grown to become an essential part of any modern data-driven process. We are well beyond the point where organizations are ignorant about the potential of using data to optimize processes and activities. The growing awareness of this potential has triggered the need for well-thought data pipelines, in which quality assessment and improvement play a key role. At the same time, the intensified use of data as a resource has created new challenges. Some notable examples include all privacy-related matters and the transfer of certain biases in datasets to models learned on those datasets. It is thus safe to say that on one hand, much progress has been made to a wide variety of problems and this paper aims to provide a concise overview of those developments. On the other hand, this paper also aims to identify some important challenges on the road ahead.

As a practical guidance throughout the paper, data quality will be discussed on two distinct levels: the *macro-level* and the *micro-level*. The positioning of these levels in a typical data management set-up, as well as the goals and methodology are shown in Fig. 1.

© Springer Nature Switzerland AG 2021
T. Andreasen et al. (Eds.): FQAS 2021, LNAI 12871, pp. 127–141, 2021.
https://doi.org/10.1007/978-3-030-86967-0_10

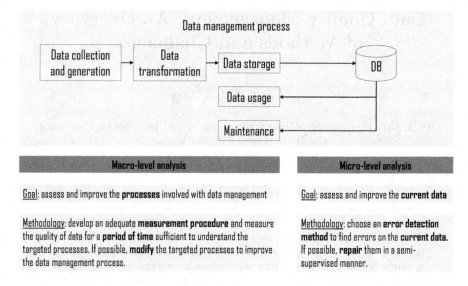

Fig. 1. The data management process with positioning of macro-level and micro-level analysis of data quality.

When talking about data quality on the *macro-level*, we are concerned with the different *processes* that are involved with management of data. In a typical set-up, data are generated, collected, preprocessed or transformed and then stored in a database. Data remain in this database (potentially subjected to maintenance) and can be consulted for a variety of tasks. Sub-optimality of each one of these processes can lead to deterioration of data quality. The main goal of macro-level analysis is therefore to gain insight in these processes and in particular their connection with quality of data in the database.

A typical methodology to tackle this is to carefully design a *measurement procedure* that can be used to monitor the data for a longer period of time, after which decisions regarding process optimization can be taken. Typically, making changes to processes are far from trivial and very costly. The analysis should therefore be done carefully, collect a sufficient amount of measurements over a sufficient period of time so that decisions are well-supported.

Example 1. A typical example of macro-level analysis is when an organisation collects customer address and contact data. Such data are known to become outdated at a certain pace. These data are usually important for several business units like marketing and customer-relationship management (CRM), but it is particularly hard to keep them up-to-date. In this situation, the typical macro-level trade-off appears: how much should an organization invest in keeping these address and contact data up-to-date in such a way the investment still pays off? Such a question is not easily answered, but it goes without a saying that the first step is to gain insight in the extent to which data are still up-to-date.

When talking about data quality on the *micro-level*, we are less concerned with processes that act on data. Instead, micro-level analysis puts an emphasis on the current state of the database and aims to identify errors or artefacts on this database. The artefacts in question are usually very detailed, addressing a single row in a table or even a single value of an attribute, but more general scope are possible. For example, issues with referential integrity in between two tables can be considered as artefacts on the micro-level as well.

Example 2. A typical example of micro-level analysis deals with violations of constraints that data should meet. For example, in a census survey, if a person indicates to be a minor then the yearly income of that person is upper bounded, depending on the precise laws that apply in the country where the census is executed. In a similar spirit, when the same clinical trial is executed in different sites, we expect that certain reported parameters in the design are equal.

It should be noted from the start that the borderline between macro-level and micro-level analysis as introduced here, is not a crisp one. One particular example is when we consider *aggregates* of micro-level errors. Consider for example the presence of NULL-values in the columns of table. A typical micro-level analysis aims to *estimate* values that can be used to fill in missing data. This process is known as *imputation*. However, we could also count the amount of missing data in each column and based on these numbers, we could evaluate whether or not there is a problem with the collection of data for some particular columns. This simple example illustrates that macro-level and micro-level analysis can exploit similar techniques and tools. The main reason we do make the distinction, is because of the difference in the goals and therefore unavoidably also in the methodology. Macro-level analysis operates on an abstract, process-based level, whereas micro-level analysis operators on the data we have at our disposal right now.

The remainder of this paper is organised as follows. In Sect. 2, the common macro-level methodology is introduced and is shown to consist of a *measurement* phase (Sect. 2.1) and an *analysis* phase (Sect. 2.2). In Sect. 3, the common micro-level methodology is treated similarly where we now detail techniques for error *detection* (Sect. 3.1) and error *repair* (Sect. 3.2). In Sect. 4 a short discussion is presented to outline some important challenges for future research. Finally, Sect. 5 wraps up this paper with a brief conclusion.

2 Macro-level Data Quality Management

As explained in the introduction, analysis of data quality at a macro-level aims to grasp the life-cycle of data. From it's origin to it's current state, data are handled by many different processes. Systematic flaws in these processes can cause severe data quality issues over a long period of time. It is therefore key to identify these flaws and correct processes where necessary to create a sustainable data life-cycle.

The hypothesis that modification of data processes can improve data quality is not new. It has been coined and empirically verified in two recent studies

[30, 31]. In particular, these studies provide empirical evidence that an investment in the data collection process positively impacts the quality of data.

On a high level, the main methodology used in macro-level analysis is to develop carefully designed *measurement procedures* [41] to monitor the data, typically but not necessarily, over a longer period of time (Fig. 1). With these measurement procedures, the idea is that some measurable characteristics of the data can be used to learn something about the processes. This learning requires some particular methods that allow to analyse the measurements we collected. Figure 2 shows a schematic overview of this macro-analysis of data quality.

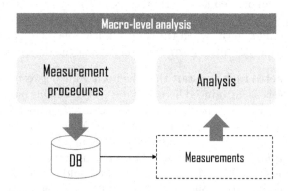

Fig. 2. A schematic overview of macro-level analysis.

In what follows, we discuss some common approaches to develop measurement procedures Sect. 2.1 as well as some approaches to analyse collected measurements.

2.1   Measurement Procedures

Data quality can be measured in several ways. Often, a measurement procedure can be linked to one or more data quality dimensions like accuracy, consistency or completeness [2]. It this paper, we largely omit this link and give a preference to the notion of a measurement procedure because of it's more rigorous nature.

Procedures Based on Rules. Perhaps the most simple method to devise a measurement procedure is to compile a set of rules to which data must adhere. The idea is simple: if data fail some of these rules, then such failure indicates a deterioration of quality. There are several ways in which this deterioration can be quantified. One way is to simply count failing rules, which has been formalized in [48] and been applied in numerous cases [32, 47]. In a more general approach, one can use a capacity function to map sets of rules to levels of quality [9].

The appeal in this approach is that composition of rules is very intuitive and because of this, it has been applied numerous times. A first example is given by the *FAIR principles* that dictate data should Findable, Accessible, Interoperable and Reusable [58]. Other examples include the *five star data model* (five rules to make data more open) and the database *normal forms* (levels of design quality that are obtained if certain criteria are met [15]). Also simple micro-level constraints (e.g., NOT NULL constraints) can be a useful basis for measurement when combined with a suitable analysis technique (Sect. 2.2).

Despite their intuitive nature and easy usage, rule-based approaches towards measurement have some downsides. First of all, rule-based approaches make it difficult if not impossible to quantify differences. For example, failure to meet some FAIR principles does not convey any information about how difficult it is to modify the data in such a way that these principles would be met. A second drawback is that it can be difficult to decide if a rule is satisfied or not. This can be mitigated by dividing abstract constraints into more simple and tangible sub-constraints. But this does not always help. For example, one of the basic criteria for data to be findable is that data are described with rich meta-data [58]. Here, the inclusion of the predicate "rich" makes it more difficult to say if this criterion is met or not. A possible solution for this, is to accept that not all rules can be evaluated with complete certainty and include a notion of (un)certainty about the satisfaction of the rule [54]. This brings us to the next approach towards measurement.

Procedures Based on Uncertainty Models. A second approach to measure data quality is to use an uncertainty model. The idea is now that some aspects of data are either not directly observable or it is very costly to do so. Examples include the reliability of data [40] and the currency of data [33,34]. The latter deals with the question whether or not data are up-to-date or not. In both cases, uncertainty plays a key role. Given some piece of data, we might have no clue about the reliability, but given some additional information (e.g., the provider, the time of generation), we might be able to estimate the reliability. This applies when data are provided by human input (e.g., accounting for fatigue and hunger, [40], pg. 43–44) as well as when data are computer-generated (e.g., accounting for the noise of a sensor). Similarly, if we are given some piece of data, we initially don't know whether it is still up-to-date, but when we know it's age, we can estimate the probability it is.

As indicated in Example 1, usage of uncertainty models can be useful to support decisions. If one is able to adequately model the (un)certainty that address data are still up-to-date, parts of the database can be targeted where data are most likely to be outdated. One drawback is that the construction of an adequate model might be far from easy. For example, the age of address and contact data might be less influential for elderly than for younger people, who are more likely to move. Another drawback is that these models allow to target specific data, but carry no information about the benefits of improving data. One can identify a number of entries, say 10, that are outdated with very high probability, but is it worth it to improve those data? Would it be worth it if it were 1000 entries? Part of the answer lies of course in the analysis strategy we use (Sect. 2.2), but in some cases, we can devise measurement procedures that already convey some information about the *magnitude* of error like approaches based on metrics.

Procedures Based on Metrics. If one is interested in the magnitude of errors, measurement of data quality naturally shifts to the mathematical construct of a metric space (D, d) where D is a set and d is a metric on D. The metric d can then be used to quantify the distances between values. This can for example be used to measure the distance between the data and the actual value it is supposed to represent [29]. A recent study has examined the extent to which junior home loan advisers make errors when entering the value of the collateral for home loans in a Belgian financial institution [28]. One of the main measurement procedures is here to compute the order of magnitude of the error made. By using these measurements, it becomes possible to focus on *large* errors that are made and this provides a very adequate basis for making decisions on which data needs to be improved.

A common downside to using metrics is the assumption that data can be cast into a system (D, d) in such a way d reflects the magnitude of errors. This is relatively easy if data are ratio-scaled numeric data [29] but might become difficult for categorical data. For example, the set of strings can be equipped with a metric like the Levenshtein distance [57] but a greater Levenshtein distance does not always imply a larger error. This does not mean it is impossible to use metrics for categorical data, but it shows one should be cautious when doing so. For example, consider the case of postal codes, which are strictly speaking nominal scaled data. However, in many countries, postal codes carry spatial information. In Belgium, a postal code allows to determine the province and in some other countries like the Netherlands, postal codes even carry more detailed information. Moreover, in the Belgium case, there are some municipalities that are part of a nearby city but are still assigned a distinct postal code. Using such information adds a certain structure to the set D. Codes in the same province imply an equivalence relation and codes of municipalities belonging administratively to a nearby city imply a partial order. These structures can be used to construct a very coarse metric that still reflects the order of magnitude.

Procedures Based on Cost. The final approach to measurement of quality, is the most generic one and accounts for the difficulty to using data for a set of tasks. With this approach, a database is considered for usage in the scope of a series of tasks [10]. To complete those tasks, users need to manipulate the data. Such manipulations can be as simple as a single SQL query and as difficult as the addition of external data sources. Each manipulation comes with a certain *cost* and the quality of data is measured as being inverse proportionate to the minimal cost one needs to pay to complete all tasks.

Working with this approach has several advantages. The notion of cost is universal and often easy to measure (e.g., amount of time, amount of resources, amount of money). Moreover, improvement of processes also come with an investment cost. So if one is able to quantify the improvement of certain steps as a cost, one can immediately compare this improvement with the investment cost.

The methodology also does not rely on any assumptions like the existence of an uncertainty model or a suitable metric, but is more generic in nature. This genericness is at the same time also a drawback, in the sense that the set-up of a full scale cost-based measurement requires quite some effort. This can be mitigated by *estimating* costs, but in that case one should be aware of the fact that estimates come with a certain margin of error.

2.2 Methods for Analysis

Having explained the most common measurement procedures for data quality, this section provides an overview of approaches to *analyse* collected measurements and draw some conclusions from them.

A first series of methods is based on the idea of *root cause analysis*. As indicated by the name, when a large collection of data quality measurements have been collected and there is a disturbing or significant deterioration of quality, one might be interested in finding out what causes this deterioration. A well-know family of techniques that can provide some insights in the collected measurements is bundled under the umbrella term *data profiling* [39]. The main idea with data profiling is to collect statistics about the data at hand that summarize some aspects about them. For example, with simple rule-based measurements, aggregates and distributions of these measurements can provide some useful insights in the collection of data. For example, monitoring the distributions over a longer period of time can learn something about the stability of data collection. In a similar spirit, one can use micro-level measurements to check if errors in a database occur purely at *random* [4,25]. If errors don't occur at random, this might be an indication that some data generation or transformation process introduces *systematic* errors and this can be a call for action to track down the problem and modify the process accordingly. Another instrument for analysis is *visualisation* of measurements. A recent study constructed embeddings of a database based on a selection of attributes and projected data quality measurements on this embedding by using colourings [28]. This technique produced an easy-to-interpret visualization of different data quality measurements, which were produced by counting of errors as well as a metric-based approach. Other popular visualisation techniques for root-cause analysis are Ishikawa diagrams as demonstrated in [53]. Finally, a helpful tool for root cause analysis can be provided by data lineage [37], where the idea is to track down how data was generated and manipulated, from it's origin to the current state. This enables a form of debugging for data.

Besides root cause analysis, another important instrument in analysis is a *cost-benefit* analysis. In the example with contact and address data, we can use an uncertainty model to prioritize which data entries need to be validated. Suppose by this method, we have a targeted set of entries we suspect to be outdated. Recollecting these data can now be done in several ways. An external and trusted data source can be consulted or the data can be recollected by contacting customers, assuming some contact information like a phone number or an email address is still valid. However, in anyway we proceed, a certain cost will be involved in improving data quality. The question is then: "Is this cost worth it?". Several techniques can be used to answer this question. In statistics, the concept of *influential errors* is used to identify those errors that have a significant impact on statistics of interests [19]. To identify them, score functions are used to estimate the importance of errors. This is an example where we try to weigh the *cost* for fixing errors against the benefits we can draw from them. This line of thinking naturally leads us to the cost-based framework for measurement of data quality, where cost-benefit analysis is intrinsically available.

3   Micro-level Data Quality Management

Data quality on the micro-level is concerned with errors to individual data items. Micro-level analysis consists of two phases: *detection* of errors and *repair* or errors as illustrated in Fig. 3. In the bulk of approaches, error detection is based on a specific constraint formalism [1,20]. Given such a formalism, Fan and Geerts identified five fundamental problems [20], of which *error detection* and *repair* are two. The other three are *coherence* (whether a set of constraints is internally consistent), *minimality* (whether a set of constraints has any redundancy) and *discovery* (automated generation of constraints). The latter three problems are often studied in function of either detection or repair. Discovery of constraints allows to reduce manual configuration of error detection. Coherence is verified before error detection in order to ensure consistent data exists. Minimality is often used to simplify repair methods.

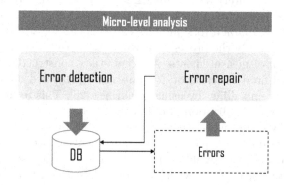

Fig. 3. A schematic overview of micro-level analysis.

3.1   Error Detection

In the most common scenario, error detection departs from a fixed set of constraints. In the past decades, an abundance of different constraint formalisms has been proposed and studied. These formalisms can be characterized by considering the number of attributes and the number of tuples they affect, as illustrated in Fig. 4.

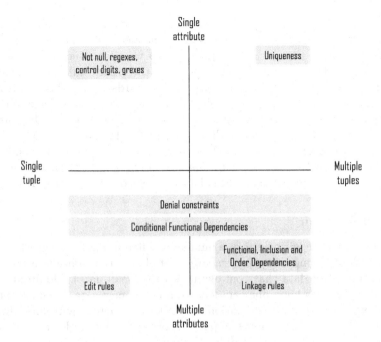

Fig. 4. Types of constraint formalisms organized by the number of attributes and number of tuples they affect.

The most common distinction is made between the number of tuples to which constraints apply. Constraints that affect a single tuple at once are known as *tuple-level* constraints. Some tuple-level constraints are specifically designed to deal with a *single* attribute. The most simple example here is a NOT NULL constraints in a database, but more advanced constraints like regular expressions [36], control digits [17,18,26,56] and group expressions or grexes [11] are heavily used. The latter concept provides an elegant and simple syntax of regex group predicates and has been implemented within the ledc framework[1]. When tuple-level constraints deal with *multiple* attributes in a single tuple, the most notable concept is that of an edit rule *edit rules* [19,23].

When constraints affect multiple tuples at once they are called *relation-level* constraints. This type of constraints has been heavily studied in the field of databases of the past four decades under the umbrella term of dependencies [1]. Two famous examples of dependencies used in data quality management are *functional dependencies* (FDs) and *inclusion dependencies* (INDs) [6]. Next to these fundamental cornerstones of the relational model, other types of dependencies have been used. For example, *order dependencies* have been proposed to enforce monotonicity across tuples. Other examples include generalizations of FDs like *conditional functional dependencies* (CFDs) [7,16,21] and *denial con-*

---

[1] ledc is short for Lightweight Engine for Data quality Control.

straints [14] (DCs). Despite the overwhelming amount of generalizations [12], not all relation-level constraints initiate from the idea of dependencies. The most notable example is that of *linkage rules*, which were introduced by Fellegi and Sunter as a part of their Bayesian solution to the record linkage problem [24], which is today still the predominant approach towards solving this problem [59].

Perhaps the most important evolution in the field of error detection is the emphasis on trying to *learn* constraints in a data-driven manner. This has been done for FDs [35,44], INDs [45], CFDs [13,22], DCs [14], edit rules [5,49,50] and other types of constraints [42,46]. In this evolution, we can also include techniques from the field of *outlier detection* that do not explicitly use a constraint formalism, but where the learned model can be encoded as a set of rules [8,43].

3.2   Error Repair

When it comes to repairing errors, a number of different methodologies have been proposed [38]. The main idea is to *modify* a set of data that contains errors (dirty data) into a set of data that contains no errors (clean data). Modification can mean several things here: one can delete data, add new data or update present data. Regardless of which operations are allowed, there is virtually always a desire to *minimize* the changes applied in order to obtain clean data. Again, minimality can be expressed in different manners [38].

When dealing with tuple-level constraints like edit rules, the most common approach is the *set-cover* method, where minimal-cost changes can be found by minimal-cost (set) covers of failing rules [23]. The actual repair can then be done by regression imputation or donor imputation methods [19] when errors occur at random. When errors are systematic and can be explained by specific error mechanisms, dedicated corrections mechanisms can be used [52].

In case of relation-level constraints, the set cover method can not be applied and other techniques are used. One example is a generalization of the Chase algorithm which has been implemented in the Llunatic framework [27]. In this approach, a Chase tree of possible repairs is gradually built and pruned to keep the search space manageable. Other approaches like HoloClean use probabilistic inference [51] to find repairs of dirty data. In case of duplicate tuples, HumMer has been proposed as a data fusion tool [3]. Hereby, usage of dedicated fusion operators like subsumption allows to suppress redundancy in the final result.

4   Discussion

In the previous, an overview of the most important techniques in both macro-level and micro-level analysis of data quality has been given. In this section, a non-exhaustive list of challenges is presented.

Standards of Measurement. Section 2.1 presented a number of methods to devise a measurement procedure for data quality. These methods are quite different in where they can be applied, what scales they produce and what information the measurements they produce will convey. In the past, much of the debate involving quality has revolved around the notion of dimensions. It has been argued that the semantics of these dimensions are not always clear [29]. To become more mature, the focus of the data quality field should shift to the more fundamental and rigorous notion of *measurement theory*.

Decision Making. Whereas there are several approaches to get some insights from a collection of data quality measurements, the connection between data quality measurement and decision making has not been investigated deeply. The FAIR principles are a good way to orient towards better data management, but to date, there are no concrete measurement approaches that qualify the differences between datasets well. One way to proceed towards better decision making, is to invest more resources in empirical studies on this topic. A recent study quantified the differences between different versions of the same database in terms of tasks that need to be fulfilled [55]. One outcome of this study is a concrete recommendation of the utility of database design phases in terms of improved data quality. This is a direct application of the cost-based measurement paradigm we explained in Sect. 2.1. More studies like this are necessary to gain better insights in the costs of data quality issues. Such insights can help an organisation to prioritize investments to improve data quality.

Expressiveness Versus Complexity. A recent survey shows that there exists an abundance of dependency-like constraints, conjointly referred to as *relaxed functional dependencies* (RFDs) [12]. A general observation here is that much research is directed towards *more expressive* formalisms. However, these formalisms tend to be more complex with regard to the study of their fundamental properties. In particular, *repair* of violations and *discovery* of constraint are significantly more complex [20]. These problems are more simple for tuple-level constraints, but these formalisms are usually less expressive. The question is then which is most important: expressiveness or mitigation of complexity? One argument in favour of complexity reduction is that in real-life datasets, a significant amount of the constraints can be captured by simple tuple-level constraints [49]. This naturally leads to the question if expressiveness of tuple-level constraints can be increased while maintaining their appeal in mitigated complexity. This latter translates to preservation of the set cover methodology. An interesting research question is thus whether mixtures of tuple-level constraints and simple relation-level constraints like key constraints would lead to a better balance between expressiveness and complexity. A optimal balance between expressiveness and complexity can lead to scalable tools that can still deal with a wide range of common errors.

Learning Approaches. There has been a strong emphasis on learning approaches for micro-level analysis. However, many learning approaches still deal with scalability issues. This is for example clearly demonstrated in an empirical study on the discovery of functional dependencies [44]. One important challenge is the search for methodologies that can overcome these scalability issues. Especially scalability in terms of attributes is troublesome. Solutions in this direction could find reasonable partitions of attributes in such a way constraints are likely to involve within-class attributes only.

Error Mechanisms. A final challenge is that much of the literature on error repair assumes error occur at random. However, empirical research has already shown that certain error patterns are far more common than others. For example, single digit errors and adjacent transposition errors have been found to be more common than other errors in identification numbers [18,56]. In addition, statistical surveys often deal with certain types of systematic errors like unit errors, rounding errors and swap errors [19]. It has been argued accounting for this wide variety of mechanisms can help in finding better repairs [52]. This involves not only the incorporation of error mechanisms into repair algorithms. An interesting research problem is the automated discovery of which error mechanisms are prevalent in a given dataset.

5   Conclusion

In this paper, we have presented an overview of state-of-the-art techniques for data quality management in different research disciplines. We guided this overview by making a distinction between macro-level analysis and micro-level analysis. The former deals with assessment and optimization of data quality processes while the latter deals errors in data. We have provided a general methodology for both levels and presented an overview of common approaches. Finally, we have presented a number of interesting research questions for future research.

References

1. Abiteboul, S., Hull, R., Vianu, V. (eds.): Foundations of Databases: The Logical Level, 1st edn. Addison-Wesley Longman Publishing Co., Inc., Boston (1995)
2. Batini, C., Cappiello, C., Francalanci, C., Maurino, A.: Methodologies for data quality assessment and improvement. ACM Comput. Surv. **41**(3), 16–52 (2009)
3. Bilke, A., Bleiholder, J., Naumann, F., Böhm, C., Draba, K., Herschel, M.: Automatic Data Fusion with Hummer, vol. 3, pp. 1251–1254 (2005)
4. Boeckling, T., Bronselaer, A., De Tré, G.: Randomness of data quality artifacts. In: Medina, J., Ojeda-Aciego, M., Verdegay, J.L., Perfilieva, I., Bouchon-Meunier, B., Yager, R.R. (eds.) IPMU 2018. CCIS, vol. 855, pp. 529–540. Springer, Cham (2018). https://doi.org/10.1007/978-3-319-91479-4_44
5. Boeckling, T., Bronselaer, A., De Tré, G.: Mining data quality rules based on T-dependence. In: Proceedings of the 11th Conference of the European Society for Fuzzy Logic and Technology (EUSFLAT 2019), vol. 1, pp. 184–191 (2019)
6. Bohannon, P., Fan, W., Flaster, M., Rastoqi, R.: A cost-based model and effective heuristic for repairing constraints by value modification. In: Proceedings of the 2005 ACM SIGMOD International Conference on Management of Data, pp. 143–154 (2005)
7. Bohannon, P., Fan, W., Geerts, F., Jia, X., Kementsietsidis, A.: Conditional functional dependencies for data cleaning. In: Proceedings of the 23rd International Conference on Data Engineering, pp. 746–755 (2007)

8. Brabant, Q., Couceiro, M., Dubois, D., Prade, H., Rico, A.: Extracting decision rules from qualitative data via sugeno utility functionals. In: Medina, J., et al. (eds.) IPMU 2018. CCIS, vol. 853, pp. 253–265. Springer, Cham (2018). https://doi.org/10.1007/978-3-319-91473-2_22

9. Bronselaer, A., De Mol, R., De Tré, G.: A measure-theoretic foundation for data quality. IEEE Trans. Fuzzy Syst. **26**(2), 627–639 (2017)

10. Bronselaer, A., Nielandt, J., Boeckling, T., De Tré, G.: Operational measurement of data quality. In: Medina, J., Ojeda-Aciego, M., Verdegay, J.L., Perfilieva, I., Bouchon-Meunier, B., Yager, R.R. (eds.) IPMU 2018. CCIS, vol. 855, pp. 517–528. Springer, Cham (2018). https://doi.org/10.1007/978-3-319-91479-4_43

11. Bronselaer, A., Nielandt, J., De Mol, R., De Tré, G.: Ordinal assessment of data consistency based on regular expressions. In: Carvalho, J.P., Lesot, M.-J., Kaymak, U., Vieira, S., Bouchon-Meunier, B., Yager, R.R. (eds.) IPMU 2016. CCIS, vol. 611, pp. 317–328. Springer, Cham (2016). https://doi.org/10.1007/978-3-319-40581-0_26

12. Caruccio, L., Deufemia, V., Polese, G.: Relaxed functional dependencies - a survey of approaches. IEEE Trans. Knowl. Data Eng. **28**(1), 147–165 (2016)

13. Chiang, F., Miller, R.J.: Discovering data quality rules. In: Proceedings of the VLDB Endowment, pp. 1166–1177 (2008)

14. Chu, X., Ilyas, I., Papotti, P.: Discovering denial constraints. In: Proceedings of the VLDB Endowment, pp. 1498–1509 (2013)

15. Codd, E.F.: A relational model of data for large shared data banks. Commun. ACM **13**(6), 377–387 (1970)

16. Cong, G., Wenfei, F., Geerts, F., Jia, X., Ma, S.: Improving data quality: consistency and accuracy. In: Proceedings of the VLDB Conference, pp. 315–326 (2007)

17. Damm, M.: Check digit systems over groups and anti-symmetric mappings. Arch. Math. **75**(6), 413–421 (2000). https://doi.org/10.1007/s000130050524

18. Damm, M.: Total anti-symmetrische Quasigruppen. Ph.D. thesis, Philipps-Universität Marburg (2004)

19. De Waal, T., Pannekoek, J., Scholtus, S.: Handbook of Statistical Data Editing and Imputation. Wiley, Hoboken (2011)

20. Fan, W., Geerts, F.: Foundations of Data Quality Management. Morgan & Claypool Publishers, San Rafael (2012)

21. Fan, W., Geerts, F., Jia, X., Kementsietsidis, A.: Conditional functional dependencies for capturing data inconsistencies. ACM Trans. Database Syst. **33**(2), 1–48 (2008)

22. Fan, W., Geerts, F., Lakshmanan, L., Xiong, M.: Discovering conditional functional dependencies. In: Proceedings of the IEEE International Conference on Data Engineering, pp. 1231–1234 (2009)

23. Fellegi, I., Holt, D.: A systematic approach to automatic edit and imputation. J. Am. Stat. Assoc. **71**(353), 17–35 (1976)

24. Fellegi, I., Sunter, A.: A theory for record linkage. J. Am. Stat. Assoc. **64**(328), 1183–1210 (1969). https://doi.org/10.1080/01621459.1969.10501049

25. Fisher, C.W., Lauria, E.J.M., Matheus, C.C.: An accuracy metric: percentages, randomness, and probabilities. J. Data Inf. Qual. **1**(3), 16:1-16:21 (2009)

26. Gallian, J.: Error detection methods. ACM Comput. Surv. **28**, 504–517 (1996)

27. Geerts, F., Mecca, G., Papotti, P., Santoro, D.: Cleaning data with LLUNATIC. VLDB J. **29**(4), 867–892 (2019). https://doi.org/10.1007/s00778-019-00586-5

28. Haegemans, T., Reusens, M., Baesens, B., Lemahieu, W., Snoeck, M.: Towards a visual approach to aggregate data quality measurements. In: Proceedings of the International Conference on Information Quality (ICIQ), October 2017

29. Haegemans, T., Snoeck, M., Lemahieu, W.: Towards a precise definition of data accuracy and a justification for its measure. In: Proceedings of the International Conference on Information Quality (ICIQ), pp. 16:1–16:13 (2016)
30. Haegemans, T., Snoeck, M., Lemahieu, W.: Entering data correctly: an empirical evaluation of the theory of planned behaviour in the context of manual data acquisition. Reliab. Eng. Syst. Saf. **178**, 12–30 (2018)
31. Haegemans, T., Snoeck, M., Lemahieu, W.: A theoretical framework to improve the quality of manually acquired data. Inf. Manag. **56**, 1–14 (2019)
32. Heinrich, B., Kaiser, M., Klier, M.: Does the EU insurance mediation directive help to improve data quality? - a metric-based analysis. In: European Conference on Information Systems, pp. 1871–1882 (2008)
33. Heinrich, B., Klier, M.: Metric-based data quality assessment - developing and evaluation a probability-based currency metric. Decis. Support Syst. **72**, 82–96 (2015)
34. Heinrich, B., Klier, M., Kaiser, M.: A procedure to develop metrics for currency and its application in CRM. ACM J. Data Inf. Qual. **1**(1), 5:1-5:28 (2009)
35. Huhtala, Y., Kärkkäinen, J., Porkka, P., Toivonen, H.: TANE: an efficient algorithm for discovering functional and approximate dependencies. Comput. J. **42**(2), 100–111 (1999)
36. IEEE: ISO/IEC/IEEE 9945:2009 information technology - portable operating system interface (posix®) base specifications, issue 7 (2009)
37. Ikeda, R., Widom, J.: Data lineage: a survey. Technical report, Stanford University (2009)
38. Ilyas, I.F., Chu, X.: Trends in cleaning relational data: consistency and deduplication. Found. Trends Databases **5**(4), 281–393 (2015). https://doi.org/10.1561/1900000045
39. Johnson, T.: Data Profiling, pp. 604–608. Springer, Heidelberg (2009)
40. Kahneman, D.: Thinking, Fast and Slow. Penguin Books, London (2011)
41. Krantz, D., Luce, D., Suppes, P., Tversky, A.: Foundations of Measurement: Additive and Polynomial Representations, vol. I. Academic Press, Cambridge (1971)
42. Kruse, S., Naumann, F.: Efficient discovery of approximate dependencies, vol. 11, pp. 759–772 (2018)
43. Liu, F.T., Ting, K.M., Zhou, Z.H.: Isolation-based anomaly detection. ACM Trans. Knowl. Discov. Data **6**, 1–39 (2008)
44. Papenbrock, T., et al.: Functional dependency discovery: an experimental evaluation of seven algorithms. In: Proceedings of the VLDB Endowment, vol. 8, pp. 1082–1093 (2015)
45. Papenbrock, T., Kruse, S., Quiané-Ruiz, J.A., Naumann, F.: Divide and conquer based inclusion dependency discovery. In: Proceedings of the VLDB Endowment, vol. 8, pp. 774–785 (2015)
46. Pena, E.H.M., de Almeida, E.C., Naumann, F.: Discovery of approximate (and exact) denial constraints. Proc. VDLB Endow. **13**(3), 266–278 (2019)
47. Pipino, L., Lee, Y., Wang, R.: Data quality assessment. Commun. ACM **45**(4), 211–218 (2002)
48. Pipino, L.L., Wang, R.Y., Kopcso, D., Rybolt, W.: Developing measurement scales for data-quality dimensions (chap. 3). In: Wang, R.Y., Pierce, E.M., Madnick, S.E., Fisher, C.W. (eds.) Information Quality, pp. 37–51. M.E. Sharpe (2005)
49. Rammelaere, J., Geerts, F.: Cleaning data with forbidden itemsets. IEEE Trans. Knowl. Data Eng. **32**, 1489–1501 (2019)

50. Rammelaere, J., Geerts, F., Goethals, B.: Cleaning data with forbidden itemsets. In: 33rd IEEE International Conference on Data Engineering, ICDE 2017, San Diego, CA, USA, 19–22 April 2017, pp. 897–908. IEEE Computer Society (2017). https://doi.org/10.1109/ICDE.2017.138
51. Rekatsinas, T., Chu, X., Ilyas, I., Ré, C.: HoloClean: holistic data repairs with probabilistic inference. In: Proceedings of the VDLB Endowment, pp. 1190–1201. VLDB (2017)
52. Scholtus, S.: A generalised Fellegi-Holt paradigm for automatic editing. In: UN/ECE Work Session on Statistical Data Editing 2014 (2014). https://doi.org/10.13140/2.1.2211.7446
53. Shaheen, N., Manezhi, B., Thomas, A., Alkelya, M.: Reducing defects in the datasets of clinical research studies: conformance with data quality metrics. BMC Med. Res. Methodol. 19, 1–8 (2019). https://doi.org/10.1186/s12874-019-0735-7
54. Timmerman, Y., Bronselaer, A.: Measuring data quality in information systems research. Decis. Support Syst. 126, 113–138 (2019). https://doi.org/10.1016/j.dss.2019.113138
55. Timmerman, Y., Bronselaer, A., De Tré, G.: Quantifying the impact of EER modeling on relational database success: an experimental investigation. In: Dobbie, G., Frank, U., Kappel, G., Liddle, S.W., Mayr, H.C. (eds.) ER 2020. LNCS, vol. 12400, pp. 487–500. Springer, Cham (2020). https://doi.org/10.1007/978-3-030-62522-1_36
56. Verhoeff, J.: Error Detecting Decimal Codes. The Mathematical Centre, Amsterdam (1969)
57. Levenstein, V.: Binary codes capable of correcting deletions, insertions and reversals. Physics Doklady 10(8), 707–710 (1966)
58. Wilkinson, M.D., et al.: The fair guiding principles for scientific data management and stewardship. Sci. Data 3(1), 1–9 (2016)
59. Xu, H., Li, X., Grannis, S.: A simple two-step procedure using the Fellegi-Sunter model for frequency-based record linkage. J. Appl. Stat., 1–16 (2021). https://doi.org/10.1080/02664763.2021.1922615

J-CO, A Framework for Fuzzy Querying Collections of *JSON* Documents (Demo)

Paolo Fosci⬤ and Giuseppe Psaila⁽✉⁾⬤

University of Bergamo, Viale Marconi 5, 24044 Dalmine, BG, Italy
{paolo.fosci,giuseppe.psaila}@unibg.it
http://www.unibg.it

Abstract. This paper accompanies a live demo during which we will show the *J-CO Framework*, a novel framework to manage large collections of *JSON* documents stored in *NoSQL* databases. *J-CO-QL* is the query language around which the framework is built; we show how it is able to perform fuzzy queries on *JSON* documents.

This paper briefly introduces the framework and the cross-analysis process presented during the live demo at the conference.

Keywords: Collections of JSON documents · Framework for managing JSON data sets · Fuzzy querying · Live demo.

1 Introduction

In the era of Big Data, classical relational technology has shown its limitations. In fact, apart from very large volumes of data, the main characteristic of them is their *variety*, both in terms of content and in terms of structure [11]. In order to easily represent complex data, *JSON* (JavaScript Object Notation) has become the *de-facto* standard for sharing and publishing data sets over the Internet. In fact, it is able to represent complex objects/documents, with nesting and arrays; its simple syntactic structure makes it possible to easily generate and parse *JSON* data sets within procedural and object-oriented programming languages.

Straightforwardly, *NoSQL* DBMSs [7] for managing *JSON* documents have been developed and have become very popular. They are called *JSON Document Stores*, since they are able to natively store *JSON* documents in a totally schema-free way. The most popular one is *MongoDB*, but some others, which are attracting more and more users, are *AWS DocumentDB* and *CouchDB*.

However, although these systems are quite effective in storing very large collections of *JSON* documents, there is not a standard query language that allows for retrieving and manipulating data: each system has its own query language. Furthermore, they do not give a unified view of document stores: if data are provided by various JSON stores, they must be managed separately, by exporting data from one document store, to import them into another one.

These considerations motivated the development of the *J-CO Framework* (where *J-CO* stands for *JSON CO*llections). The goals we targeted during its development are manifold:

© Springer Nature Switzerland AG 2021
T. Andreasen et al. (Eds.): FQAS 2021, LNAI 12871, pp. 142–153, 2021.
https://doi.org/10.1007/978-3-030-86967-0_11

- we wanted a framework able to retrieve data from and store data to any *JSON Document Store*, independently of its query language;
- we wanted to provide a unique tool, provided with a non-procedural query language, able to integrate and transform collections of *JSON* documents;
- we wanted to provide native support to spatial operations, to cope with very frequent geo-tagging of *JSON* documents, such as in *GeoJSON* documents.

Furthermore, the *J-CO Framework* aims at being a constantly evolving laboratory project, in which to address novel problems concerning the management of *JSON* documents that can be solved either by defining new statements in the query language, or by extending the underlying data model, so as to support new features, or both. For example, we are currently extending the data model to support fuzzy sets [12], to deal with various forms of uncertainty and imprecision that can affect data (a first step is presented in [10] and applied in [6]).

The development of the *J-CO Framework* started at the end of 2016 stimulated by our participation to the *Urban Nexus* project [4]. Funded by the University of Bergamo, in this project computer scientists and geographers worked together to identify a data driven approach to study mobility of city users, but integrating many (possibly big) data sources, including data published in Open Data portals. The need for providing analysts with a tool to easily integrate and analyze so heterogeneous data sets gave the idea to develop the *J-CO Framework*. Since its birth, [2], the framework has significantly evolved, as far as both the query language [1,3] and the components of the framework [8] are concerned.

During the live demo, we showed how the *J-CO Framework* easily works on *JSON* data by exploiting fuzzy sets. In this accompanying paper, Sect. 2 briefly presents the *J-CO Framework*; Sect. 3 briefly describes the features of its query language; Sect. 4 shows a sample query (presented during the live demo too) that illustrates its capability. Finally, Sect. 5 draws the conclusions.

2   The *J-CO Framework*

The *J-CO Framework* is designed to provide analysts and data scientists with a powerful tool to integrate, transform and query data represented as *JSON* documents collected in various *JSON* Stores. It is based on three distinct layers, depicted in Fig. 1.

- *Data Layer.* In principle, this layer encompasses any *JSON Document Store*. Currently, we encompass *MongoDB*, *ElasticSearch* and *J-CO-DS*, a lightweight *JSON* store developed within the *J-CO* project, designed to be able to manage very large *JSON* documents, such as *GeoJSON* layers [5].
- *Engine Layer.* This layer encompasses the *J-CO-QL Engine*, i.e., the software tool that processes collections of *JSON* documents retrieved from *JSON* stores, by executing queries written in the *J-CO-QL* language; results are stored again into some *JSON* store.
- *Interface Layer.* This layer encompasses *J-CO-UI*, the user interface of the framework. It provides functionalities to write queries step-by-step, possibly rolling back queries, as well as to inspect intermediate results of the process.

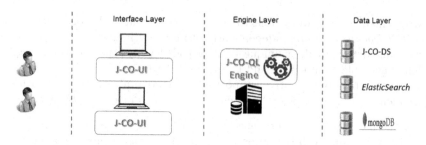

Fig. 1. Layers for the *J-CO Framework*.

The *J-CO-QL Engine* and the *J-CO-UI* are independent applications, so that they can be executed on different machines: for example, the *J-CO-QL Engine* on a powerful cloud virtual machine, while the *J-CO-UI* on the PC of the analyst. The *J-CO-QL Engine* can access any *JSON Document Store* through a standard internet connection. Thus, *J-CO* is actually a platform-independent framework: this choice allows for further extending the framework in the future, for example by providing a parallel version of the engine possibly based on the Map-Reduce paradigm. The reader can find a detailed description of the *J-CO Framework* in [9].

3   The Query Language: *J-CO-QL*

J-CO-QL is the query language around which the framework is built. We do not describe the language in details here; the interested reader can refer to our works [1,3,9]; in Sect. 4, we report the simple query shown during the live demo and shortly explain the statements.

The aim of *J-CO-QL* is to provide a powerful tool to perform complex transformations on collections of *JSON* documents. More in details, the main features of the language are the following ones:

- *High-level Statements.* The language provides high-level statements, i.e., statements suitable to specify complex transformations without writing procedural programs;
- *Native Support to Spatial Operations.* The language natively manages geotagging in *JSON* documents and, consequently, its statements provide constructs for this purpose. In this demo, this feature is not highlighted, but the interested reader can refer to [1,9];
- *Managing Heterogeneous Documents. JSON* document stores are schema free, consequently, they can store heterogeneous *JSON* documents all together in the same collection. *J-CO-QL* statements are able to deal with heterogeneous documents in one single instruction. In this demo, this feature is not highlighted, but the interested reader can refer to [1,9];
- *Independence of the Data Source.* The language is tied neither to any data source nor to any query language provided by any data source. This way,

in principle, any data source could be accessed to get and save collections of *JSON* documents, because all processing activities are performed by the *J-CO-QL Engine*, with no intervention of *JSON* stores;
- *Simple and Clear Execution Semantics.* The language relies on a simple and clear execution semantics, based on the notion of *process state*. We briefly introduce it hereafter.

Execution Semantics. A *Process State* describes the current state of the execution of a query process. It is a tuple $s = \langle tc, IR, DBS \rangle$. Specifically, tc is called *temporary collection* and is the collection produced by the last executed instruction, which will be the input for the next instruction. IR is the *Intermediate-Result Database*, i.e., a process-specific database where to temporarily store collections that constitute intermediate results for the process. *DBS* is a set of *database descriptors* $dd = \langle url, dbms, name, alias \rangle$, whose fields, respectively, describe the connection URL, the specific DBMS (i.e., `"MongoDB"`, `"ElasticSearch"` and `"J-CO-DS"`), the name of the database and the alias used within the *J-CO-QL* query in place of its actual name.

A *query* q is a sequence (or *pipe*) of instructions $(i_1, i_2, , \ldots, i_n)$, where an instruction i_j is the application of a *J-CO-QL* statement.

The *initial process state* is $s_0 = \langle \emptyset, \emptyset, \emptyset \rangle$. Given an instruction $i_j \in q$, it can be seen as a function such that $i_j(s_{j-1}) = s_j$; in other words, an instruction (and the applied statement) can possibly change the temporary collection tc, the intermediate result database IR, and the database descriptors, that, in turn, can be used as input by the next instruction.

4 Demo: Cross-Analyzing Weather Measurements

We now show the main analysis task that was shown during the demo at the conference. Specifically, we showed how *J-CO-QL* can be used to cross-analyze weather measurements and rank them by means of user-defined fuzzy operators.

4.1 Dataset

All the investigated data have been downloaded from the *Open Data Portal of Regione Lombardia*, the administrative body of the region named Lombardia in northern Italy (https://dati.lombardia.it/). The data consist of measurements provided by atmospheric sensors that detect values related to temperatures, rain, wind speed and direction, solar radiation, humidity and others. Each sensor is specialized in providing one kind of measure (e.g., temperature) several times each day. The sensors are organized into weather stations located in various sites in Lombardia region. For this demo, we only considered temperature and rain data detected in a time period that covers one week from 1 March 2021 to 7 March 2021 in Bergamo area (see Fig. 2).

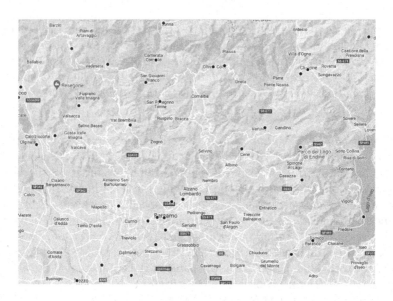

Fig. 2. Map of sensors.

The *Open Data Portal of Regione Lombardia*, provides the data in *JSON* format. Thus, we stored the downloaded data into a *MongoDB* database. Before conducting this experiment, all the data passed through a *pre-processing phase*, since stations and sensors data are provided together in a *de-normalized way*, meaning that while a station is a group of sensors in the same place and a sensor is a device able to measure a certain kind of physical quantity, the Open Data Portal provides a document for each sensor reporting in the same document also all the information about the station in which the sensor is located. Instead, measurement data are provided separately. Moreover, all field names are in Italian, so, they had to be translated into English. The pre-processing phase was performed by using a *J-CO-QL* script that we do not discuss here, since it is out of the scope of this paper and of the *live demo* during the conference. The queries submitted to the Open data portal to get the data are the following ones:

- https://www.dati.lombardia.it/resource/nf78-nj6b.json;
- https://www.dati.lombardia.it/resource/647i-nhxk.json?$where=
  data >= "2021-03-01" AND data <"2021-03-08".

After the pre-processing phase, the data set contains two distinct collections of *JSON* documents:

- The `Temperatures` collection contains 26,215 documents. Each document represents a different temperature measurement in a precise moment. An example of document is shown in Fig. 3a;
- The `Rain` collection contains 32,362 documents. Each document represents a different rain measurement in a precise moment. Since the considered time

Listing 1. *J-CO-QL* cross-analysis process (part 1): Fuzzy operators.

```
1:  CREATE FUZZY OPERATOR Has_Medium_Temperature
        PARAMETERS temperature TYPE Float, altitude TYPE Integer
        PRECONDITION temperature >= -273 AND altitude >= 0
        EVALUATE temperature + 0.006*altitude
        POLYLINE (-30, 0), (0, 0), (5, 1), (15, 1), (25, 0), (50, 0);

2:  CREATE FUZZY OPERATOR Has_Persistent_Rain
        PARAMETERS rain TYPE Integer
        PRECONDITION rain > 0
        EVALUATE rain
        POLYLINE (0, 0), (0.5, 0), (1, 0.2), (1.5, 0.9), (1.7, 1), (2, 1);
```

period was quite dry in the area of interest, we discarded more than 99% of the documents that were reporting a *zero value* as a measurement. The choice was made also considering the need to speed-up the execution time during the live demo at the conference. Thus, the actual collection used for this demo contains only 238 meaningful documents. An example of document is shown in Fig. 3b.

```
{                                              {
    "stationId" : "595",                           "stationId" : "821",
    "stationName" : "Filago v.Don Milani",         "stationName" : "Azzone Dezzo di Scalve",
    "province" : "BG",                             "province" : "BG",
    "latitude" : "45.63386450908066",             "latitude" : "45.97808314682598",
    "longitude" : "9.556084255790864",            "longitude" : "10.103188671004808",
    "altitude" : "190",                            "altitude" : "767",
    "sensorId" : "5863",                           "sensorId" : "8171",
    "type" : "Temperature",                        "type" : "Rain Precipitation",
    "unit" : "°C",                                 "unit" : "mm",
    "dateTime" : "2021-03-07T23:00:00",            "dateTime" : "2021-03-06T08:10:00",
    "measure" : 3.1                                "measure" : 0.2
}                                              }
```

   (a) **Temperatures** document.   (b) **Rain** document.

Fig. 3. Examples of documents in **Temperatures** and **Rain** collections.

In Fig. 3, the reader can see an example of documents contained respectively in the **Temperatures** collection and in the **Rain** collection. *JSON* documents in both collections have the same structure. Each document describes the weather station through its unique identifier and name (respectively, the **stationId** and the **stationName** fields), as well as the geographic area and the exact *WGS84* coordinates of the weather station are provided (respectively, the **province**, the **latitude**, the **longitude** and the **altitude** fields). Each document describes also the sensor through its unique identifier (the **sensorId** field), its type (the **type** field) and the unit of measure used for sensor measurements (the **unit** field). Finally, the exact date-time and value of measurement are reported (respectively, the **dateTime** and the **measure** fields).

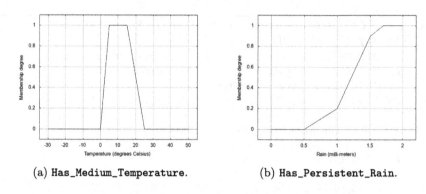

(a) **Has_Medium_Temperature.**   (b) **Has_Persistent_Rain.**

Fig. 4. Membership Functions of Fuzzy Operators in Listing 1

4.2 Creating Fuzzy Operators

The *J-CO-QL* language provides a specific construct to create novel fuzzy operators, so as to use them within queries to evaluate the extent of the belonging of *JSON* documents to fuzzy sets. Listing 1 reports the instructions that create two fuzzy operators, named **Has_Medium_Temperature** and **Has_Heavy_Rain**, respectively.

Let us consider the instruction that defines the **Has_Medium_Temperature** operator.

First of all, it defines the list of formal parameters necessary to the operator to provide a membership degree. Specifically, the operator receives two formal parameters, named **temperature** and **altitude**, which denote a measured temperature and the altitude of the measuring point, respectively.

The **PRECONDITION** clause specifies a precondition that must be met in order to correctly evaluate the membership degree. In the example, the temperature is considered valid if above -273 *degree Celsius* (that is, 0 *Kelvin*), as well as the altitude is considered valid if no less than 0 **meter** above the sea level.

The **EVALUATE** clause defines the function whose resulting value is used to get the actual membership degree. In the example, the temperature is compensated when the altitude increases (due to the altitude, temperatures become lower).

The value returned by the function specified in the **EVALUATE** clause is used as x-value; the corresponding y-value, given by the polyline function, is the final membership degree provided by the fuzzy operator.

The **POLYLINE** clause defines the polyline function depicted in Fig. 4a.

The second fuzzy operator defined in Listing 1 is the **Has_Persistent_Rain** operator. It receives only one parameter, whose value is directly used (see the simple function specified in the **EVALUATE** clause) to get the membership degree through the polyline depicted in Fig. 4b. Notice that the polyline is not a simple trapezoidal function: this way, we allow for specifying possibly complex membership functions to cope with complex real situations.

Listing 2. *J-CO-QL* cross-analysis process (part 2): Joining Collections.

```
3:  USE DB FQAS_Source
        ON SERVER MongoDB 'http://127.0.0.1:27017';
4:  USE DB FQAS_Destination
        ON SERVER MongoDB 'http://127.0.0.1:27017';

5:  JOIN OF COLLECTIONS
        Temperatures@FQAS_Source AS T, Rain@FQAS_Source AS R
        CASE WHERE .T.stationId = .R.stationId
            AND .T.dateTime = .R.dateTime
            AND .R.measure > 0
        GENERATE { .stationId: .T.stationId,
                    .stationName: .T.stationName,
                    .province: .T.province,
                    .latitude: .T.latitude,
                    .longitude: .T.longitude,
                    .altitude: .T.altitude,
                    .dateTime: .T.dateTime,
                    .temperatureSensorId: .T.sensorId,
                    .temperatureUnit: .T.unit,
                    .temperatureMeasure: .T.measure,
                    .rainSensorId: .R.sensorId,
                    .rainUnit: .R.unit,
                    .rainMeasure: .R.measure  }
        DROP OTHERS;
```

4.3   J-CO-QL Cross-Analysis Process

The *J-CO-QL* instructions that create the two fuzzy operators (Listing 1) are the first part of the script that specifies the cross-analysis process. In Listing 2, we report the second part, which actually starts the analysis process.

On lines 3 and 4, we ask to connect to two databases managed by the *MongoDB* server installed on the PC to be used for the demo. They are called **FQAS_Source** and **FQAS_Destination**: the former contains the source data to analyze, the latter will contain the output data.

The **FQAS_Source** database contains the **Temperatures** collection, which describes measurements of temperatures, and the **Rain** collection, which describes measurements of rain, as described in Sect. 4.1. The **JOIN** instruction on line 5 keeps the two collections from the database and joins them, in order to pair temperature and rain measurements made by the same station in the same moment. The two collections are aliased as **T** and **R**, respectively.

Within the instruction, the **CASE WHERE** clause specifies the join condition: among all pairs of input documents, only those referring to the same station and to the same moment, as well as having a rain measurement greater than zero, are kept. For each pair of input documents, a novel document is built, where two fields named **T** and **R** (the collection aliases) are present: the former contains the input document coming from the T collection, the latter contains the input document coming from the R collection. This motivates the *dot notation* used within the condition (e.g., `.T.stationId`, where the initial dot denotes that we refer to the root-level T field).

For each selected document, the `GENERATE` action restructures the output document; specifically, we flatten it. The output document is inserted into the output temporary collection, which will be used as input collection by the next instruction.

Notice the final `DROP OTHERS` option. It specifies that all documents obtained by pairing input documents that do not satisfy the condition must be discarded from the output temporary collection.

An example of document in the temporary collection is shown in Fig. 5a.

```
{                                              {
    "stationId" : "1221",                          "stationId" : "1209",
    "stationName" : "Casnigo Campo Sportivo",      "stationName" : "Rota d'Imagna",
    "province" : "BG",                             "province" : "BG",
    "latitude" : "45.811360742715465",            "latitude" : "45.839840095961094",
    "longitude" : "9.865590362771156",            "longitude" : "9.511348909108976",
    "altitude" : "502",                            "altitude" : "674",
    "dateTime" : "2021-03-06T07:10:00.000",       "dateTime" : "2021-03-06T06:10:00",
    "temperatureSensorId" : "9024",               "temperatureSensorId" : "9034",
    "temperatureUnit" : "°C",                      "temperatureUnit" : "°C",
    "temperatureMeasure" : 4.7,                    "temperatureMeasure" : 4.2,
    "rainSensorId" : "9113",                       "rainSensorId" : "9123",
    "rainUnit" : "mm",                             "rainUnit" : "mm",
    "rainMeasure" : 0.8                            "rainMeasure" : 1.6,
}                                                  "~fuzzysets" : {
                                                       "Medium_Temperature" : 0.84,
                                                       "Persistent_Rain" : 0.949999976158142,
                                                       "Wanted" : 0.84
                                                   }
                                               }
```

(a) Document after `JOIN` (line 5).   (b) Document after `FILTER` (line 8).

Fig. 5. Examples of documents in the temporary collection.

Listing 3 reports the fuzzy part of the cross-analysis process. It is based on four different applications of the `FILTER` statement, whose general goal is to filter the temporary collection. Since [10], the `FILTER` statement has been extended to provide constructs for performing fuzzy evaluations of documents.

On line 6, we evaluate the extent to which documents belong to the fuzzy set called `Medium_Temperature`. First of all, the `CASE WHERE` condition selects documents with the fields named `temperatureMeasure` and `altitude`. For those documents, the `CHECK FOR FUZZY SET` clause evaluates the desired fuzzy set, by using the fuzzy expression specified in the `USING` sub-clause, which provides the membership degree; in this case, the membership degree is provided by the `Has_Medium_Temperature` fuzzy operator, defined in Listing 1. As an effect, the output document is obtained by extending the input one with a novel field named `~fuzzysets`, which in turn contains a field named `Medium_Temperature`, whose numerical value is the membership degree of the document to the fuzzy set.

The `FILTER` instruction on line 7 evaluates the extent to which documents belong to the fuzzy set named `Persistent_Rain`, by using the operator named

Listing 3. *J-CO-QL* cross-analysis process (part 3): Evaluating Fuzzy Sets.

```
6:  FILTER
        CASE WHERE WITH .temperatureMeasure, .altitude
          CHECK FOR FUZZY SET Medium_Temperature
            USING Has_Medium_Temperature(.temperatureMeasure, .altitude)
        DROP OTHERS;

7:  FILTER
        CASE WHERE WITH .rainMeasure
          CHECK FOR FUZZY SET Persistent_Rain
            USING Has_Persistent_Rain(.rainMeasure)
        DROP OTHERS;

8:  FILTER
        CASE WHERE KNOWN FUZZY SETS Medium_Temperature, Persistent_Rain
          CHECK FOR FUZZY SET Wanted
            USING (Medium_Temperature AND Persistent_Rain)
          ALPHA-CUT 0.75 ON Wanted
        DROP OTHERS;

9:  FILTER
      CASE WHERE WITH .~fuzzysets.Wanted
          GENERATE {  .stationId, .stationName, .province, .dateTime,
                      .latitude, .longitude, .altitude,
                      .rank: MEMBERSHIP_OF (Wanted) }
          DROPPING ALL FUZZY SETS
        DROP OTHERS;

10: SAVE AS DetectedWeatherStations@FQAS_Destination;
```

Has_Persistent_Rain, defined in Listing 1. Within the ~fuzzysets field, output documents now have a novel field, denoting the membership degree to the Persistent_Rain fuzzy set.

The FILTER instruction on line 8 combines the two previously evaluated fuzzy sets, to obtain the membership degree to the Wanted fuzzy set, whose value will be used to rank documents. In the WHERE condition, we use the predicate named KNOWN FUZZY SETS, which is true if the specified fuzzy sets have been evaluated for the current document. If so, the Wanted fuzzy set is evaluated, by means of the expression within the USING sub-clause: notice that it is based on the fuzzy AND conjunction applied to the previously checked fuzzy sets. In fact, the WHERE clause is a pure Boolean condition, while the USING clause is a fuzzy condition. Finally, the ALPHA-CUT sub-clause discards all documents whose membership degree to the Wanted fuzzy set is less than the specified threshold of 0.75.

An example of document in the temporary collection, after the FILTER instruction on line 8, is shown in Fig. 5b. Notice the ~fuzzysets field, whose fields denotes the membership degrees of the document to the homonym fuzzy sets (i.e., `Medium_Temperature`, `Persistent_Rain` and `Wanted`).

The final `FILTER` instruction on line 9 prepares the final output collection of the process. In particular, the `rank` field is added, assigning it the membership degree of the `Wanted` fuzzy set by means of the `MEMBERSHIP_OF` built-in function. The `DROPPING ALL FUZZY SETS` option asks to drop fuzzy sets from the documents (i.e., the `~fuzzysets` field is removed).

Finally, the `SAVE AS` instruction at line 10 saves the final temporary collection into the `FQAS_Destination` database, with name `DetectedWeatherStations`. An example of document in this collection is shown in Fig. 6.

```
{
    "stationId" : "119",
    "stationName" : "San Giovanni Bianco C.",
    "province" : "BG",
    "dateTime" : "2021-03-06T05:10:00",
    "latitude" : "45.86969089938538",
    "longitude" : "9.639112837494569",
    "altitude" : "622",
    "rank" : 0.759999993443489
}
```

Fig. 6. Example of document in the `DetectedWeatherStation` collection.

5   Conclusions

During the live demo at FQAS 2021 Conference, we showed the *J-CO Framework* and the capability of its query language, called *J-CO-QL*, to retrieve and manipulate collections of *JSON* documents, by evaluating the extent of their belonging to fuzzy sets.

This paper accompanies the live demo, so as to describe it in the conference proceedings. Thus, it briefly presents the main characteristics of the *J-CO Framework* and its query language. The main goal of the framework is to provide analysts with a unifying tool to manage, query and transform big collections of *JSON* documents stored in *JSON* storage systems based on different technologies and provided with different query languages. The platform-independent design of the framework is the key factor to achieve this goal.

During the live demo, we presented a cross-analysis process of meteorological data, to show a typical, yet simplified, application of the *J-CO Framework*. The paper reports and explains the *J-CO-QL* query written to perform the cross-analysis; in particular, the way fuzzy sets are evaluated on *JSON* documents, based on the definition of fuzzy operators tailored on the application context.

The reader interested to learn more about the framework is kindly invited to read the related papers in bibliography and to get in touch with the authors. All the software developed within the project and the data used for this demo, and for other works, are freely accessible in the *GitHub* repository of the project (https://github.com/zunstraal/J-Co-Project/).

References

1. Bordogna, G., Capelli, S., Ciriello, D.E., Psaila, G.: A cross-analysis framework for multi-source volunteered, crowdsourced, and authoritative geographic information: the case study of volunteered personal traces analysis against transport network data. Geo-spat. Inf. Sci. **21**(3), 257–271 (2018)
2. Bordogna, G., Capelli, S., Psaila, G.: A big geo data query framework to correlate open data with social network geotagged posts. In: Bregt, A., Sarjakoski, T., van Lammeren, R., Rip, F. (eds.) GIScience 2017. LNGC, pp. 185–203. Springer, Cham (2017). https://doi.org/10.1007/978-3-319-56759-4_11
3. Bordogna, G., Ciriello, D.E., Psaila, G.: A flexible framework to cross-analyze heterogeneous multi-source geo-referenced information: the J-CO-QL proposal and its implementation. In: Proceedings of the International Conference on Web Intelligence, pp. 499–508. ACM, Leipzig (2017)
4. Burini, F., Cortesi, N., Gotti, K., Psaila, G.: The urban nexus approach for analyzing mobility in the smart city: towards the identification of city users networking. Mob. Inf. Syst. **2018**, 1–18 (2018)
5. Butler, H., Daly, M., Doyle, A., Gillies, S., Hagen, S., Schaub, T., et al.: The GeoJSON format. Internet Engineering Task Force (IETF) (2016)
6. Fosci, P., Marrara, S., Psaila, G.: Soft querying GeoJSON documents within the J-CO framework. In: 16th International Conference on Web Information Systems and Technologies (WEBIST 2020), pp. 253–265. SCITEPRESS-Science and Technology Publications, Lda (2020)
7. Nayak, A., Poriya, A., Poojary, D.: Type of NOSQL databases and its comparison with relational databases. Int. J. Appl. Inf. Syst. **5**(4), 16–19 (2013)
8. Psaila, G., Fosci, P.: Toward an analyst-oriented polystore framework for processing JSON geo-data. In: IADIS International Conference Applied Computing 2018, pp. 213–222. IADIS, Budapest, Hungary (2018)
9. Psaila, G., Fosci, P.: J-CO: a platform-independent framework for managing geo-referenced JSON data sets. Electronics **10**(5) (2021). https://doi.org/10.3390/electronics10050621, https://www.mdpi.com/2079-9292/10/5/621
10. Psaila, G., Marrara, S.: A first step towards a fuzzy framework for analyzing collections of JSON documents. In: IADIS International Conference Applied Computing 2019, pp. 19–28. IADIS, Cagliari, Italy (2019)
11. Uddin, M.F., Gupta, N., et al.: Seven V's of big data understanding big data to extract value. In: Proceedings of the 2014 Zone 1 Conference of the American Society for Engineering Education, pp. 1–5. IEEE (2014)
12. Zadeh, L.A.: Fuzzy sets. Inf. Control **8**(3), 338–353 (1965)

Data-Driven Approaches

Detecting Environmental, Social and Governance (ESG) Topics Using Domain-Specific Language Models and Data Augmentation

Tim Nugent[1]([✉]), Nicole Stelea[1], and Jochen L. Leidner[1,2,3]

[1] Refinitiv Labs, London, UK
[2] Department of Business and Economics, Coburg University of Applied Sciences,
Friedrich-Streib-Str. 2, 96450 Coburg, Germany
[3] Department of Computer Science, University of Sheffield,
211 Portobello, Sheffield S1 4DP, UK

Abstract. Despite recent advances in deep learning-based language modelling, many natural language processing (NLP) tasks in the financial domain remain challenging due to the paucity of appropriately labelled data. Other issues that can limit task performance are differences in word distribution between the general corpora – typically used to pre-train language models – and financial corpora, which often exhibit specialized language and symbology. Here, we investigate two approaches that can help to mitigate these issues. Firstly, we experiment with further language model pre-training using large amounts of in-domain data from business and financial news. We then apply augmentation approaches to increase the size of our data-set for model fine-tuning. We report our findings on an Environmental, Social and Governance (ESG) controversies data-set and demonstrate that both approaches are beneficial to accuracy in classification tasks.

Keywords: Topic classification · Meta-data for information systems · Financial applications · Sustainability · Environmental · Social & Governance (ESG) · Corporate social responsibility (CSR) · Information retrieval

1 Introduction

Recent advances in deep learning have led to state-of-the-art performance across a broad range of natural language processing (NLP) tasks [8]. The introduction of distributed representations and models pre-trained using large corpora mean that traditional, task-specific feature engineering is no longer required, and neural approaches that employ such techniques typically outperform more conventional machine learning models. Despite these advances, many NLP tasks in

This research was conducted while all authors.

T. Andreasen et al. (Eds.): FQAS 2021, LNAI 12871, pp. 157–169, 2021.
https://doi.org/10.1007/978-3-030-86967-0_12

the financial domain remain challenging due to the paucity of appropriately labelled data. In particular, annotated data for supervised learning remains scarce, although *data augmentation* has been proposed as one method to address this problem. Data augmentation originated in computer vision, and enables practitioners to increase the diversity of data for model training without collecting new examples. It enables both model accuracy and generalization to be improved, while controlling for over-fitting [4]. Besides insufficient data, having data that is sampled from a different subject domain or textual genre can also limit performance: differences in word distributions between the corpora, as they are typically used to pre-train language models, and financial corpora, which often exhibit specialized language and notation conventions (*e.g.* company ticker symbology) can lead to a drop in task performance. In this paper, we investigate two approaches to mitigate these issues: *domain adaptation* and *data augmentation*. Firstly, we experiment with further language model pre-training using large amounts of in-domain data from business and financial news. We then apply augmentation approaches to increase the size of our dataset for model fine-tuning. We report our findings on an Environmental, Social and Governance (ESG) controversies dataset, and demonstrate that both approaches are beneficial to performance in automatic classification tasks. ESG data can provide investors with company-specific metrics that attempt to quantify a company's environmental footprint, the degree to which they conduct their business in a socially responsible manner, and to what extent they are well-governed. Examples of ESG controversies include news stories about toxic waste spills (Environmental), human rights violations (Social), and corrupt CEOs (Governance)[1]. ESG controversies can be highly impactful on financial markets with recent estimates indicating they have wiped $500bn off the value of US companies over the past five years[2]. Companies have already recognized that investors are taking ESG information into account, which has also led to framing of stories in ESG terms more favorably ("green") than facts suggest, a practice known as *greenwashing*. Recently, the United Nations defined the seventeen *UN Sustainable Development Goals* to promote global improvement of the human condition [20]. Predictive models that can accurately classify news into ESG-related controversy categories, and also relate them to the UN SDGs, may be able to inform investment decision-making using news as actionable intelligence. This may be especially useful in an industry where ESG metrics are often published only annually or quarterly, providing investors with the ability to dynamically adjust their portfolios in response to emerging ESG news trends.

---

[1] Note that our definition is company- and investment -centric and differs from consumer/citizen-relevant controversies dealt with by [9] and [5], for example.

[2] https://www.ft.com/content/3f1d44d9-094f-4700-989f-616e27c89599   (accessed 2020-06-30).

2   Related Work

2.1   Bidirectional Transformer Models (BERT)

Bidirectional Encoder Representations from Transformers (BERT, [8]) is a neural language model capable of learning word representations from large volumes of unannotated text. Unlike earlier approaches, BERT embeddings are highly contextual due to its deep and bidirectional (*i.e.* left-to-right and right-to-left) formulation. BERT pre-training uses a masked language model that learns to predicts words randomly masked from a sequence, and whether two sentences in a document naturally follow each other (next sentence prediction). It leverages a "transformer" encoder-decoder architecture which uses attention mechanisms to forward a more complete picture of the whole sequence to the decoder at once, rather than sequentially. Fine-tuned BERT models have been used to substantially improve performance in many downstream NLP tasks.

2.2   Domain-Specific BERT Variants

Domain-specific adaptation of BERT has been conducted before, notably in the scientific domain and in the financial sub-domain of securities filings: AllenAI's SciBERT [3], a pre-trained model variant of BERT, was trained on large-scale labeled scientific data, and leverages unsupervised pretraining on a large multi-domain corpus of scientific publications. It was shown to improve performance in sequence tagging, sentence classification and dependency parsing. In the biomedical domain, BioBERT [18] was pre-trained on large-scale biomedical corpora. Again, this in-domain variant of BERT outperforms vanilla BERT on biomedical named entity recognition (0.62% F1 improvement), biomedical relation extraction (2.80% F1 improvement) and biomedical question answering (12.24% mean reciprocal rank improvement). To support computational analysis of financial language, in particular Security and Exchange Commission (SEC) quarterly and annual filings, [7] present FinBERT, a variant of BERT trained on decades of annual reports (Form 10-K, 1999–2019) and tested on quarterly reports (10-Qs). FinBERT outperforms BERT on several NLP performance tasks ($\approx$30% reduction in loss on next sentence prediction; $\approx$25% reduction in loss in predicting masked words). The authors report a model pre-trained using financial news outperforms the standard version of BERT during fine-tuning experiments. Another model, *also* called FinBERT, targets the specific task of financial sentiment analysis as applied to a financial subset of the Thomson Reuters Corpus 2 (TRC2) dataset [1].

2.3   Responsible Investing and ESG Data

Recently, there has been an increasing interest in incorporating ESG factors into investment decisions. [13] investigate how high quality ESG data can map onto investment decision-making processes. [12] is a meta-study of over 2,200 studies linking ESG factors with financial performance. [24] provides a categorization of the 17 UN Sustainable Development Goals into three ordinal classes indicating opportunity size [20].

2.4   Automatic Controversy Classification

[21] propose a system for company risk profiling, which is related to, but also different from controversy classification: while all controversies also represent a risk, many but not all risks are controversial. Additionally, our method classifies documents, while theirs classifies sentences. [9] and [14] describe attempts to detect controversies in Wikipedia, whereas our approach is aimed at controversies reported in financial and business news. [5] detect controversies in news, but the application is geopolitical security rather than financial investing. We are not aware of any previous attempts to train a deep learning model on a large financial news archive (*i.e.* several decades of data), and to the best of our knowledge, there is also no prior work on automatic ESG controversy classification.

3   Methods

3.1   Financial Corpus

For pre-training, we start with the cased BERT-base model which consists of 12 layers, 12 attention heads, 768 hidden units, and a total of 110M parameters. This is trained using English Wikipedia and the BookCorpus [32] totalling approximately 3,300M words. Our financial corpus for further pre-training is the well-known *Reuters News Archive (RNA)*, which consists of all Reuters articles published between 1996 and 2019[3]. We filter the corpus using metadata to ensure that only English language articles with Reuters topic codes that matched company news, corporate events, government finances or economic news were retained. Additionally, we excluded articles using topic codes and headline keywords that were news summaries, highlights, digests, and market round-ups. Such articles typically contain list or bullet points of unrelated news headlines which are unsuitable for next sentence prediction. Many financial news articles also contain "structured" data in the form of ASCII tables containing market data; we excluded these using a heuristic approach based on the fraction of non-alphabetical characters (>0.1). The resulting filtered corpus consists of 2.2M articles and 715M words. We converted this corpus into TensorFlow record format for masked LM and next sentence prediction at sequence lengths of 128 and 512 tokens with a duplication factor of 10 and masked LM probability of 0.15. We performed sentence boundary disambiguation using spaCy, but post-processed the results to correct errors around Reuters Instrument Codes (RICs) which are present in almost all articles. These symbols are used to identify financial instruments or indices and are made up of the security's ticker symbol, optionally followed by a period and exchange code based on the name of the associated stock exchange, all enclosed within angle brackets. For example, the RIC <IBM.N> refers to IBM being traded on the New York Stock Exchange.

---

[3] To obtain the data for replication, it can be licensed from Reuters at https://www.reutersagency.com/en/products/archive/ (accessed 2020-06-30).

3.2 Pre-training

We performed pre-training using a maximum sequence length of 128 for 5M steps, using 50,000 warm-up steps, a learning rate of 1e-5 and a batch size of 256. We then additionally pre-train using a maximum sequence length of 512 for a further 1M steps, since long sequences are mostly needed to learn positional embeddings which can be learned relatively quickly. Pre-training was run on Google Cloud Tensor Processing Units (TPUs).

3.3 ESG Dataset

Table 1. Counts of each ESG controversy type, with mappings to the UN Sustainable Development Goals (SDGs) where available.

ESG controversy	UN SDG	Count
Accounting		386
Anti-competition		2945
Business ethics	16	4672
Consumer complaints		1386
Customer health & Safety	3	1479
Diversity & opportunity	5, 9	904
Employee health & safety	3	1427
Environmental	2, 3, 6, 11, 12, 13, 14, 15	571
General shareholder rights		694
Human rights	1,2,8	340
Insider dealings		422
Intellectual property		1875
Management compensation		398
Management departures		4082
No controversy		5501
Privacy		791
Public health	3, 11	633
Responsible marketing	1, 3, 4	1134
Tax fraud		481
Wages or working condition	8	1484

Our multi-class ESG dataset is a commercial offering provided by Refinitiv[4], consisting of 31,605 news articles each annotated into one of 20 ESG controversy

---

[4] https://www.refinitiv.com/en/financial-data/company-data/esg-research-data (accessed 2020-06-30).

Table 2. Examples of back-translated paraphrases generated using a range of softmax temperature settings. The first example is the original sentence from an article concerning mining company AngloGold Ashanti ⟨ANGJ.J⟩.

Temp	Paraphrase
–	Human rights legal group says gold mining in Ghana rife with abuse, land grabs, pollution
0.6	According to the human rights group, diamond mining in Ghana is subject to abuse, mountaineering and pollution
0.7	The human rights group asserts that gold mining in Ghana is a source of violence, friction and pollution
0.8	Ghana's human rights legislation had been consistent in affirming that the gold mines in Ghana were the target of abuse, land extraction and pollution
0.9	According to information provided by the human rights legal group, gold mining in Ghana is of paramount importance for fighting beautiful weather, property damage and pollution

categories by analysts with backgrounds in finance and sustainable investing. Each article concerns an ESG controversy that a specific company is implicated in, with the entire dataset covering a total of 4137 companies over the time range 2002−2019. Included among these 20 is a negative class generated by sampling articles relating to companies in our dataset in the same date range whose headlines did not match a controversy article. There is significant class imbalance in the dataset, with only half of topics having >1,000 examples. Articles are processed by substituting company names identified using a named entity tagger with a placeholder. Additionally, we map 9 of these categories to 14 of the 17 UN Sustainable Development Goals (SDGs)[5], resulting in a multi-label dataset consisting of 21,126 labels across 12,644 news articles. The ESG dataset along with the UN SDG mapping can be found in Table 1.

3.4 Data Augmentation

We apply a back-translation approach for data augmentation [10,25] to our training sets using the open-source Tensor2Tensor implementation [26,28]. Back-translating involves translating text in language A into another language B, before translating it back into language A, therefore creating an augmented example of the original text. This enables diverse paraphrases to be generated that still preserve the semantics of the original text, and can result in significant improvements to tasks such as question answering [30]. We use the English-French and French-English models from WMT'14[6] to perform back-translation on each sentence in our training set. We controlled the diversity-validity trade-off of the generated paraphrases using a random sampling strategy controlled by

---

[5] https://sustainabledevelopment.un.org (accessed 2020-06-30).

[6] https://www.statmt.org/wmt14/translation-task.html (accessed 2020-06-30).

a tunable softmax *temperature* instead of beam search for the generation [28], ensuring diversity while preserving semantic meaning. A temperature setting of 0 results in identical paraphrases, while a setting of 1 results in diverse but incomprehensible paraphrases which risk altering the ground-truth label. We generated paraphrases using temperature settings in the range 0.6−0.9. Articles were split into sentences and paraphrases were generated for each sentence, before being recombined into articles. We generated 3 augmented articles at each temperature setting. Example paraphrases at these softmax temperatures are shown in Table 2.

3.5   Fine-Tuning

We fine-tune using cross-entropy loss after softmax activation for the multi-class task [31], and after sigmoidal activation for the multi-label task, respectively. Fine-tuning was run for 40 epochs with a dropout probability of 0.1, batch size of 64, maximum sequence lengths of 128, 256 and 512 tokens, and learning rates of 1e-5 and 1e-6. We used 30% of the data for our test set, maintaining chronological ordering.

3.6   Baseline Methods

For baseline comparison, we used a support vector machine (SVM) classifier with RBF kernel since SVMs are known to perform relatively well on small news-based datasets [22]. We use a one-vs-one scheme with TFIDF features and sub-linear term frequency scaling. The radial basis function's gamma and regularization parameters are optimized using a grid search. We also used a hierarchical attention network (HAN) classifier [29] using GLoVe word embeddings [23] which has been shown to outperform SVMs, CNNs, and LSTMs on document classification tasks [22].

4   Results

4.1   ESG Dataset Fine-Tuning

Fine-tuning results for the multi-class ESG dataset are shown in Table 3. Here we can see that the baseline SVM approach (RBF gamma parameter 0.01, regularization parameter 1.0, F1 = 0.75) and the HAN model (GLoVE embeddings of dimension 200, F1 = 0.77) are both outperformed by all BERT models, each of which achieved highest performance using a maximum sequence length of 512 tokens, a learning rate of 1e-6 and a cased vocabulary. The relatively small improvement of the HAN over the SVM seems to demonstrate that the task is a challenging problem even for relatively recent deep learning architectures. $BERT_{BASE}$, which is pre-trained using general domain English Wikipedia and the BookCorpus only, improves on the HAN model by 0.01 in terms of absolute F-score (F1 = 0.78).[7] BERT$_{RNA}$, our method further pre-trained on RNA, improves on BERT$_{BASE}$ performance by 0.04 (F1 = 0.82) which suggests that the additional pre-training using a financial domain corpus is effective in improving the performance of downstream classification tasks. The magnitude of improvement here is approximately in line with the performance gains we see elsewhere when additional domain-specific pre-training has been used [18]. BERT$_{RNA-AUG}$, our method trained on RNA and fine-tuned using the augmented training set, achieves F1 = 0.84 when data is generated using a softmax temperature of 0.9, emphasising the importance of high diversity among training examples. This demonstrates that our back-translation approach is also effective, and that both approaches can be used in combination to achieve highest performance. Results for individual ESG controversies are shown in Table 4. These show that the highest relative improvement in F1-score between BERT$_{RNA}$ and BERT$_{BASE}$ typically occurs in classes with amongst the lowest number of training examples, such as Accounting, Management Compensation, Public Health, Insider Dealings, and Human Rights controversies. We see an improvement in F1 score in 18 out of 20 classes, of which 16 are significant at the $p < 0.05$ level, 2 at the $p < 0.01$ level, and 13 at the $p < 0.001$ level using McNemar's test. Comparing BERT$_{RNA-AUG}$ with BERT$_{RNA}$, relative improvements are much smaller although we still see the largest gains in Accounting and Public Health controversies, and at least some improvement in 15 classes. 10 classes are significant at the $p < 0.05$ level, and of these 3 at the $p < 0.01$ level, and 5 at the $p<0.001$ level. Two classes – Insider Dealings and Wages or Working Condition controversies – actually see a slight reduction in performance, which suggests that the diversity-validity trade-off is slightly too high for these classes.

Table 3. ESG dataset fine-tuning performance using. Our method is BERT$_{RNA}$, and BERT$_{RNA-AUG}$ uses data augmentation. HAN is the hierarhical attention network; best performance was achieved using GLoVe embeddings of dimension 200. Precision, recall and F1 scores are all weighted metrics accounting for class imbalance.

Model	Precision	Recall	F1
SVM$_{TF-IDF}$	0.76	0.75	0.75
HAN$_{GLoVE-200}$	0.77	0.77	0.77
BERT$_{BASE}$	0.79	0.78	0.78
BERT$_{RNA}$	0.82	0.82	0.82
BERT$_{RNA-AUG}$	0.84	0.84	**0.84**

4.2   Qualitative Analysis

We also performed a qualitative analysis by comparing the BERT$_{BASE}$ and BERT$_{RNA}$ confusion matrices and inspecting the off-diagonal values. Some of

---

[7] F-score or F1 is the harmonic mean between precision and recall.

Table 4. ESG dataset fine-tuning F1 performance by BERT models for individual classes. BASE is the pre-trained using general domain English Wikipedia and the BookCorpus, RNA is our model further pre-trained on RNA, and RNA-AUG is our model further pre-trained on RNA and fine-tuned using the augmented training set. Asterisks indicate statistical significance compared to the model in the previous column using McNemar's test at p-values of $< 0.05(^*)$, $0.01(^{**})$ and $0.001(^{***})$

ESG controversy	BASE	RNA	RNA-AUG
Accounting	0.08	0.29***	0.40***
Anti-competition	0.79	0.84***	0.84
Business ethics	0.65	0.70***	0.71
Consumer complaints	0.48	0.53*	0.59***
Customer health & safety	0.70	0.74	0.76
Diversity & opportunity	0.85	0.86**	0.88
Employee health & safety	0.81	0.85	0.87
Environmental	0.59	0.66***	0.70**
General shareholder rights	0.54	0.65***	0.71*
Human rights	0.53	0.67***	0.70**
Insider dealings	0.62	0.80***	0.79
Intellectual property	0.92	0.92***	0.94*
Management compensation	0.57	0.76***	0.82***
Management departures	0.96	0.97	0.97
No controversy	0.99	0.99	1.00
Privacy	0.79	0.84***	0.84
Public health	0.37	0.48***	0.57***
Responsible marketing	0.62	0.69***	0.73***
Tax fraud	0.58	0.71***	0.73**
Wages or working condition	0.84	0.86**	0.89

the more interesting misclassifications by $BERT_{BASE}$ that were corrected by $BERT_{RNA}$ were Accounting controversies and Management Departures controversies, for example: *The Finnish company swung to a net loss of 1.6 billion euros in the first quarter, hit by falling sales and heavy restructuring charges. Nokia said Colin Giles, head of sales, would leave the firm in June, as it restructures the sales team. Nokia's first-quarter cellphone sales fell 24% from a year ago. The company said Giles was leaving to spend more time with his family and would not be replaced.* Management Departures are often associated with negative earnings reports which, although are typically not controversial, often include similar references to financial losses as are found in actual Accounting controversies, for example: *Three former Deutsche Bank employees have filed complaints with the U.S. securities regulators claiming the bank failed to recognize up to $12 billion of unrealized losses during the financial crisis.* It appears that BERT$_{RNA}$ is able to learn to distinguish between such cases. Other examples include misclassifications between Public Health controversies and Customer Health & Safety controversies; these are often hard to distinguish and occasionally overlap. The following example was correctly predicted as Public Health controversy by BERT$_{RNA}$ and incorrectly predicted as Customer Health & Safety controversy by BERT$_{BASE}$: *A wireless service provider has agreed to drop its lawsuit against the county over proposed wireless antennas in Hacienda Heights under one condition – that it approve a permit that residents have vehemently opposed for almost four years. Between September 2008 and February 2009, the permit was approved twice by county officials and appealed both times by dozens of residents, including 13-year resident John Chen. "Our residents and community are really, really concerned about health problems", said Chen, President Broadmoor Monaco Crest Homeowners Association.*

4.3   UN SDG Dataset Fine-Tuning

Fine-tuning results for the multi-label UN SDGs dataset are shown in Table 5. Similar to the ESG results, we are able to improve on BERT$_{BASE}$ (F1 = 0.75) using BERT$_{RNA}$ by 0.03 (F1 = 0.78) – slightly less than the corresponding improvement in the ESG dataset. BERT$_{RNA-AUG}$ further improves over BERT$_{RNA}$ by 0.05 (F1 = 0.83), which is slightly more than in the ESG dataset. Again, best model performance was achieved using a maximum sequence length of 512 tokens, a learning rate of 1e−6, and a softmax temperature of 0.9 in the case of BERT$_{RNA-AUG}$. Due to the mapping in Table 1, the broad Environmental ESG category corresponds exclusively to 5 different UN SDGs (6, 12, 13, 14, 15) and performance is highly correlated between them. If we treat these as a single class during validation, the relative performance of the three methods are unchanged with F1 scores 0.76, 0.79 and 0.85 for BERT$_{BASE}$, BERT$_{RNA}$ and BERT$_{RNA-AUG}$, respectively.

Table 5. UN SDGs dataset fine-tuning performance. Our method is BERT$_{RNA}$, and BERT$_{RNA-AUG}$ uses data augmentation.

Model	Loss	Precision	Recall	F1
BERT$_{BASE}$	0.23	0.84	0.70	0.75
BERT$_{RNA}$	0.16	0.85	0.73	0.78
BERT$_{RNA-AUG}$	0.07	0.85	0.83	**0.83**

5   Discussion and Future Work

We have introduced BERT$_{RNA}$, a domain-specific version of the BERT language model which has been further pre-trained using a 715M word corpus consisting of financial and business articles from Reuters News Archive. We have demonstrated that fine-tuning $BERT_{RNA}$ for two downstream classification task – multi-class ESG controversy and multi-label UN SDGs detection – can result in an improvement in performance compared to the general domain $BERT_{BASE}$ model. Furthermore, we have applied a back-translation approach to the limited dataset and have demonstrated that such techniques can further boost classification performance, and have also invested the linguistic behaviour of the different layers in both the pre-trained and fine-tuned models. Taken together, these results indicate that domain-specific language models and data augmentation can both help to mitigate the challenges associated with building machine learning models using small datasets. These approaches and the associated performance gains may be especially important in the financial industry, which is highly adversarial, and could form the basis for alpha-generating NLP/NLU systems [11]. To the best of our knowledge, this is the first use of a finance-domain neural language model applied to ESG controversy prediction. While these results are encouraging, there are a number of areas where we believe further work could enable additional performance gains. One aspect which we did not address is the use of a domain-specific vocabulary. BERT's general domain vocabulary is constructed using WordPiece tokenization [27], which effectively deals with out-of-vocabulary issues by representing words using sub-word units ("wordpieces"). While financial and business vocabulary is closer to BERT's general domain vocabulary than for example, the life sciences, the use of acronyms and abbreviations (EBITDA, CAGR, P/E, *etc.*) in news is common. A domain-specific vocabulary may be of benefit here since many of these terms provide strong clues as to the subject of news articles. Another area of focus could be to extend the financial pre-training corpus beyond Reuters News to include other news sources, as well as additional sources of financial text such as SEC company filings and transcripts of earnings calls. Reuters News has specific style guide-lines[8], so we may be sacrificing stylistic diversity by using only a single source. The rich metadata provided in RNA does however allow us to filter the contents to ensure high quality and relevance, and this information is much more limited elsewhere. Geo-spatial meta-data enrichment [19] could be applied to enable spatial analysis. A closer inspection of the underlying mechanisms that contribute to the performance gains of domain-specific models may also yield useful insight. An analysis of the self-attention head patterns could reveal whether certain linguistic features are more or less prevalent in finance [6,16], while extensions to the underlying transformer architecture may enable the processing of longer financial texts than is currently possible [15]. There are also more advanced methods for data augmentation available, such as the unsupervised data augmentation [28], which uses weighted supervised cross-entropy and unsupervised consistency training loss, and combines well with BERT fine-tuning. Other loss functions such as cosine loss are also reported to benefit deep learning on small data-sets [2]. Although we have tested our model here on ESG and UN SDGs classification problems, one may extend this validation to a much broader range of financial NLP tasks. Examples include analysis of financial sentiment, named

---

[8] http://handbook.reuters.com (accessed 2020-06-39).

entity recognition or relation extraction. The approach we outline can also be applied to many of the BERT variants that have emerged recently [17].

References

1. Araci, D.: FinBERT: financial sentiment analysis with pre-trained language models. arXiv preprint arXiv:1908.10063 (2019)
2. Barz, B., Denzler, J.: Deep learning on small datasets without pre-training using cosine loss. In: IEEE Winter Conference on Applications of Computer Vision, WACV 2020, IEEE (2020)
3. Beltagy, I., Lo, K., Cohan, A.: SciBERT: a pretrained language model for scientific text. In: Proceedings of the 2019 Conference on Empirical Methods in Natural Language Processing and the 9th International Joint Conference on Natural Language Processing (EMNLP-IJCNLP), pp. 3606–3611 (2019)
4. Bloice, M.D., Stocker, C., Holzinger, A.: Augmentor: an image augmentation library for machine learning. Technical report, ArXiv preprint server (2017). https://arxiv.org/pdf/1708.04680.pdf
5. Choi, Y., Jung, Y., Myaeng, S.-H.: Identifying controversial issues and their subtopics in news articles. In: Chen, H., Chau, M., Li, S., Urs, S., Srinivasa, S., Wang, G.A. (eds.) PAISI 2010. LNCS, vol. 6122, pp. 140–153. Springer, Heidelberg (2010). https://doi.org/10.1007/978-3-642-13601-6_16
6. Clark, K., Khandelwal, U., Levy, O., Manning, C.D.: What does BERT look at? An analysis of BERT's attention. In: Proceedings of the 2019 ACL Workshop BlackboxNLP: Analyzing and Interpreting Neural Networks for NLP, pp. 276–286. ACL, Florence (2019). https://doi.org/10.18653/v1/W19-4828
7. Desola, V., Hanna, K., Pri Nonis: FinBERT: pre-trained model on sec filings for financial natural language tasks. Technical report, University of California at Berkeley (2019). https://doi.org/10.13140/RG.2.2.19153.89442
8. Devlin, J., Chang, M.W., Lee, K., Toutanova, K.: BERT: pre-training of deep bidirectional transformers for language understanding. In: Proceedings of the 2019 Conference of the North American Chapter of the Association for Computational Linguistics: Human Language Technologies, pp. 4171–4186. Association for Computational Linguistics, Minneapolis (2019). https://doi.org/10.18653/v1/N19-1423
9. Dori-Hacohen, S., Jensen, D., Allan, J.: Controversy detection in Wikipedia using collective classification. In: Proceedings of SIGIR, New York, NY, USA, pp. 797–800 (2016)
10. Edunov, S., Ott, M., Auli, M., Grangier, D.: Understanding back-translation at scale. arXiv preprint arXiv:1808.09381 (2018)
11. Feuerriegel, S., Prendinger, H.: News-based trading strategies. Decis. Support Syst. **90**, 65–74 (2016)
12. Friede, G., Busch, T., Bassen, A.: ESG and financial performance: aggregated evidence from more than 2000 empirical studies. J. Sustain. Financ. Invest. **5**(4), 210–233 (2015). https://doi.org/10.1080/20430795.2015.1118917
13. In, S.Y., Rook, D., Monk, A.: Integrating alternative data (also known as ESG data) in investment decision making. Glob. Econ. Rev. **48**(3), 237–260 (2019). https://doi.org/10.1080/1226508X.2019.1643059
14. Jang, M., Foley, J., Dori-Hacohen, S., Allan, J.: Probabilistic approaches to controversy detection. In: Proceedings of the 25th ACM International on Conference on Information and Knowledge Management, CIKM 2016, pp. 2069–2072. ACM, New York (2016). https://doi.org/10.1145/2983323.2983911

15. Kitaev, N., Kaiser, L., Levskaya, A.: Reformer: the efficient transformer. arXiv preprint arXiv:2001.04451 (2020)
16. Kovaleva, O., Romanov, A., Rogers, A., Rumshisky, A.: Revealing the dark secrets of BERT. arXiv preprint arXiv:1908.08593 (2019)
17. Lan, Z., Chen, M., Goodman, S., Gimpel, K., Sharma, P., Soricut, R.: ALBERT: a lite BERT for self-supervised learning of language representations. arXiv preprint arXiv:1909.11942 (2019)
18. Lee, J., et al.: BioBERT: pre-trained biomedical language representation model for biomedical text mining. arXiv preprint arXiv:1901.08746 (2019)
19. Leidner, J.L.: Survey of textual data & geospatial technology. In: Werner, M., Chiang, Y.-Y. (eds.) Handbook of Big Geospatial Data. Springer, Cham (2021). https://doi.org/10.1007/978-3-030-55462-0_16
20. Lu, Y., Nakicenovic, N., Visbeck, M., Stevance, A.S.: Policy: five priorities for the UN Sustainable Development Goals. Nat. News **520**(7548), 432 (2015)
21. Nugent, T., Leidner, J.L.: Risk mining: company-risk identification from unstructured sources. In: Domeniconi, C., et al. (eds.) IEEE International Conference on Data Mining ICDM, 12–15 December 2016, Barcelona, Spain, pp. 1308–1311 (2016)
22. Nugent, T., Petroni, F., Raman, N., Carstens, L., Leidner, J.L.: A comparison of classification models for natural disaster and critical event detection from news. In: 2017 IEEE International Conference on Big Data (Big Data), pp. 3750–3759. IEEE (2017)
23. Pennington, J., Socher, R., Manning, C.D.: GloVe: global vectors for word representation. In: Proceedings of EMNLP (2014)
24. Schramade, W.: Investing in the UN sustainable development goals: opportunities for companies and investors. J. Appl. Corp. Fin. **29**(2), 87–99 (2017)
25. Sennrich, R., Haddow, B., Birch, A.: Improving neural machine translation models with monolingual data. arXiv preprint arXiv:1511.06709 (2015)
26. Vaswani, A., et al.: Tensor2Tensor for neural machine translation. CoRR abs/1803.07416 (2018)
27. Wu, Y., et al.: Google's neural machine translation system: bridging the gap between human and machine translation. arXiv preprint arXiv:1609.08144 (2016)
28. Xie, Q., Dai, Z., Hovy, E., Luong, M.T., Le, Q.V.: Unsupervised data augmentation. arXiv preprint arXiv:1904.12848 (2019)
29. Yang, Z., Yang, D., Dyer, C., He, X., Smola, A., Hovy, E.: Hierarchical attention networks for document classification. In: Proceedings of NAACL-HLT, pp. 1480–1489. ACL, San Diego (2016). https://doi.org/10.18653/v1/N16-1174
30. Yu, A.W., et al.: QANet: combining local convolution with global self-attention for reading comprehension. arXiv preprint arXiv:1804.09541 (2018)
31. Zhang, Z., Sabuncu, M.R.: Generalized cross entropy loss for training deep neural networks with noisy labels. arXiv preprint arXiv:1805.07836 (2018)
32. Zhu, Y., et al.: Aligning books and movies: towards story-like visual explanations by watching movies and reading books. In: Proceedings of IEEE ICCV, pp. 19–27 (2015)

A Novel Approach for Supporting Italian Satire Detection Through Deep Learning

Gabriella Casalino[1], Alfredo Cuzzocrea[2(✉)], Giosué Lo Bosco[3,5],
Mariano Maiorana[3], Giovanni Pilato[4], and Daniele Schicchi[5]

[1] Department of Computer Science, University of Bari, Bari, Italy
gabriella.casalino@uniba.it
[2] iDEA Lab, University of Calabria, Rende, Italy
alfredo.cuzzocrea@unical.it
[3] Department of Mathematics and Computer Science, University of Palermo,
Palermo, Italy
giosue.lobosco@unipa.it, mariano.maiorana@community.unipa.it
[4] ICAR-CNR, National Research Council of Italy, Palermo, Italy
giovanni.pilato@cnr.it
[5] Department of Science for Technological Innovation,
Euro-Mediterranean Institute of Science and Technology, Palermo, Italy
danieleschicchi@iemest.eu

Abstract. Satire is a way of criticizing people (or ideas) by ridiculing them on political, social, and morals topics often used to denounce political and societal problems, leveraging comedic devices such as parody exaggeration, incongruity, etc.etera. Detecting satire is one of the most challenging computational linguistics tasks, natural language processing, and social multimedia sentiment analysis. In particular, as satirical texts include figurative communication for expressing ideas/opinions concerning people, sentiment analysis systems may be negatively affected; therefore, satire should be adequately addressed to avoid such systems' performance degradation. This paper tackles automatic satire detection through effective deep learning (DL) architecture that has been shown to be useful for addressing sarcasm/irony detection problems. We both trained and tested the system exploiting articles derived from two important satiric blogs, *Lercio* and *IlFattoQuotidaino*, and significant Italian newspapers. Experiments show an optimal performance achieved by the network capable of detecting satire in a context where it is not marked.

Keywords: Satire detection · Deep learning · Natural language processing

1 Introduction

Satire is a way of criticizing people (or ideas) by ridiculing them on political, social, and morals topics. Most of the time, such a language form is utilized to influence people's opinions. It is a figurative form of language that leverages

© Springer Nature Switzerland AG 2021
T. Andreasen et al. (Eds.): FQAS 2021, LNAI 12871, pp. 170–181, 2021.
https://doi.org/10.1007/978-3-030-86967-0_13

comedic devices such as *parody* (i.e. to imitate techniques and style of some person, place or thing), *exaggeration* (i.e. to represent something beyond normality make it ridiculous), *incongruity* (i.e. to present things that are absurd concerning the context), *reversal* (i.e. to present the opposite of normal order), *irony/sarcasm* (i.e. to say something that is the opposite of what a person mean). Moreover, satire masks emotions like irritation and disappointment by using ironic content.

The easy way of denouncing political and societal problems exploiting humor has brought consensus to satire that has been widely accepted. It leads people to constructive social criticism, to participate actively in the socio-political life, representing a sign of democracy. Unfortunately, the ironic nature of satire tends to mislead subjects that can believe the humorous news as they were real; therefore, satirical news can be deceptive and harmful.

Detecting satire is one of the most challenging computational linguistics tasks, natural language processing, and social multimedia sentiment analysis. It differs from irony detection since satire *mocks* something or someone, while irony is intended to be a way for causing laughter. Tackling such a task means both to pinpoint linguistic entities that characterize satire and look at how they are used to express a more complex meaning. Another yet interesting paradigm consists in coupling these aspects with the emerging *big data trend*, as to cover some advanced topics such as graph analytics (e.g., [10]) and cybersecurity (e.g., [7]).

As satirical texts include figurative communication for expressing ideas/opinions concerning people, sentiment analysis systems may be negatively affected. In this case, satire should be adequately addressed to avoid performances degradation of such systems, mainly if sarcasm/irony is used [1]. Moreover, reliably detecting satire can benefit many other research areas where figurative language usage can be a problem, such as *Affective Computing* [17]. An autonomous way of detecting satire might help computers interpret human interaction and notice its emotional state, improving the human-computer experience.

In this paper, we tackle automatic satire detection through effective deep learning (DL) architecture that has been shown to be effective for addressing the sarcasm/irony detection problem. The Neural Network (NN) exploits articles derived from two important satiric blogs, *Lercio* and *Il Fatto Quotidaino*, and major Italian newspapers. The dataset has been specifically created for the task, and it includes news concerning similar topics. Experiments show an optimal performance achieved by the network that is capable of performing well on satire recognition. The network demonstrates the ability to detect satire in a context where it is not marked as in Il Fatto Quotidaino. In fact, in this special case, news are so realistic that they seem to be true [17]. An autonomous way of detecting satire might help computers interpret human interaction and notice its emotional state, improving the human-computer experience.

The structure of this paper is organized as follows: in Sect. 2 we present the satire detection topic showing some related works. Section 3 describes the methodology we used to tackle the task and it contains details for replicating the system. Finally Sects. 5 and 6 respectively show experiments and comments on results. Finally, we give the conclusion and future works in Sect. 7.

2   Related Works

Satire is a fascinating topic extensively studied in literature [13,16,18]. Its automatic detection is an emerging task that has been introduced by Burfoot and Baldwin [6], where they presented their first solution: a Support Vector Machine-based system that relied on bag-of-words features.

Although the importance of the task, it has been tackled mainly for the English language. The Italian one, like other languages, have suffered the prominence of such a language. Few works tackle the satire detection problem for Italian text and a lack of resources to support the development of a computational system for such a problem. Nonetheless, Barbieri and Saggion [2] have proposed a language-independent framework for detecting satiric Tweets. They harvested data from popular satirical Twitter accounts. Then they have trained a Support Vector Machine for the classification task by taking into account both language-independent intrinsic word features and language-dependent word-based features. The experimentation reveals the effectiveness of their system for English, Spanish and Italian Tweets. To the best of our knowledge, it is the most relevant work that tackles the Italian language problem, but it differs from ours because of the different type of text we address. Our system analyzes full articles extracted from online *satirical journals* that are different from Tweets in several respects.

A key element of satire is *irony*. Automatically detecting irony is a related research topic that has been widely studied in the past [1,3,11]. The literature concerned such a task is a good support for the satire detection one, but it is limited because of the principal characteristic of the satire: it is utilized for mocking something of someone. Therefore, they are different tasks that have to be dealt with separately.

3   Methodology

Recognizing *satire* can be modeled as a classification task subdividing *satiric* and *non-satiric* articles in two different classes. Such a task has been widely tackled by using machine learning algorithms, and it has been shown that it is important to consider various aspects related to the application domain. For what concerns the subject problem, many factors should be taken into account: the way the text is represented and how it is structured (Sect. 3.1), the model's architecture for tackling the task and its tuning (Sect. 3.2 and 3.3). Le Hoang Son et al. [14] have introduced a deep learning model that promises optimal performances for detecting sarcasm/irony. We believe that such a network can also help recognizing the main aspects of the satire; a detailed description is given in Sect. 3.2.

3.1 Preprocessing

The preprocessing phase deals with the input arrangement to make it analyzable to the model as best as possible. Most of the time, the text is changed by removing punctuation marks, stop-words, etc. In this case, since the articles have been harvested from online resources we focused on the removal of the *author's name, HTML tags, hyperlinks,* and *hashtags*. Subsequently, the input text is split into tokens (i.e., words and punctuation marks) using NLTK [1]. To level out the lengths of the articles, we have analyzed the cumulative frequency of the length of the texts, and then we have selected a value $L = 4500$ words such that we considered 95% of the entire set of articles. Finally, each token is mapped to a 300-dimensional space by a pre-trained embedding tool that relies on FastText [5,12]. Therefore, each article is represented by a matrix of real values of size $(L, 300)$. We crop texts longer than L, and we pad with 0s texts that are shorter.

3.2 Architecture

The network's architecture is inspired from the one presented by Le Hoang Son et al. [14], that exploits *Bidirectional Long Short Term Memory* (BiLSTM), *Soft Attention Mechanism, Convolutional* NNs, and *Fully Connected* NNs. Moreover, such a model consider five different auxiliary characteristics that have been shown to be relevant to sarcasm/irony detection: number of exclamation marks (!), number of question marks (?), number of periods (.), number of capital letters, number of uses of *or*. A complete model representation is given in Fig. 1.

Input Layer. The first network's layer is the *Input* layer which manage the pre-processed text in order to allow the analysis by the BiLSTM.

BiLSTM Layer. BiLSTM is composed of two LSTM layers which examine respectively the input sequence in *forward* (from the first token x_0 to the last one x_T) and *backward* (from the last token x_T to the first one x_0) ways. LSTM *cell*, is a neural unit created specifically for overcoming the vanish/exploding gradient problem [4] that affects the training phase by using the backpropagation through time algorithm. The *cell* is composed of a set of *gates* (i.e. input, forget, and output gate) which control the flow of information. The *forget* gate deals with choosing the information part should be kept and what should be gotten rid, the *input* gate proposes new information that is worth to be considered, and the *output* gate mix the contributes given by both the *input* and *forget* gates for creating the final cell's output. LSTM cell leverages two *feedback* loops (i.e. internal and external) which allow to track the sequence of elements the cell has already analyzed through a sequence of internal states $h_1, \ldots, h_T$. The final output of the LSTM cell is its final internal state that is strictly dependent of the previous ones. The formulation of a LSTM unit, named *memory unit*, is described in by the following equations [15]:

---

[1] www.nltk.org.

$$f_t = \sigma(W_f x_t + U_f h_{t-1} + b_f)$$
$$i_t = \sigma(W_i x_t + U_i h_{t-1} + b_i)$$
$$o_t = \sigma(W_o x_t + U_o h_{t-1} + b_o)$$
$$c_t = tanh(W_c x_t + U_c h_{t-1} + b_c)$$
$$s_t = f_t \odot s_{t-1} + i_t \odot c_t$$
$$h_t = tanh(s_t) \odot o_t$$

where f_t, i_t, o_t are respectively the input, forget and output gates, the $\odot$ is the element-wise multiplication, the b_f, b_i, b_o, b_c are bias vectors, while tanh is the hyperbolic tangent and sigma is the sigmoid function.

The analysis of the input text in these two opposite directions create two representation of the input sequence: straight and reversed. BiLSTM layer merges the output of the two LSTM layers into a single output by concatenating them. The final vector, if examined through the soft attention, allow the network to capture the salient words considering the input text totally.

Soft Attention Layer. The Soft Attention is a mechanism that weight the input sequence elements on the basis of their relevance for the classification task, suggesting on what elements leverage for classifying the input correctly. It exploits the sequence of LSTM states during the examination of the input sequence.

The attention layer's output is the *context-vector*. It is computed as the weighted sum of the *attention weights* α_t and the LSTM's states $h_0, \ldots, h_T$. The approach is described by the following formulas, considering w_α the weights matrix:

$$z_t = h_t w_\alpha$$
$$\alpha_t = \frac{e^{z_t}}{\sum_{i=1}^{T} e^{z_i}}$$
$$c = \sum_{i=1}^{T} \alpha_i h_i$$

In this case, the context-vector c is extended by concatenating the auxiliary features. Finally, one-dimensional vector C which contains the analysis of the BiLSTM layer and the Pragmatic features becomes the input of the next convolutional layer.

Convolutional Layer. We stacked three convolutional layers for the feature learning. Each convolving filter of size s slides over the input vector to compute a localized feature vector v_j for each possible word through a nonlinear activation function. For each filter, a transition matrix T is generated. Such a matrix is iteratively applied to a part of the input vector to compute the features as following :

$$v_j = f(\langle T, F_{j:j+s-1} \rangle + b_a)$$

where $\langle \cdot, \cdot \rangle$ is the inner product, $F_{g,l}$ is the part of the input vector which includes elements from position g to position l, b_a is a bias related to the specific filter, and f is a non linear function.

The output of the convolutional layers is a vector of features $v = v_1, v_2, \ldots, v_{n-s+1}$ where n is the length of the input vector.

A max-pooling layer then processes the convolutional layer's output. Such a layer extracts the largest computed feature for each filter, considering only the most relevant ones. The output layer then analyzes the output vector that included the selected features.

Output Layer. The output layer is a Fully Connected NN activated by Softmax. Such a layer takes as input the features extracted by the max-pooling layer. Employing the Softmax activation function computes the probability that the input text belongs to the either *satiric* or *non-satiric* class.

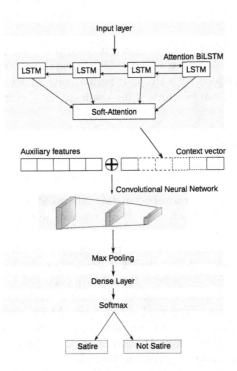

Fig. 1. The representation of the Neural Network's architecture. The first layer manages the input in order to make it available for analysis. BiLSTM layer analyses the input in the forward and backward way to give a complete representation of the text. The attention mechanism is exploited for detecting the most relevant words for accomplishing the classification task. Its output is concatenated to the auxiliary features and then it is given as input to the convolutional layer. Such a layer extract prominent features, which are processed by a fully connected layer activated by softmax.

Table 1. List of the model's hyperparameters.

Embedding size	300
LSTM neurons	500
Batch size	10
Convolutional layers	3
Kernel size	3
Convolutional activation function	ReLU
Dropout BiLSTM	0.2
Dropout ConvNet	0.4
Optimization algorithm	Adam
Learning rate	0.0001
Dense layer neurons	350

3.3 Parameters

Hyperparameters have been chosen empirically and taking inspiration from [1, 14]. Different tries have shown that taking a small learning rate and using a small minibatch coupled with Dropout regularization factors helps the network improve its performance by diminishing the loss. A complete list of them can be found in Table 1.

4 Experiments

4.1 Corpus

Satiric texts has been extracted from two famous Italian sites named *Lercio*[2] and *IlFattoQuotidaino*[3]. Both of them include satiric news written according to the *news satire* format.

The gathering process has been carried out by exploiting the RDF Site Summary (RSS): a technology that makes it possible to distribute web contents in a standardized, computer-readable format. We collected 7354 articles (2195 full articles and 5159 texts related to satiric *memes*) from Lercio and 943 full articles from IlFattoQuotidaino. Afterward, we used the RAKE algorithm [19] to extract a set of keywords from the satiric texts. Finally, such keywords have been used to filter newspaper articles from the *Event Registry*[4] site. A complete set of the RAKE's parameters used are given in Table 2.

Event Registry collects and annotate news published by over 30'000 news publishers, and it provides tools for selecting articles on the basis of *topic, language, keywords, article location* and so on. We focused on *Italian current news* that best matched the keywords extracted from the satiric news.

The final dataset is a mixture of satiric news extracted from Lercio and IlFattoQuotidaino coupled with Newspaper articles which concern similar topics.

---

[2] www.lercio.it.

[3] www.ilfattoquotidaino.it.

[4] https://eventregistry.org/.

Table 2. RAKE's parameters used for extracting keywords from the satiric texts.

Parameter	Value
Mininum characters	3
Maximum words	2
Language	It
Mininum frequency	2
Stopwords	NLTK stopwords

Table 3. Averaged system results on Lercio and regular newspapers.

Measures	Epochs			
	5	10	15	20
Accuracy	.9445	.9620	**.9885**	.9855
Recall	.9620	.9820	.998	**.9920**
Precision	.9294	.9442	**.9793**	.9792
F1-Score	.9455	.9628	**.9886**	.9856

5   Experiments

The network has been trained and tested exploiting a dataset composed of 1'000 Lercio's full articles and 1'000 full regular articles extracted from newspapers. We leveraged on cross-validation methodology K-Fold with $K = 5$. We evaluate the network's behavior for each fold by using Accuracy, Recall, Precision, and F1-Score. The final network's behavior has been evaluated by averaging the partial results achieved for each fold. Moreover, we used 400 articles extracted from IlFattoQuotidaino *only* for testing.

Table 3 shows the results computed considering the averaged performance of the network on Lercio and regular newspapers on varying of the number of epochs. Similarly, table 4 contains the performances of the network on IlFatto-Quotidaino.

5.1   Baseline Models

The main model was compared with a set of competitors derived rearranged its layers. To doing so, it makes clear whether the problem's complexity is overestimated leaving room for the usage of fewer complex models. We trained and tested five different NNs systems according to the methodology used for the main model. We assembled the baselines leveraging on LSTMs, Convolutional NNs, Attention Mechanism, and Fully Connected NNs as follows:

- *sAttBiLSTMConvNet* is the main model as described in Sect. 3.2;
- *sBiLSTMConvNet* is structured as the main model except for the attention mechanism. The auxiliary features are concatenated to the output of the

Table 4. Averaged system results on IlFattoQuotidaino and regular newspapers.

Measures	Epochs			
	5	10	15	20
Accuracy	.9512	.955	.9887	**.9912**
Recall	.9325	**.9975**	.9975	.990
Precision	.9688	.9194	.9803	**.9925**
F1-Score	.9503	.9569	.9888	**.9912**

Table 5. Averaged systems results on Lercio and regular newspapers: models comparison.

Model	Accuracy	F1-score
sAttBLSTMConvNet	**.9885**	**.9886**
sBiLSTMConvNet	.9445	.9442
S-LSTM	.5930	.7107
BiLSTM	.9580	.9670
BiLSTM-Att	.9305	.9344
SVM	.8389	.8579

BiLSTM layer, and the resulting vector is given as input to the convolutional layer;

– *S-LSTM* is a simple NN that relies on the Input layer that manages the input articles linked to an LSTM cells layer. The last layer analyzes the input sequence only in the forward direction. The final output is then processed by a fully connected NN activated by softmax;

– *BiLSTM* is a NN composed of the Input layer and a Bidirectional LSTM layer. The output of such a layer is then given as input to the final fully connected layer that is activated by the softmax activation function. Auxiliary features are concatenated to the output of the Bidirectional LSTM layer.

– *BiLSTM-Att* is a BiLSTM that exploits the Attention Mechanism and that output the final result through the fully connected layer activated by softmax. Auxiliary features are concatenated to the context vector.

Moreover, we used a Support Vector Machine for tackling the satire classification problem. In this case, the articles are represented as the averaged vector computed exploiting the tokens embedding described in Sect. 3.1.

Table 5 compares the results achieved by the models on Lercio considering 5-Fold cross-validation. It contains the best performance achieved by each model. For what concern the *sAttBLSTMConvNet* we have chosen the model trained for 15 epochs.

6   Discussion

The testing phase is made harder by the lack of data and benchmarks that standardize experimentation. Furthermore, few models tackle the same tasks; therefore it is hard to carry on an extended comparison. Although such difficulties, the cross-validation methodology allows us to measure the network's performances and generalizing capabilities beyond the training set. Moreover, many different full models' are tested in the same way.

Experiments' verdict outlines a relevant performance achieved by the sAttBLSTMConvNet for tackling the task of *satire detection*. The model achieves 98.9% of accuracy and F1-Score on Lercio achieving respectively +3% and +2% compared to the second-best model *BiLSTM*.

LSTM is the worst model; it is not capable of detecting the satire as well as other models, suggesting the need for more efficiency to approximate the input space and to find the right threshold between approximation and generalization. The other models achieve relevant performance, which is almost comparable to the ones achieved by sAttBLSTMConvNet. Experiments show the importance of the attention mechanism, which get decreasing the sBiLSTMConvNet's performance. Surprisingly, a simpler model as BiLSTM achieves the second most relevant results.

Another significant contribution is given by relating the sAttBLSTMConvNet's performance to the analysis of the corpora. Lercio and IlFattoQuotidiano treat satire in different ways: the former makes use of *exaggeration* heavily, the latter tends to use a *soft* satire. From a human-being perspective, satire is easy to recognize in Lercio but more complex in IlFattoQuotidiano since their authors write articles similar to those published in regular newspapers. We believed that the satire included in the IlFattoQuotidiano news could be detected mainly by human-beings since their articles are often mistaken for *real* news or *fake* news. Results in Table 4 show a different trend, further demonstrating the primary model's effectiveness.

7   Conclusion and Future Works

Satire aims at criticizing either something or someone leveraging on comedic devices. Its automatically detection is a non-trivial task that have to consider the components it is composed such as *parody, exaggeration, reversal, irony/sarcasm* which often are related to stand-alone research topics.

In this paper, we have introduced a powerful DL model that tackles the satire detection problem by examining lexical, syntactical, and auxiliary features. To support the analysis by the system, we exploited an effective pre-trained embedding tool based on FastText. The system has been widely tested, and results show its capability to detect the soft satire and the more marked one.

Future work will further analyze the network's behavior by exploiting incremental data [9] and clustering [8]. Moreover, we are going to study how satire might affect the text comprehension [20] and if it might be reproduced through automatic creative processes [21].

Acknowledgement. Gabriella Casalino acknowledges funding from the Italian Ministry of Education, University and Research through the European PON project AIM (Attraction and International Mobility), nr. 1852414, activity 2, line 1.

References

1. Alcamo, T., Cuzzocrea, A., Lo Bosco, G., Pilato, G., Schicchi, D.: Analysis and comparison of deep learning networks for supporting sentiment mining in text corpora. In: 22th International Conference on Information Integration and Web-based Applications and Services (iiWAS2020) (2020)
2. Barbieri, F., Ronzano, F., Saggion, H.: Do we criticise (and laugh) in the same way? Automatic detection of multi-lingual satirical news in Twitter. In: Twenty-Fourth International Joint Conference on Artificial Intelligence (2015)
3. Barbieri, F., Saggion, H.: Automatic detection of irony and humour in Twitter. In: ICCC, pp. 155–162 (2014)
4. Bengio, Y., Simard, P., Frasconi, P.: Learning long-term dependencies with gradient descent is difficult. IEEE Trans. Neural Netw. **5**(2), 157–166 (1994). https://doi.org/10.1109/72.279181
5. Bojanowski, P., Grave, E., Joulin, A., Mikolov, T.: Enriching word vectors with subword information. CoRR abs/1607.04606 (2016)
6. Burfoot, C., Baldwin, T.: Automatic satire detection: Are you having a laugh? In: Proceedings of the ACL-IJCNLP 2009 Conference Short Papers, pp. 161–164 (2009)
7. Campan, A., Cuzzocrea, A., Truta, T.M.: Fighting fake news spread in online social networks: actual trends and future research directions. In: 2017 IEEE International Conference on Big Data, BigData 2017, Boston, MA, USA, 11–14 December 2017, pp. 4453–4457. IEEE Computer Society (2017)
8. Casalino, G., Castellano, G., Mencar, C.: Incremental adaptive semi-supervised fuzzy clustering for data stream classification. In: 2018 IEEE Conference on Evolving and Adaptive Intelligent Systems (EAIS), pp. 1–7 (2018). https://doi.org/10.1109/EAIS.2018.8397172
9. Casalino, G., Castiello, C., Del Buono, N., Mencar, C.: A framework for intelligent twitter data analysis with non-negative matrix factorization. Int. J. Web Inform. Syst. **14**(3), 334–356 (2018)
10. Cuzzocrea, A., Song, I.: Big graph analytics: the state of the art and future research agenda. In: Proceedings of the 17th International Workshop on Data Warehousing and OLAP, DOLAP 2014, Shanghai, China, 3–7 November 2014, pp. 99–101. ACM (2014)
11. Di Gangi, M.A., Lo Bosco, G., Pilato, G.: Effectiveness of data-driven induction of semantic spaces and traditional classifiers for sarcasm detection. Nat. Lang. Eng. **25**(2), 257–285 (2019). https://doi.org/10.1017/S1351324919000019
12. Grave, E., Bojanowski, P., Gupta, P., Joulin, A., Mikolov, T.: Learning word vectors for 157 languages. In: Proceedings of the International Conference on Language Resources and Evaluation (LREC 2018) (2018)
13. Highet, G.: Anatomy of Satire. Princeton University Press, Princeton (2015)
14. Hoang Son, L., Kumar, A., Raj Saurabh, S., Arora, A., Nayyar, A., Abdel-Basset, M.: Sarcasm detection using soft attention-based bidirectional long short-term memory model with convolution network. IEEE Access **7**, 23319–23328 (2019)
15. Hochreiter, S., Schmidhuber, J.: Long short-term memory. Neural Comput. **9**(8), 1735–1780 (1997)

16. Hodgart, M.J.C.: Die Satire, vol. 42. Transaction Publishers (1969)
17. Picard, R.W.: Affective Computing. MIT Press, Cambridge (2000)
18. Pollard, A.: Satire, vol. 6. Taylor & Francis (2017)
19. Rose, S., Engel, D., Cramer, N., Cowley, W.: Automatic keyword extraction from individual documents. Text Min.: Appl. Theory **1**, 1–20 (2010)
20. Schicchi, D., Lo Bosco, G., Pilato, G.: Machine learning models for measuring syntax complexity of English text. In: Samsonovich, A.V. (ed.) BICA 2019. AISC, vol. 948, pp. 449–454. Springer, Cham (2020). https://doi.org/10.1007/978-3-030-25719-4_59
21. Schicchi, D., Pilato, G.: WORDY: a semi-automatic methodology aimed at the creation of neologisms based on a semantic network and blending devices. In: Barolli, L., Terzo, O. (eds.) CISIS 2017. AISC, vol. 611, pp. 236–248. Springer, Cham (2018). https://doi.org/10.1007/978-3-319-61566-0_23

DocTalk: Combining Dependency-Based Text Graphs and Deep Learning into a Practical Dialog Engine

Yifan Guo[✉], Weilun Sun, Ali Khan, Tam Doan, and Paul Tarau

Department of Computer Science and Engineering, University of North Texas, Denton, USA

Abstract. Today's deep learning dominates the field of natural language processing (NLP) with text graph-based approaches being another promising approach. However, both have inherent weaknesses. We present our system called DocTalk that brings together a model that combines the strength of the two approaches. DocTalk's symbiotic model widens its application domain, enhanced with automatic language detection and effective multilingual summarization, keyword extraction, and question answering on several types of documents. Taking advantage of DocTalk's flexibility, we built it into a dialog engine, coupled with an easy-to-use web interface.

Keywords: Symbiotic graph-based and neural NLP · Multilingual web-based dialog engine · Dependency-graph-based summary and keyword extraction · Document-centered query-answering system

1 Introduction

Deep learning systems have been successful at a wide variety of tasks ranging from parsing to factoid question answering on short documents. However, they have limited success on complex and lengthy documents, for which summarization and query answering have more practical uses. On the other hand, text graph-based systems have been used successfully for extractive summarization and query answering on lengthy documents and short documents alike. Their success, however, is limited on high level information extraction and knowledge representation tasks, requiring inference steps. To make NLP more practical and accessible, our system utilizes both approaches and combines their respective strengths, circumventing many limitations intrinsic to each approach and consequently remaining viable for a much wider variety of applications.

Taking advantage of Doctalk's flexibility, we build it into a dialog agent that digests a text document (e.g. a textbook, a scientific paper, a story, a legal document) and enables the user to interact with its most relevant content elements. We will start with an overview of the system, including the main tools and functions of each module.

© Springer Nature Switzerland AG 2021
T. Andreasen et al. (Eds.): FQAS 2021, LNAI 12871, pp. 182–195, 2021.
https://doi.org/10.1007/978-3-030-86967-0_14

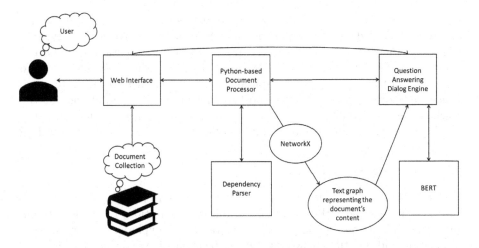

Fig. 1. System architecture

Figure 1 summarizes the architecture of our system. Our system implements a visually-appealing web interface that allows the users to not only easily adjust several parameters of the system, but also input documents of their choice. After a document is uploaded, it is forwarded to the Python-based document processor, which creates a text graph representation of the text that could be used for summarization, keyword extraction, and query answering. Afterwards, the text graph is forwarded to the Dialog Engine, enabling direct interaction via its web interface. To avoid query answering using solely machine learning, which has limited success with long documents, the engine first uses ranking algorithms on text graphs built from dependency trees to retrieve sentences that most likely contain the answer. BERT [4], a deep learning model that works well on small text documents, then determines the answer using the retrieved sentences. Both retrieved sentences and BERT's answer are directed to the web interface and presented to the user as "long answer" and "short answer" respectively.

The rest of the paper is organized as follows: Sect. 2 describes the Python-based document processor. Section 3 describes the question answering dialog engine. Section 4 describes the web interface and includes interaction examples. Section 5 provides empirical evaluation. Section 6 discusses some real-world applications. Section 7 overviews related work and background information. Section 8 concludes the paper.

2   The Python-Based Document Processor

The Python-based document processor relies on Stanford Stanza [9][1] for extracting dependency trees that it aggregates together into a document graph along

---

[1] Working as a client to the CoreNLP server for English documents.

the lines of [13]. Using the lemmatization, part-of-speech tagging, named-entity-recognition, and dependency parsing from Stanza, we derive various types of edges and incorporate the edges into a text graph representation of the text using Python's NetworkX library. Besides dependency links between lemmas of the words in the text, the text graph also connects lemmas to the sentences in which they occur. By selecting the most salient sentences via additional filtering mechanisms and PageRank [8], our document processor provides summarization and keyword extraction. The text graph is also utilized later for query answering.

2.1   Creating TextGraph

Unlike approaches that develop special techniques for each individual task, we present a unified algorithm to obtain graph representations of documents and show that this unified representation is suitable for keyphrase extraction, summarization and question answering. Our implementation is available at https://github.com/Yifan-G/DocTalk. In our implementation, we organize the information gleaned from Stanford Stanza's dependency trees into various types of edges, which would form a unified text graph.

Entity-Oriented Text Graph Representation. In order to represent the main idea or plotline of a document, we focus on the entities present in the document and their influence on each other by extracting *SVO* and *has_instance* edges.

SVO edges, short for subject-verb-object edges, play an important role in the text graph. Each SVO edge connects two nodes representing a subject and an object with a verb, all in a lemmatized form. An example would be 'senate' have 'power' in Fig. 2. We redirect some dependency edges towards nouns because we consider nouns to representative of the content of the text when focusing on summarization and extracted keyphrases and when asking questions about a document.

In order to orient the text graph around key content elements, we try to recognize the nodes that represent real-world entities and identify them with *has_instance* edges that connect a node representing an entity to another node representing the category of the entity. An example is 'organization' *has_instance* 'senate' in Fig. 2. Through the inclusion of *has_instance* edges, we add weight to nodes representing real-world entities, increasing their influence over the keyword extraction and summarization process.

Text Graph Expansion Using Syntactic Relations. To incorporate relational edges that are overlooked by Stanza, we extract WordNet relations between lemmas and include them as edges in the text graph. For every token that is not a noise word, we utilize the *NLTK* toolkit's WordNet package to find its *synonyms*, *hypernyms*, and *meronyms*. If the related word is in the same sentence as the original token, we organize them as follows:

1. synonym relations into the form of (original token, is_like, synonym)
2. hypernym relations into the form of (original token, kind_of, hypernym)
3. meronym relations into the form of (original token, part_of, meronym).

Some of these relations, along with other types of relations, are shown in Fig. 2. As a result of expanding the text graph with edges reflecting accurately syntactic and semantic relations between words, the text graph is completed with both entity-oriented edges and relational edges.

So far, text graph expansion is only utilized for English documents. However, thesaurus in other languages could be implemented to enable multilingual text graph expansion.

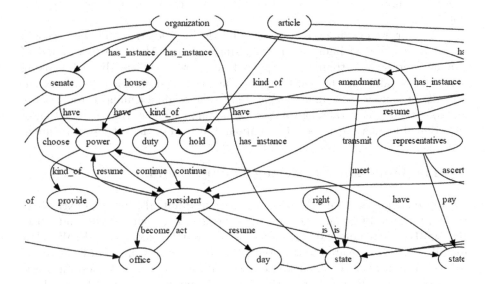

Fig. 2. Part of the dependency graph for the constitution of the United States

2.2   Summarization and Keyword Extraction

Summarization. We rely on *NetworkX's* digraph centrality algorithms (by default, PageRank) to provide an initial ranking value indicating the importance of each sentence in regards to the document. Since the initial ranking value provided by *NetworkX* depends on the number of nodes adjacent to the sentence node, longer sentences are intrinsically prioritized due to containing more nodes. Consequently, short and medium-sized sentences containing important information would be overlooked if only the PageRank ranking value is used.

To prevent that, a post-ranking normalization is applied to the ranking value, deprioritizing both excessively long and excessively short sentences. We compute the new ranking value as:

$$\text{new ranking value} = \frac{\text{ranking value}}{1 + |\text{sentence length} - \text{average sentence length}| + \text{sentence length}}$$

The scaling ensures that sentences that are as close as possible to the average sentence length are prioritized. This also helps with discarding the noisy or fragmented sentences incorrectly extracted by our *pdftotext*[2] converter.

Keyword Extraction. Given their position in the dependency graph, with links pointed to them from their dependents, verbs and nouns are usually the highest ranked. With the intuition that texts more likely center around nouns and keyphrases always contain a nominal component, we only center a keyphrase around a lemma if more than half of its occurrences in the text are tagged as nouns.

Moreover, we prioritize compounds, with the intuition that compounds could reveal more detailed information than single words. After the first round of lemma filtering, we attempt to expand lemmas with sufficiently high ranking values into compounds by collecting their adjacent nodes, which could be compounds containing the lemmas (connected to the original lemmas through *as_in* edges). As long as the ranking value of a compound is higher than 1/16 of that of the original lemma, we collect the compound instead of the single-word lemma.

3   The Question Answering Dialog Engine

After a question is inputted, it is parsed using Stanford Stanza to extract its tokens, lemmas, POS tags and dependency edges. The nouns, verbs, and adjectives in the original question are stored as our original question words. We additionally find words related to the original question words using WordNet. Afterwards, we feed both the expanded question words and original question words into our ranking algorithm (e.g., the NetworkX implementation of Personalized Pagerank) which provides a ranking value for each sentence that indicates the relevance of the sentence to the original question words and expanded question words, discovering sentences that likely contain the answer. Lastly, sentences with the highest ranking values are combined in the order in which they occur in the text and forwarded to BERT, which returns a short answer to the question.

3.1   Question Word Expansion

We find the synonyms, hypernyms, hyponyms, meronyms, and holonyms of each original question word using NLTK's WordNet and save the words that exist in the original text as expanded question words. The intuition behind expanding the original question words is twofold. First, the procedure counters the effect of grammatical mistakes and ambiguity. By retrieving and considering the related words, the model could potentially 'guess' the user's intended meaning

---

[2] https://poppler.freedesktop.org/.

and answer the question even when the question is not grammatically or linguistically accurate. Second, the expansion of original question words possibly recalls more information relevant to the answer. Due to the short length of questions, they often contain little information, which makes it difficult to find the answers. However, by finding words related to the original question words, we gain more information relevant to the question and consequently have more to work with. The approach is especially critical when an entity is referred to using multiple names in a document.

3.2 Ranking Algorithm

In our ranking algorithm, the ranking value of each sentence is dependent on three aspects (*lshared*, *important* and *unusual*) and calculated by the equation:

$$\text{ranking value} = lshared * important * unusual,$$

where *lshared* is the number of original question words and expanded question words in the sentence, which measures the relevance of the sentence to the question and *important* is calculated by the equation:

$$important = e^{\frac{\text{the original ranking value of the sentence}}{1+|\text{sentence length}-\text{average sentence length}|+\text{sentence length}}}$$

The original ranking value of the sentence is calculated in the summarization process and uninfluenced by the question asked. It indicates the general importance of a sentence based on its influence. The denominator below the original ranking value serves to scale the ranking value against the sentence's length, ensuring that the sentence is informative as opposed to just lengthy (with the intuition described in the summarization section).

Lastly, *unusual* is calculated using the following equation:

$$unusual = sigmoid(1 - \frac{\text{the harmonic mean of(the occurrences of question word)}}{\text{number of sentences}})$$

The *unusual* value prioritizes sentences that do not contain a large amount of original question words and expanded question words. It serves to mitigate the dominance of sentences with high values in the previous two aspects and consequently foster the discovery of sentences that do not appear relevant to the question but still contain important information.

Through taking all three aspects into account, Talker fosters both the discovery of sentences closely related to the question and less relevant sentences that could provide interesting information.

3.3 BERT Short Answer

After importing the BERT transformer[3] in our Python code base, we combine a maximum of 4 highest ranked sentences into a document that is short enough for

---

[3] https://huggingface.co/transformers/main_classes/pipelines.html#transformers.QuestionAnsweringPipeline.

effective processing using BERT. We then feed the shortened document and the question to the pretrained BERT model, which then generates a short answer to the question. The short answer is outputted along with a confidence level, which is the estimated probability that the short answer is correct.

If no short answer is outputted or if the confidence level is lower than the threshold value of 0.1, we set the short answer displayed to "No Answer". Otherwise, we display the short answer generated by BERT.

4   The Interactive Web Interface

Our dialog agent is built around both the extractive summarization algorithm as well as the question answering algorithm. The dialog agent is built with *streamlit*[4], a Python package that allows us to turn Python code into a web app without writing additional HTML or Javascript. The main window in the center of the web interface holds the results of the analysis. The sidebar at the left allows users to upload a document to process and select a task (either summarization or question answering).

Users can upload documents up to 200 megabytes. Once a document is uploaded, the interface will automatically detect the language that the document is written in. The interface will then process the document and output the summary and keywords in the main window (Fig. 3).

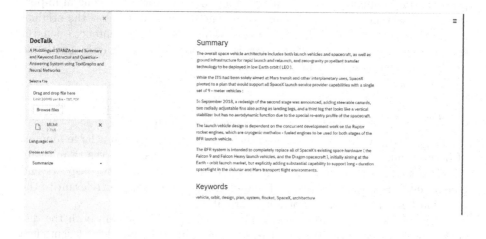

Fig. 3. Summary of an article about SpaceX's "Big Falcon Rocket"

---

[4] https://streamlit.io/.

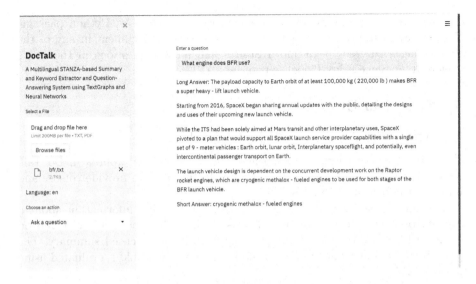

Fig. 4. Question answering based on an article about SpaceX's "Big Falcon Rocket"

When the question-answering task is chosen from the select box at the bottom-left corner, a text box appears prompting the user to enter a question about the content of the uploaded document. The interface then outputs the answer to the question (Fig. 4).

As shown above, the algorithm provides both a short and long answer. Moreover, the system is capable of multilingual summarization and question answering, in languages including English, Chinese (Fig. 5), Russian, and Spanish.

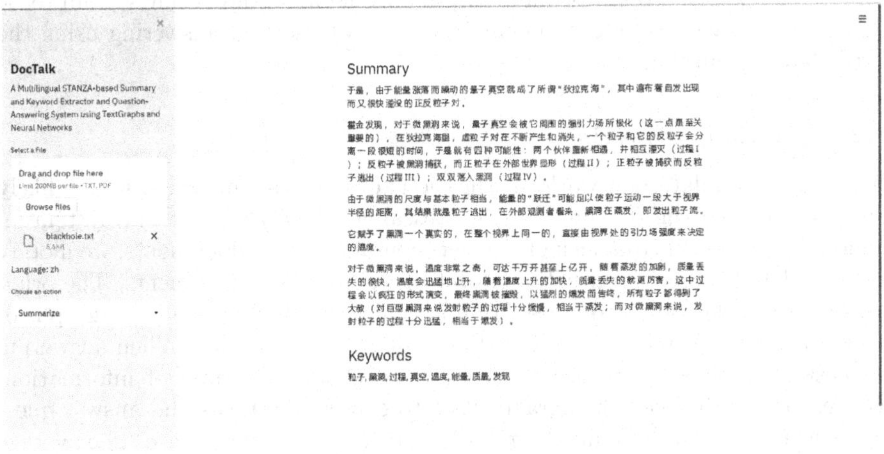

Fig. 5. Summarization of a Chinese article about blackholes

Language is automatically detected using the *langdetect*[5] Python package. We plan as future work to enable a user to upload a document in any of the 68 languages covered by Stanford Stanza and answer questions in the user's preferred language using Google's translate API.

5   Empirical Evaluation

5.1   Query-Specific Information Retrieval

To enable effective question answering using the combined approach, DocTalk retrieves sentences relevant to the query in the first step to provide concise and important information to BERT in the second step.

In order to assess our system's ability for extracting information about a specific topic, we test the first step of our system on the proof-extraction version of Liar-PLUS [6]. We pick the top 4 sentences as our focused summary. The performance of our model and other models is shown in Table 1, evaluated using *py-rouge 1.1*[6].

Table 1. Comparison with other models on Liar-PLUS dataset

Model	Validation			Test		
	ROUGE-1	ROUGE-2	ROUGE-L	ROUGE-1	ROUGE-2	ROUGE-L
Lead-4	30.85	8.08	22.48	31.28	8.17	22.75
Biased TextRank [6]	44.73	26.29	36.58	44.88	26.65	36.69
DocTalk	**44.50**	**26.10**	**38.06**	**44.49**	**26.10**	**38.19**

Our system's performance on extracting information relevant to a specific topic is comparable to recent models, proving the first step of our system to be effective. An effective first step enables successful question answering using the extracted information.

5.2   Question Answering

In order to simulate real-world applications of our system, which would likely be on relatively long documents (e.g., research papers) we test our system on long documents. Due to a lack of datasets containing long documents, we modify SQuAD 1.1 [11] into a synthetic dataset containing long documents. The original SQuAD 1 dataset is composed of question answering pairs on paragraphs of text. Those paragraphs are retrieved by splitting long articles. When answering a question, models only need to process one short paragraph of information. We recombine the pre-split paragraphs into complete articles and answer questions using full articles, simulating our intended real-world use-case. The average length of the paragraphs and articles are shown in Table 2.

---

[5] https://github.com/Mimino666/langdetect.
[6] https://github.com/Diego999/py-rouge.

Table 2. Average sentence count/document, average word count/document, total number of questions, and total number of documents for the two versions of SQuAD 1.1

Dataset	Avg sentence count	Avg word count	Num questions	Num articles
SQuAD-paragraphs	5.03	143.33	10570	2067
SQuAD-articles	217.35	6174.56	10570	48

In order to evaluate the advantage of our combined approach, we test both DocTalk with BERT and BERT by itself on the modified dataset. When testing DocTalk with BERT, we feed the 4 highest ranked sentences to BERT. The F1 and EM score of the tests are shown in Table 3.

Table 3. Performance of different setups on SQuAD-articles

Setup	F1	EM
DocTalk with BERT	68.21	61.46
BERT	57.72	52.12

As shown in Table 3, the performance of our combined approach surpasses that of BERT by itself, proving our symbiotic approach to be effective.

6   Discussion

Due to taking a symbiotic deep learning and graph based approach, DocTalk circumvents the intrinsic limitations in each. It produces a question specific summary of a long document using a graph-based approach from which it generates a salient short answer using deep learning. Consequently, it achieves a synergy that makes it applicable to a much wider variety of documents than the two approaches alone.

Furthermore, DocTalk utilizes three separate answer sentence rankers, each based on different criteria, when selecting the answer sentences. This allows for the discovery of a wide variety of sentences as candidate answer sentences, which subsequently increases the practicality of the question answering dialog engine. As a result of the underlying dependency graph-based processor and WordNet-based query expansion, DocTalk has access to richer semantic information, such as various types of relations, a feature also helping focusing in key content elements of long documents.

One potential application of the DocTalk system is as a teaching aid. In an online learning setting, it can function as a virtual teaching assistant [15] by expediently and accurately answering questions regarding content covered, saving both instructors and students time.

DocTalk is not limited to the classroom setting, since it provides summarization and answers regarding long, technical documents. Ranging from researchers who want to find something specific within a lengthy research paper to car owners who need to identify a specific feature of their vehicle from the user's manual, DocTalk's generated summary and answers provide additional clarification and save time. Specifically, the question-answering feature enables interaction with the content and quick retrieval of information, facilitating in-depth understanding.

7   Related Work

The DocTalk dialog agent is novel as it contains a text graph built from dependency links that integrates words and sentences in the same text graph, resulting in a unified algorithm that enables keyword extraction, summarization, and interactive question answering. A comprehensive overview of graph-based natural language processing can be found in [10].

As the simplest but possibly still the most popular graph-based algorithm, TextRank [7] extracts keyphrases using word co-occurrence relations controlled by distance between words and computes sentence similarity as content overlap giving weights to the links that refine the original PageRank algorithm [8]. Our main innovations with respect to TextRank, besides the use of dependency-tree based graphs, is the addition of SVO relations extracted from the text as well as relations extracted from WordNet.

In extractive text summarization, sentences are ranked based on their relative importance to understanding the overall document before being considered for use in a summary. The various methods to accomplish this task can be separated into two main categories: supervised machine learning and graph-based text processing. An example in the former category is [12], which ranks sentences obtained during extractive summarization through reinforcement learning. Recent advances in natural language processing have also enabled abstractive summarization (e.g., [2]), usually tested on the CNN/DailyMail dataset, which consists of very short news articles.

Question Answering, like summarization, comes in many forms, including multiple choice and short answers. An example of multiple choice answering is [1], which incorporates both shallow lexical methods and logical reasoning into a unified framework, achieving strong results. On the other hand, [14] first obtains the question-aware passage representation and then refines the representation through a self-matching attention mechanism.

Dialog engines have been used extensively in many fields, including e-commerce, customer service, and virtual assistants. For instance, [3] presents a customer service chatbot that leverages large-scale and publicly available e-commerce data, such as data from in-page product descriptions and user-generated content from e-commerce websites. [5] presents a chatbot that aims to foster conversations and emphasizes user-centric and content-driven design. Like most of the dialog engines, their focus is primarily on providing information about relatively short documents (such as product descriptions and online logs based on conversations with real-world users).

While neural networks are prevalent in the field of summarization, question answering, and dialog engines, the DocTalk system presents a symbiotic neural and graph-based approach to the common tasks of summarization and question answering with an emphasis on longer documents (ex. scientific papers, legal documents, textbooks) as opposed to the short datasets used by the models overviewed.

DocTalk's dependency-based text graph is built in a way similar to [13]. However, instead of using a bridge to a logic-programming system for relational reasoning tasks, we rely here on graph algorithms and a deep-learning component to achieve similar outcomes. While the system described in [13] interacts via English text or voice, DocTalk provides a Web-app interface supporting user-uploaded documents in multiple languages.

8 Conclusion

The key idea of the paper evolved from the pursuit of a synergy between graph-based approaches and deep learning-based approaches in NLP. By using a combination of the two approaches, we effectively avoid many of their intrinsic limitations and take advantage of their respective strengths. Consequently, our model is capable of effective question answering on a wider variety of texts compared to solely deep-learning based approaches, and it is also capable of more intelligent question answering than solely graph-based approaches.

Moreover, we create a unified graph representation of the text that contains both words and sentences from dependency links. Due to the various types of edges present and the sentences contained, the unified text graph is simultaneously applicable to summarization, keyword extraction, and question answering. For question answering, we utilize three algorithmic approaches (text graph weight analysis, subgraph centrality, and closeness weight analysis) to extract a comprehensive collection of answer sentences.

We couple our model with a visually appealing web interface and automatic language detection. It supports summarization, keyword extraction, and question answering in languages including English, Spanish, Chinese, and Russian. Its applications range from assistive technologies to social media monitoring, education, and interactive knowledge extraction from complex legal and technical documents.

References

1. Angeli, G., Nayak, N., Manning, C.D.: Combining natural logic and shallow reasoning for question answering. In: Proceedings of the 54th Annual Meeting of the Association for Computational Linguistics (Volume 1: Long Papers), pp. 442–452. Association for Computational Linguistics, Berlin, August 2016. https://doi.org/10.18653/v1/P16-1042. https://www.aclweb.org/anthology/P16-1042

2. Choi, H., et al.: VAE-PGN based abstractive model in multi-stage architecture for text summarization. In: Proceedings of the 12th International Conference on Natural Language Generation, pp. 510–515. Association for Computational Linguistics, Tokyo, October-November 2019. https://doi.org/10.18653/v1/W19-8664. https://www.aclweb.org/anthology/W19-8664

3. Cui, L., Huang, S., Wei, F., Tan, C., Duan, C., Zhou, M.: SuperAgent: a customer service chatbot for E-commerce websites. In: Proceedings of ACL 2017, System Demonstrations, pp. 97–102. Association for Computational Linguistics, Vancouver, Canada, July 2017. https://www.aclweb.org/anthology/P17-4017

4. Devlin, J., Chang, M.W., Lee, K., Toutanova, K.: BERT: pre-training of deep bidirectional transformers for language understanding. In: Proceedings of the 2019 Conference of the North American Chapter of the Association for Computational Linguistics: Human Language Technologies, Volume 1 (Long and Short Papers), pp. 4171–4186. Association for Computational Linguistics, Minneapolis, June 2019. https://doi.org/10.18653/v1/N19-1423. https://www.aclweb.org/anthology/N19-1423

5. Fang, H., et al.: Sounding board: a user-centric and content-driven social chatbot. In: Proceedings of the 2018 Conference of the North American Chapter of the Association for Computational Linguistics: Demonstrations, pp. 96–100. Association for Computational Linguistics, New Orleans, June 2018. https://doi.org/10.18653/v1/N18-5020. https://www.aclweb.org/anthology/N18-5020

6. Kazemi, A., Pérez-Rosas, V., Mihalcea, R.: Biased TextRank: unsupervised graph-based content extraction. In: Proceedings of the 28th International Conference on Computational Linguistics, pp. 1642–1652. International Committee on Computational Linguistics, Barcelona, December 2020. https://doi.org/10.18653/v1/2020.coling-main.144. https://www.aclweb.org/anthology/2020.coling-main.144

7. Mihalcea, R., Tarau, P.: TextRank: bringing order into text. In: Proceedings of the 2004 Conference on Empirical Methods in Natural Language Processing, pp. 404–411. Association for Computational Linguistics, Barcelona, July 2004. https://www.aclweb.org/anthology/W04-3252

8. Page, L., Brin, S.: The anatomy of a large-scale hypertextual web search engine. Comput. Netw. ISDN Syst. **30**, 107–117 (1998). http://citeseer.nj.nec.com/brin98anatomy.html

9. Qi, P., Zhang, Y., Zhang, Y., Bolton, J., Manning, C.D.: Stanza: a Python natural language processing toolkit for many human languages. In: Proceedings of the 58th Annual Meeting of the Association for Computational Linguistics: System Demonstrations (2020). https://nlp.stanford.edu/pubs/qi2020stanza.pdf

10. Rada, M., Dragomir, R.: Graph-Based Natural Language Processing and Information Retrieval. Cambridge University Press (2011). https://www.academia.edu/2958437/Graph_based_natural_language_processing_and_information_retrieval

11. Rajpurkar, P., Zhang, J., Lopyrev, K., Liang, P.: SQuAD: 100,000+ questions for machine comprehension of text. In: Proceedings of the 2016 Conference on Empirical Methods in Natural Language Processing, pp. 2383–2392. Association for Computational Linguistics, Austin, November 2016. https://doi.org/10.18653/v1/D16-1264. https://www.aclweb.org/anthology/D16-1264

12. Shashi, N., Shay, B.C., Mirella, L.: Ranking sentences for extractive summarization with reinforcement learning. In: North American Chapter of the Association for Computational Linguistics 2018 (2018). https://arxiv.org/abs/1802.08636

13. Tarau, P., Blanco, E.: Interactive text graph mining with a prolog-based dialog engine. Theory Pract. Log. Program. 1–20 (2020). https://doi.org/10.1017/S1471068420000137

14. Wang, W., Yang, N., Wei, F., Chang, B., Zhou, M.: Gated self-matching networks for reading comprehension and question answering. In: Proceedings of the 55th Annual Meeting of the Association for Computational Linguistics (Volume 1: Long Papers), pp. 189–198. Association for Computational Linguistics, Vancouver, July 2017. https://doi.org/10.18653/v1/P17-1018. https://www.aclweb.org/anthology/P17-1018

15. Zylich, B., Viola, A., Toggerson, B., Al-Hariri, L., Lan, A.: Exploring automated question answering methods for teaching assistance. In: Bittencourt, I.I., Cukurova, M., Muldner, K., Luckin, R., Millán, E. (eds.) AIED 2020. LNCS (LNAI), vol. 12163, pp. 610–622. Springer, Cham (2020). https://doi.org/10.1007/978-3-030-52237-7_49

A Comparative Study of Word Embeddings for the Construction of a Social Media Expert Filter

Jose A. Diaz-Garcia$^{(\boxtimes)}$ ⓘ, M. Dolores Ruiz ⓘ, and Maria J. Martin-Bautista ⓘ

Department of Computer Science and A.I., University of Granada, Granada, Spain
joseangeldiazg@ugr.es, {mdruiz,mbautis}@decsai.ugr.es

Abstract. With the proliferation of fake news and misinformation on social media, being able to differentiate a reliable source of information has become increasingly important. In this paper we present a new algorithm for filtering expert users in social networks according to a certain topic under study. For the algorithm fine-tuning, a comparative study of results according to different word embeddings as well as different representation models, such as Skip-Gram and CBOW, is provided alongside the paper.

Keywords: Word embeddings · Pre-processing · Expertise · Social media mining

1 Introduction

Nowadays, the world could not be understood without social networks. They have become an irreplaceable source of information, and are used daily by millions of people to obtain information on a wide range of topics such as investments, what their friends have done, travelling, etc. This great success has led to social networks also being used for dubious moral purposes, such as the spread of misinformation to influence various factors, such as the opinions of other users. Identifying this fake information, or information of poor value, is therefore a very important task. In [7] we explored the possibility of detecting patterns of real and fake news on twitter using association rules. The paper opened a new direction in our research, because in order to narrow down the dissemination of misinformation, the main goal will be to detect the origin of the fake information.

In this paper, we present a new algorithm for pre-processing a Twitter dataset according to the user expertise on a given topic under study. The algorithm is tested with a dataset [13] of Tweets related to COVID-19 [11,22], composed of millions of Tweets and with a large amount of noise, low-value or fake information. Our topic of study, therefore, will be medicine, and on this experimental dataset the main objectives of our algorithm will be:

- Discover which users are relevant on the social network according to their Tweets about a topic.

© Springer Nature Switzerland AG 2021
T. Andreasen et al. (Eds.): FQAS 2021, LNAI 12871, pp. 196–208, 2021.
https://doi.org/10.1007/978-3-030-86967-0_15

- Reduce fake information by keeping only those accounts that are trustworthy.
- Dimensionality reduction of a large dataset by keeping only the information relevant to a given topic.

To achieve these objectives, the system will be based on the assumption that if a user has expertise in an area, his or her content will be useful and will contain relevant information on the topics related to that area. This assumption can be verified that have analysed the potential of Twitter in the professional environment [5,8,9]. Besides, the social network has increased its usage by professionals in diverse areas that makes it the ideal place to disseminate research or obtain relevant information. It is also a widely used place for networking between different people, connecting users with the same interests. Therefore, a person who is an expert in a certain field, or who practices a certain profession, and has a good ratio of followers and content, will be a person who generates useful content for the community. Obviously, this assumption can include fake accounts, whose biographies are false or copies of real ones. Detecting these accounts is an investigation that currently lies outside the scope of our study.

To obtain which users are relevant, we will focus on Twitter biographies, on which we will train word embedding. The word embedding corresponds to the current state-of-the-art in Natural Language Processing [14,15]. The underlying technique is to represent all the words within a given vocabulary in a vector space as vectors. With these vectors, operators such as addition or subtraction can be applied, so that for example the words *king − man + woman* would result in the word *queen*. In brief, if *king* and *queen* are the words and **king** and **queen** their embeddings, the distance in vector space between **king** and **queen** is a quantitative indicator of the semantic relation between *king* and *queen*. In this particular case the difference in distances would be very small because only the gender changes.

There are a multitude of models and representations for word embedding, so for fine-tuning our algorithm we have compared Word2Vec [16,17] and Fast-Text [4], since they are the most widespread and relevant in terms of versatility and performance at present. The main difference between Word2Vec and Fast-Text is that the latter decomposes each of the input words in the neural network into n-grams, for example for the word *matter*, and $n = 3$ we would have *<ma, mat, att, tte, ter, er>* and the final representation would be the sum of the vectors associated with each n-gram. This representation is very interesting to discern out-of-vocabulary words or words with low presence in the dataset. Word2Vec takes each word as a vector, its objective involves locating similar words together in a vector representation space. To do this, words are represented by vectors according to their features, context or nearby words within a given text. The distance of vectors is computed by means of a similarity measure, such as cosine similarity. This measure is the most widespread, and will place totally different words, separated by an angle of 90°. A word that is separated from another word by an angle close to zero will imply that they are very similar words. Word2Vec does not consume as much memory and resources as FastText (which for each word stores a vector per n-gram), although it is more sensitive to out-of-vocabulary words. For each of these embedding models, we have two representations, Skip-Gram and Continuous Bag of Words (CBOW) [16,18]. Skip-Gram tries to predict the context words surrounding the word in question, i.e. it predicts context based on a word. On the other hand, CBOW predicts a word based on the surrounding context words, i.e. it predicts a word based on the context.

The main contribution of the paper to the state-of-the-art is: the comparison and detailed study of the performance of different word embedding algorithms and their internal representations for the task of retrieving similar search terms in social networks. We also consider the best of the options found in the experimentation for the definition of an algorithm to exploit the potential of word embedding for the retrieval of experts on Twitter.

The paper is organized as follows: Next section is devoted to related work. In Sect. 3 we go into detail in the algorithm. In Sect. 4, we provide a discussion and comparison of the performance of different word embeddings in our algorithm. Finally, in Sect. 5 we examine the conclusions and the future work.

2   Related Work

Our algorithm uses the power of semantic relations between words to increase the search space in Twitter biographies by employing word embedding techniques. Many works have demonstrated the power of word embeddings to expand search queries. In [20] Roy et al. uses the KNN algorithm on vector space generated by embeddings to obtain which terms are most similar to others and expand the search query. With a similar point of view we find the works [6] and [12]. In [6] Diaz et al. train locally embedding, namely GloVe [19] and Word2Vec, to improve search processes in information retrieval. In a very similar way but with Word2Vec+CBOW Kuzi et al. demonstrate in [12] how document retrieval actually improves with this technique. In our algorithm, we will use this potential of word embeddings, not for retrieving documents, but for locating users that are experts on a topic. As far as we know, this is the first work that addresses and uses this option in addition to word embeddings.

With regard to the expert users retrieval, we find approaches such as those of Cognos or CredSaT. Cognos [10] offers a web solution for searching experts in a certain topic, for this, it uses Twitter lists. The lists on Twitter are user-managed lists, in which users add other users related to topics. Cognos exploits this potential, even improving the search for accounts in the native recommendation system of Twitter. The CredSat [1] approach, is a Big Data solution that takes into consideration the content and the time stamp to create a ranking of expert and influential users in the social network. It also adds a semantic analysis layer with sentiment analysis on Tweets and responses used to enrich the final corpus of experts.

Finally, it is necessary to mention the works proposed by Alrubaian et al. [2,3]. These papers also deal with the analysis of expertise on Twitter, although they also model other concepts such as credibility or engagement. In terms of experience, the papers [2,3] approach the problem from the point of view of user-generated content, unlike our proposal, which addresses it from the point of view of biographies, which are widely used to add information related to the work experience of the user.

3 Expertise Filter Algorithm

In this section we go into detail in the expertise filter algorithm (Algorithm 1). The algorithm takes as input, the directory where we find the csv files with the Tweets, a list of searching related to the topic under studying and the language we are interested in.

The first step of the algorithm is a pre-processing module, in this stage the cleaning of every Tweet is carried out. For this, the algorithm eliminates URLs, hashtags, mentions, reserved words from Twitter (RT, FAV...), emojis, smileys, numbers, additional spaces and punctuation marks. Following this, all the textual terms are turned into lowercase letters. After this, the database language has been detected. During the process the system also eliminates stop-words and all those Tweets using a non-recognised language or from a language other than the one desired by the user. Finally, any empty Tweets (composed of eliminated items in previous stages of pre-processing) are removed the biography and Tweet text are tokenized.

Then, the core of the algorithm starts to operate. Let's imagine the case that concerns us related to COVID-19, where we want to obtain experts or people related to science and medicine. We introduce a list of words related to medicine, for example we can introduce: *medical, doctor*. The algorithm will start to train a word embedding model on the biographies of a part of a data partition (one of the input csv file), and in the first iteration it will obtain the 5 most similar words to medical and doctor among the corpus itself. Namely, in this case, the most similar words to *doctor* and *medical* are *itresearcher, medicine, researcher, physician, epidemic, pediatrician, epidemiologist, pediatrics, postdoctoral* and *toxicologist*. The algorithm will use these 12 words, (5 similar to medical, 5 similar to doctor, besides doctor and medical), to find users whose biographies contain any of these terms and start creating the list of experts and topic-related users. In the next iteration, the set of 12 words will be used to search for their 5 similar ones, and so we will have an exponential growth of words linked by the word embedding to the domain of the problem, which will make us have a space of words very linked to the topic and which will grow intelligently to guide our algorithm.

In each iteration, the algorithm checks if any user id is already present in the expert list to avoid processing it again, since its words and content are already in the search corpus, avoiding thus additional processing. The output of the algorithm is a clean set of data in the form of a data frame ready to be processed in the following filters.

Algorithm 1: Expertise filter algorithm

Result: Dataframe with experts in the topic
 # preprocessing, initializing the variables and data structures
cleaned-dataset=preprocess(dataset)
expert_set=[]
finaldataframe=pd.dataframe()
split cleaned-dataset into batches
for *batch in batches* **do**
    #we check if any user of the batch is already located as an expert
    if *user_id in expert_set* **then**
       | *Add all their Tweets to the final data frame and do not process them*
    else
       Process the rest of the content to locate new experts
       Get the description tokens for each Tweet
       Train the word embedding model over the description tokens
       Create a data frame with the input words and 5 most similar words to each input word
       Extend the input word list with the most similar words in the embedding
       Locate all users who have in their description any of the words
       Extend the final data frame with the Tweets of the located experts
       Extend the expert set with the new experts
    end
end

---

4 Word Embedding Comparison

For the experimentation and choice of the best word embedding and representation for our algorithm we have selected a part of the Tweets dataset related to COVID-19 composed by 3 batches of 936.427, 1.062.900 and 1.319.912 Tweets respectively (total 3.319.239 Tweets). The Tweets correspond to the first days of the pandemic, specifically from March 23, 2020 09:11 AM to March 26, 2020 12:46 PM. The code has been developed in Python 3, with the Gensim [21] word embeddings library. Both development and experimentation have been carried out on the machine whose specifications can be found in Table 1.

Table 1. Machine specifications.

Component	Features
CPU	2 GHz Intel Core i5 with 4 cores
RAM	16 GB 3733 MHz LPDDR4X
VRAM	Intel Iris Plus Graphics 1536 MB
Hard Disk	SATA SSD de 512 GB

Regarding the embeddings parameters, it has been run with a window of 5 words, words with frequencies lower than 2 have been ignored and negative sampling of 10 has been done in the case of CBOW and a hierarchical softmax in the case of Skip Gram.

Below we can see the average results of the experiments for the different factors of interest in our algorithm. Figure 1 shows the average time consumed for each of the algorithms. Figure 2 shows the average number of words found to be similar to those introduced in the execution of the algorithm. In Fig. 3, it can be seen the average number of users that the algorithm found to be relevant. Finally, Fig. 4, contains the average dataset's final size. All figures are in lineal scale. Additionally Table 2 and Table 3, contain the intervals of results in the range of minimum and maximum values obtained during the experimentation.

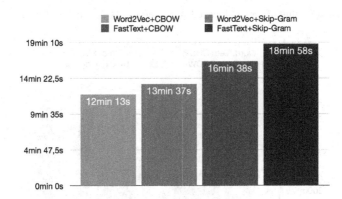

Fig. 1. Mean value of elapsed time in experiments for each of the algorithms.

Table 2. Minimum and maximum value for each variable in the Word2Vec experiments.

	W2V+CBOW	W2V+Skip-Gram
Elapsed time	Min: 11 min 7 s	Min: 13 min 1 s
	Max: 13 min 36 s	Max: 14 min 22 s
Words	Min: 209	Min: 45
	Max: 228	Max: 64
Users located	Min: 21390	Min: 7937
	Max: 23377	Max: 10044
Final dataset size	Min: 31347	Min: 12281
	Max: 34107	Max: 15239

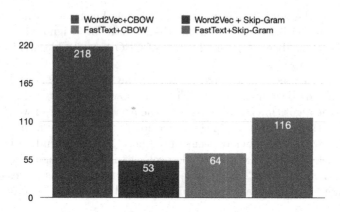

Fig. 2. Mean value of words located in experiments for each of the algorithms.

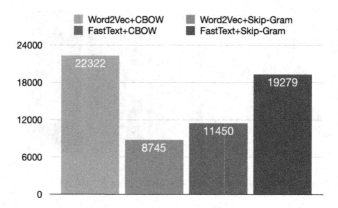

Fig. 3. Mean value of users taken as relevant in experiments for each of the algorithms.

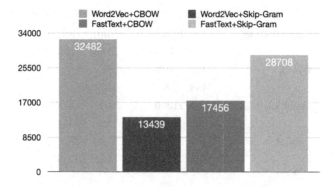

Fig. 4. Mean value of the final dataset size for each of the experiments and algorithms.

Table 3. Minimum and maximum value for each variable in the FastText experiments.

	FastText+CBOW	FastText+Skip-Gram
Elapsed time	Min: 16 min	Min: 18 min 20 s
	Max: 17 min 15 s	Max:20 min 10 s
Words	Min: 50	Min: 111
	Max: 79	Max: 125
Users located	Min: 10975	Min: 18128
	Max: 12312	Max: 20306
Final dataset size	Min: 16748	Min: 26547
	Max: 18773	Max: 31611

If we analyse the results, we can easily see how FastText is more time-consuming than Word2Vec, due to the n-gram decomposition that the algorithm performs. In terms of manageable datasets, such as the ones we are dealing with, this value is neither worrying nor prohibitive, but the execution time would undoubtedly increase a significant amount for larger datasets.

Considering the results of users and words found, we can see a divergence between the models. There are two that we can immediately discard, because they offer a very restrictive behaviour, and find fewer words related to the domain and therefore fewer results, these would be Word2Vec+Skip-Gram and Fast-Text+CBOW.

In terms of the majority of users and words found, Word2Vec+CBOW and FastText+SkipGram, are the best options. This leads us to conclude that each of the algorithms performs better with a different inference model for their words. In our problem FastText performs better at predicting context words on a one-word basis, while Word2Vec is better at predicting one word based on several context words. In our problem, where we have few context words due to the fact that Twitter texts are not very large, this makes an important difference. It is easier for the algorithm to predict context words based on a single word (Skip-Gram), than to predict a single word based on several words (CBOW), since the search space and the window within each document (Tweet) is very small. A priori it may seem that this does not influence, since Word2Vec+CBOW obtains great results, but if we obtain the ratio of users found for each word obtained, we can see how this value is 102 users per word on average in Word2Vec+CBOW, while this rises to 167 users per word in the case of FastText+SkipGram. This leads us to conclude that the words located by FastText have a higher representation in the dataset, as well as a higher relationship with the topic under study. This ratio is also improved in the case of FastText+CBOW, but after a manual check we have been able to verify that there are words that are very representative of medicine, such as *surgeon, pharmacology* or *toxicologist* among many others that are not localised by the latter option.

Therefore, the best option for our algorithm will be to use Fast-Text+SkipGram, although more time-consuming, this increase is also linked to a higher match value for the selected words and their relation to medicine, as well as a better user selection ratio. A complete result of words found by the final algorithm is: *research, doctor, surgeon, researcher, medicine, medical, lecturer, clinical, physician, epidemic, pediatrics, epidemiologist, exclinical, postdoctoral, toxicologist, epidemiolog, nonmedical, medicinal, radiotherapy, exmedical, cally, surgery, psychologist, institute, professor, ecologist, searched, paediatric, regarding, postdoc, pediatric, musicologist, chronically, oncosurgeon, clinician, paramedicine, biomedicine, postdocs, medicina, lyricologist, smedical, telemedicine, lagosmedical, cancer, marched, baemedical, medicity, laparoscopy, toxicology, labmedicine, endoscopic, issue, depressed, health, phd, fellowship, institut, chronic, ecology, organically, faculty, electoral, tanto, biomedical, infectious, biome, graphologist, clinic, surge, medica, bariatric, physically, lapar, mdspediatric, orthopaedic, treatment, technically, topical, ecological, cliched, lucina, telemark, unironically, guarding, biomed, profficinal, musicology, untouched, laparoscopic, psychologer, endemic, harding, opioid, geriatrician, dermatology, biomedic, neurobiology, logically, exdoctor, mycology, ethically, endoscopy, bandemic, mycologist, ironically, paediatrics, trichologist, psicologia, scorched* and *dicovered*; where we can see that the vast majority are words closely related to the domain of medicine and science. These terms are then used by the system to filter our dataset and keep only high value users as we can see in Fig. 5. We can measure the retrieved users by the system in an objective way. To do this, we analyse the accounts and check if their profile includes a description related to a medical professional, who also have a good ratio of followers and, in addition, are active accounts that produce content about the topic. We can observe that these users are very relevant to the topic of medicine. The algorithm even selects users verified by Twitter as in the case of the second account in Fig. 5. The vast majority of the accounts located by the algorithm are similar to those seen in Fig. 5 where the user's experience in the topic is more than evident. The power of the algorithm to automatically extend the search words is also evident, as we can see, none of the accounts shown above have the words we entered as input to the algorithm.

In contrast, a not so good result was obtained for the case of Word2Vec+Skip-Gram where the words found are very poorly relative to medicine and have hardly any meaning in many cases. The words for one of the experiments are: *doctor, researcher, medicine, medical, clinical, obstetrics, hayatabad, epidemiologist, bionerd, jeenal, traumatology, maternal, anaesthetic, traumacare, survivorship, anovus, mielipiteet, trainee, multifand, veeda, philologist, activistig, amira, ksomlive, khoutv, gmcian, teamfcb, disparity, nan, veterinary, nephrology, neurologist, learing, gastro, infant, antiaging, cruff, trialist, lowes, mdspediatric, lovehate, adequacy, kashmirim, finewine, tonga, underpinning, gmers, kaggle, psychiatric, kinnaird, sefako, maxilofacial, rheumatology, poindi, hematology, rosier, paediatrics, compounder, fetal, neetfailure, utilization, inpatient, lordgod, gynecologic,* and *muadhin*. These words lead the algorithm to get users like the ones we can see in Fig. 6.

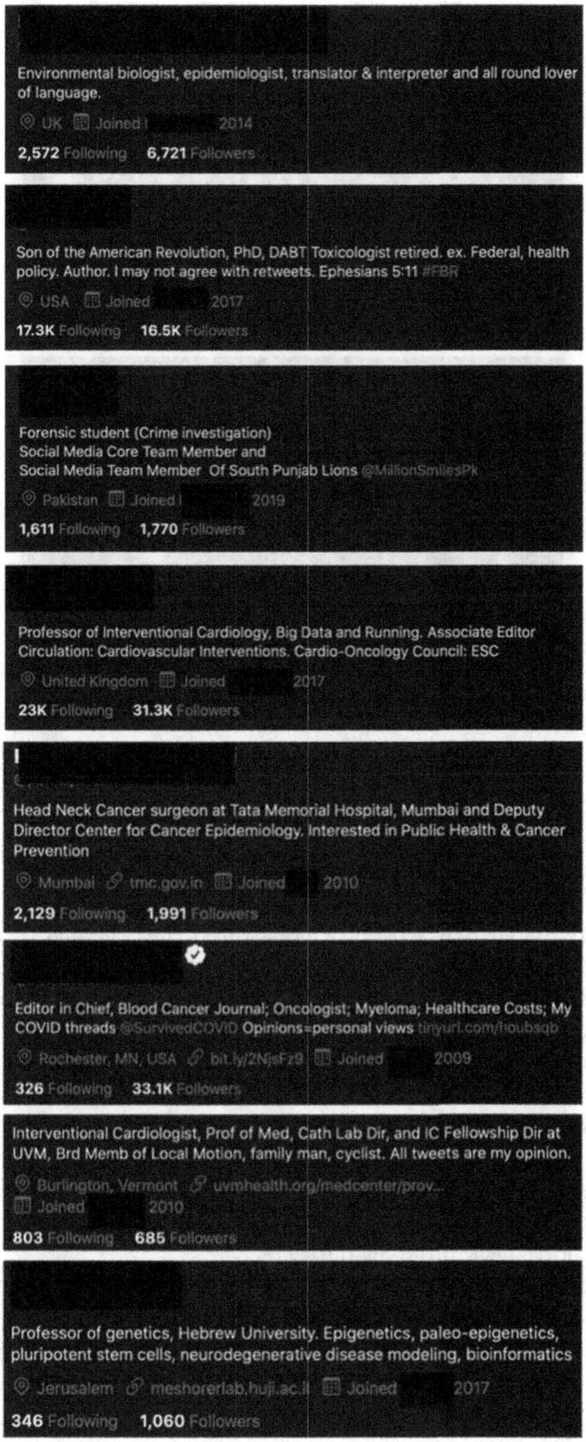

Fig. 5. Some anonymised profiles selected by the best configuration of the algorithm.

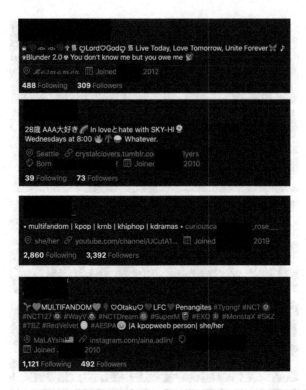

Fig. 6. Some anonymised profiles selected by the worst configuration of the algorithm.

5   Conclusion and Future Work

Throughout the paper it has been demonstrated that the algorithm works adequately, and that it meets the objectives set out in Sect. 1. Relevant users have been obtained, and the dimensionality reduction has been of great importance. This shows that the algorithm can be very useful in Big Data problems related to Twitter, as it can select the content and users relevant to a given topic under study.

As for word embedding, it has been proven to be very useful for expanding search terms, which in conjunction with Twitter biographies is very useful for locating relevant accounts. It has been shown that in terms of efficiency-accuracy ratio, FastText+SkipGram offers the best solution although n-gram decomposition can be a bottleneck in larger datasets.

In terms of future possibilities and challenges, it is worth mentioning that the algorithm is very sensitive to lies, because if someone lies in their biography it is very difficult to dismiss them as not relevant. Being able to more accurately discern lies on social networks would improve the algorithm considerably and is certainly a very promising direction of research.

Acknowledgments. The research reported in this paper was partially supported by the COPKIT project under the European Union's Horizon 2020 research and innovation program (grant agreement No. 786687), the Andalusian government and the FEDER operative program under the project BigDataMed (P18-RT-2947 and B-TIC-145-UGR18). Finally the project is also partially supported by the Spanish Ministry of Education, Culture and Sport (FPU18/00150).

References

1. Abu-Salih, B., Wongthongtham, P., Chan, K.Y., Zhu, D.: CredSaT: credibility ranking of users in big social data incorporating semantic analysis and temporal factor. J. Inf. Sci. **45**(2), 259–280 (2019)

2. Alrubaian, M., Al-Qurishi, M., Hassan, M.M., Alamri, A.: A credibility analysis system for assessing information on twitter. IEEE Trans. Dependable Secure Comput. **15**(4), 661–674 (2018). https://doi.org/10.1109/TDSC.2016.2602338

3. Alrubaian, M., AL-Qurishi, M., Alrakhami, M., Hassan, M., Alamri, A.: Reputation-based credibility analysis of twitter social network users: reputation-based credibility analysis of twitter social network users. Concurr. Comput. Pract. Exp. **29**, e3873 (2016). https://doi.org/10.1002/cpe.3873

4. Bojanowski, P., Grave, E., Joulin, A., Mikolov, T.: Enriching word vectors with subword information. arXiv preprint arXiv:1607.04606 (2016)

5. Chretien, K.C., Tuck, M.G., Simon, M., Singh, L.O., Kind, T.: A digital ethnography of medical students who use twitter for professional development. J. Gen. Intern. Med. **30**(11), 1673–1680 (2015)

6. Diaz, F., Mitra, B., Craswell, N.: Query expansion with locally-trained word embeddings. arXiv preprint arXiv:1605.07891 (2016)

7. Diaz-Garcia, J.A., Fernandez-Basso, C., Ruiz, M.D., Martin-Bautista, M.J.: Mining text patterns over fake and real tweets. In: Lesot, M.-J., et al. (eds.) IPMU 2020. CCIS, vol. 1238, pp. 648–660. Springer, Cham (2020). https://doi.org/10.1007/978-3-030-50143-3_51

8. Forte, A., Humphreys, M., Park, T.: Grassroots professional development: how teachers use twitter. In: Proceedings of the International AAAI Conference on Web and Social Media, vol. 6 (2012)

9. Gerstein, J.: The use of twitter for professional growth and development. Int. J. E-Learn. **10**(3), 273–276 (2011)

10. Ghosh, S., Sharma, N., Benevenuto, F., Ganguly, N., Gummadi, K.: Cognos: crowdsourcing search for topic experts in microblogs. In: Proceedings of the 35th International ACM SIGIR Conference on Research and Development in Information Retrieval, pp. 575–590 (2012)

11. Huang, C., et al.: Clinical features of patients infected with 2019 novel coronavirus in Wuhan, China. Lancet **395**(10223), 497–506 (2020)

12. Kuzi, S., Shtok, A., Kurland, O.: Query expansion using word embeddings. In: Proceedings of the 25th ACM International on Conference on Information and Knowledge Management, pp. 1929–1932 (2016)

13. Lamsal, R.: Coronavirus (COVID-19) tweets dataset (2020). https://doi.org/10.21227/781w-ef42

14. Levy, O., Goldberg, Y.: Dependency-based word embeddings. In: Proceedings of the 52nd Annual Meeting of the Association for Computational Linguistics (Volume 2: Short Papers), pp. 302–308 (2014)

15. Liu, Y., Liu, Z., Chua, T.S., Sun, M.: Topical word embeddings. In: Twenty-Ninth AAAI Conference on Artificial Intelligence. Citeseer (2015)
16. Mikolov, T., Chen, K., Corrado, G., Dean, J.: Efficient estimation of word representations in vector space. arXiv preprint arXiv:1301.3781 (2013)
17. Mikolov, T., Sutskever, I., Chen, K., Corrado, G.S., Dean, J.: Distributed representations of words and phrases and their compositionality. Adv. Neural. Inf. Process. Syst. **26**, 3111–3119 (2013)
18. Mikolov, T., Yih, W.t., Zweig, G.: Linguistic regularities in continuous space word representations. In: Proceedings of the 2013 Conference of the North American Chapter of the Association for Computational Linguistics: Human Language Technologies, pp. 746–751 (2013)
19. Pennington, J., Socher, R., Manning, C.D.: GloVe: global vectors for word representation. In: Empirical Methods in Natural Language Processing (EMNLP), pp. 1532–1543 (2014). http://www.aclweb.org/anthology/D14-1162
20. Roy, D., Paul, D., Mitra, M., Garain, U.: Using word embeddings for automatic query expansion. arXiv preprint arXiv:1606.07608 (2016)
21. Vrehuuvrek, R., Sojka, P., et al.: Gensim-statistical semantics in Python. Retrieved from Genism (2011)
22. Zhou, P., et al.: A pneumonia outbreak associated with a new coronavirus of probable bat origin. Nature **579**(7798), 270–273 (2020)

Aggregation for Flexible Challenge Response

Samuel Brezani[1] and Peter Vojtas[1,2(✉)] (iD)

[1] Globesy Ltd., Framborska 58, Zilina, Slovakia
[2] Department Software Engineering, Charles University, Prague, Czechia

Abstract. A real problem use-case represents a challenge. This is usually transformed (reduced) to a model. We expect the model to give a response/solution which is (at least in a degree) acceptable/meets the challenge. Moreover this challenge-response understanding has two levels – both the real world situation and model situation contains challenge side (input, query, problem…) and the response side (output, answer, solution…). We present a formal model of ChRF-Challenge-Response Framework inspired by our previous work on Galois-Tukey connections. Nevertheless, real world reduction to models needs some adaptation of this formal model. In this paper we introduce several examples extending ChRF. We illustrate this using several practical situations mainly in the area of recommender systems. Data of the model situations are motivated by Fagin-Lotem-Naor's data model with attribute preferences and multicriterial aggregation. In this realm we review our previous work on preferential interpretation of fuzzy sets; implicit behavior in/and online/offline evaluation of recommender systems. We finish with smart extensions of industrial processes. We propose a synthesis of these and formulate some open problems.

Keywords: Galois-Tukey connect · Blass-query-answer · Challenge-response framework · Recommendation · Aggregation

1 Introduction

A real problem use-case represents a challenge. This is usually transformed (reduced) to a model. We expect the model to give a response/solution which is (at least in a degree) acceptable/meets the challenge. Moreover this challenge-response understanding has two levels – both the real world situation and model situation contains challenge side (input, query, problem…) and the response side (output, answer, solution…).

We can see this phenomena in many situations. For instance, when a declarative formulation needs a procedural implementation (SQL, NLP…). Or, a human perception expects a relevant response (well, this can be difficult even between humans). Or,

This publication was realized with the support of the Slovak Operational Programme Integrated Infrastructure in the frame of the project: Intelligent systems for UAV real-time operation and data processing, code ITMS2014+: 313011V422 and co-financed by the European Regional Development Fund.

T. Andreasen et al. (Eds.): FQAS 2021, LNAI 12871, pp. 209–222, 2021.
https://doi.org/10.1007/978-3-030-86967-0_16

when a client requests some computation from a server… We consider this *"Challenge-Response in real-to-model reduction"* principle important and would like to develop it further.

These were already formally modeled by our previous work on the ChRF-Challenge-Response Framework with situations and reductions (see [13, 25]). The requirement was that the acceptable model response of reduced real world challenge will be transformed to an acceptable real world response of the original challenge.

This created a nice theory from several points of view (see Sect. 3). Nevertheless, reality sometimes needs an adaptation of our mathematically nice formal model. We illustrate this using several practical situations mainly in the area of recommender systems.

The data side of model situations is motivated by Fagin-Lotem-Naor's data model with attribute preferences and multicriterial aggregation. Second author thankfully acknowledge influence of late Peter Hajek [9]. Flexibility is obtained by offering top-k responses. We review our previous work on preferential interpretation of fuzzy sets; implicit behavior in/and online/offline evaluation of recommender systems. Second author started to study these real world situations during involvement in the project [15]. We finish the paper with smart extensions of industrial processes. We propose a synthesis of these and formulate some open problems.

Main contributions of this paper are reformulations of previous results to an adapted ChRF setting in

- data mining and identification of user model from a parametric family of models,
- interpreting implicit behavior of user,
- prediction of on-line behavior based on off-line data,
- object detection when there are no human annotated data.
- We formulate several problems both in formal and applied setting.

2 Search Reduced to a Data Model with Preference Aggregation

Our main motivation is content based recommendation (typically in real on an e-shop). Recommendation means to offer a user (customer) an ordered list of objects computed in the model situation. Depending on display, these can be top-10 (or top-k in general) in some preference ordering of objects, for each user separately.

2.1 eFLN – Extended Fagin-Lotem-Naor Approach

User object preference usually depends on preferred values of attributes (properties). In what follows we describe some special cases of preference representation. Some of them will be discussed in further sections in connection with experiments in real world situations. The object model is represented by a relational scheme $R(oid, A_1,..., A_m)$, where A_i's are attributes with domains D_i. Set of objects is a subset of Cartesian product of domains $O \subseteq \Pi D_i$.

In [7] R. Fagin, A. Lotem and M. Naor describe a system FLN where each object has assigned m-many attribute scores $x_i^o \in [0, 1]$. A Pareto order preserving (see [8]) aggregation (combination) function t: $[0, 1]^m \rightarrow [0, 1]$ assigns each object o an overall score $r(o) = t(x_1^o, \ldots, x_i^o, \ldots, x_m^o)$. So the ordering of objects is represented by natural ordering of overall score in unit interval of natural numbers as an aggregation of attribute scores (ordering on attribute values). Main motivation of [7] was to describe a middle ware system, where attribute scores are available from a web service represented by a list of object ordered descending by score either by an ordered approach or (when the ID of an object is known) by a random (direct) access. [7] proposes a top-k algorithm and proves beautiful optimality in price of sequential and random access over any possible algorithm, correctly finding top-k without random guessing.

As our interest is content based recommendation, we extend this approach by describing how these score can be obtained. Assume, for each user $u \in U$ we have an attribute preference function f_i^u: $D_i \rightarrow [0, 1]$ and an aggregation function t^u.

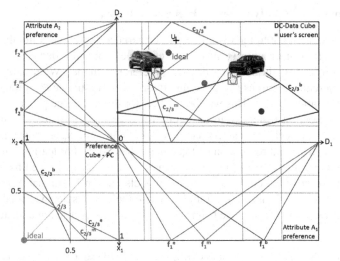

Fig. 1. We display a mockup to illustrate dynamical aspects of 3 consecutive sessions of a user (the beginning, middle and end sessions). We use a simplified linear two dimensional extended Fagin-Lotem-Naor model of preferences, see Sect. 2.1, [7], also [13]. An activity of the user can trigger learning of next preference model. New model represented by contour lines in PC and attribute preferences can be transformed to data cube representing user's screen. (Color figure online)

The overall preference $r^u(o)$ of an object o is given by

$$r^u(o) = t^u(f_1^u(oid.A_1), \ldots, f_i^u(oid.A_i), \ldots, f_m^u(oid.A_m)) \qquad (1)$$

Our system is an extension of the [7] approach as setting $f_i^u(oid.A_i) = x_i^o$ gives the original FLN system.

Illustration in Fig. 1 can serve as a mock-up of an idea where data cube-DC (NE quadrant) is the user's screen (reality), graphically calculated from preference cube-PC (via SW, NW and SE) 2/3 contour lines (motivated also by [21] and [5]).

User's action (orange and blue click) changed the preference model and showed unseen objects in the estimated highly preferred area computed by a recommender. Using a geographic intuition, we depict 2/3 contour lines of t in preference cube-PC (see SW-south-west quadrant of Fig. 1), these can be translated to areas in data cube-DC (see NE-north-east quadrant) corresponding to objects with preference at least $2/3$. For a fixed user, dynamical illustration starts with $t^b(x_1, x_2) = (x_1 + 2x_2)/3$ begin (purple) session, via medium session (t^m is average in orange) to end one (blue) with $t^e(x_1, x_2) = (2x_1 + x_2)/3$. Note that NE quadrant with DC represents a real world situation (on the user's screen) and the remaining quadrants SE with f_1, NW with f_2 and SW with aggregation represent the model situation. In the following section we introduce a general framework for reductions of real world situations to model situations. Further, several inductive aspects of eFLN will be dealt with in future sections on real world data.

2.2 Learning by Identifying user's Preference Model

In the previous paragraph, the overall object preference score was a number obtained as an aggregation of an objects attribute preference score in a deductive model. An interesting problem is the learning of user's preference model. We usually first learn attribute preference functions f_i^u and having these, we can estimate t^u. Another point is, what we know about a user. This will be our task for the rest of the paper.

Here we mention results from an unpublished preprint [16], partly published in [17]. We had real world production data with individual purchases. For learning fiu's we implemented several regression and geometric heuristics. For learning tu's we used identification of parameters of fuzzy t-conorms (S-norms, see [8]). The final model was an aggregation of individual content based models and an additional aggregation of behavioral data over all users. See Table 1. where the best results evaluated by nDCG (normalized Discount Cumulative Gain) and position resp. metric are depicted.

Table 1. Results of best methods of aggregation identification and regression [16]

Content based individual		Behavioral all users		Metrics
Aggregation	Attribute	Aggregation	Attribute	
Frank	Linear	Sugeno-Weber	Linear	nDCG
Schweizer-Sklar	Quadratic	Sugeno-Weber	Linear	Position

That is, when the overall efficiency of the system is evaluated by nDCG metric, the best results were attained by tuning parameters of Sugeno-Weber family of conorms over two inputs (for various conorm families, see [12]):

1. tuned parameters of Frank conorms over partly linear (triangle) estimation of attribute preferences of content based individual preference models optimized according to prediction of purchases;
2. aggregating the former with estimation of attribute preferences of all users.

Similar results were obtained, when the overall quality was measured by position of best object in testing data compared to its position in the prediction. It may be interesting to compare these early results with that of later publications [18, 19].

3   ChRF – Challenge-Response Framework

The origin of the Challenge-Response Framework was an old mathematical idea of Galois-Tukey connection of [24][1] in set and category theory. A. Blass in [1] interpreted this as complexity reductions in theoretical computer science (later he calls it challenge-response reductions, see [2] and Fig. 2(a)). First, we define it and discuss it formally. Later we develop it in different real world situations.

3.1   A Formal Model of Challenge-Response Framework

A Challenge-Response Situation $S = (C, R, A)$ consists of a set of challenge instances C, a set of possible responses R and a (possibly graded) binary acceptability relation $A \subseteq C \times R$. For a challenge instance $c \in C$ and a response instance $r \in R$ we read $A(c, r)$ as "r is an acceptable response to challenge c" (or also another reading "response r meets challenge c"). Please note, that acceptability relation can be a function (algorithm, process…).

Challenge-Response Reduction of a situation $S_1 = (C_1, R_1, A_1)$ to a situation $S_2 = (C_2, R_2, A_2)$ consists of a pair of functions (φ^-, φ^+) such that $\varphi^- : C_1 \to C_2$ is a reduction of S_1 challenges to S_2 challenges and $\varphi^+ : R_2 \to R_1$ is a reduction of S_2 responses to S_1 responses. A quite natural requirement of Eq. (2) says that an S_2 acceptable response r to $\varphi^-(c)$ is reduced to an S_1 acceptable response to the original challenge, in a logical formula

$$(\forall c \in C_1) \, (\forall r \in R_2) \, (A_2(\varphi^-(c), r) \Rightarrow A_1(c, \varphi^+(r))) \tag{2}$$

In case that $A_2 = \alpha$ is an algorithm the Eq. (2) changes to following requirement

$$(\forall c \in C_1) \, (A_1(c, \varphi^+(\alpha(\varphi^-(c))))) \tag{3}$$

Several aspects of this framework will be discussed. First is the logical truth value of the formula in Eq. (2).

For this, 3SAT considers reduction of the combinatorial search problem usually abbreviated as 3SAT to 3COLOR[2]. Challenge set of the 3SAT is 3CNF, i.e. the set of propositional formulas c in conjunctive normal form containing at most 3 literals. The 2^{Var} response set of 3SAT consists of truth valuations $v: Var \to 2$ of propositional variables. Acceptability relation _satisfied_ consists of pair (c, v) such that v makes c true. 3COLOR is the search problem of vertex colorability of graphs.

For correct complexity reduction we need more than sole fulfilment of Eq. (2). In a pure logical understanding it is easy to make it true. Just send all 3CNF instances to a

---

[1] Supported in 1990–91 by Alexander von Humboldt Foundation, Germany.
[2] See e.g. https://cgi.csc.liv.ac.uk/~igor/COMP309/3CP.pdf.

graph which is not 3 vertex colorable, hence $A_2(\varphi^-(c), r)$ will be false and the whole implication will be true (false implies * is always true). A. Blass in [1] assumes that acceptability relations have domains $dom(A) = C$. In this case there are no uncolorable graphs. In [13] and [25]) we discuss the possibility to extend each response set with an extra element "nar = no acceptable response" and extend the acceptability relations by $A(c, nar)$ for each $c \in C \setminus dom(A)$. It is shown that Eq. (2) with this nar-extended situation fulfills complexity reduction requirements.

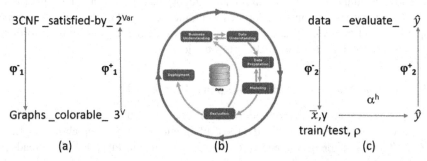

Fig. 2. ChRF illustration. Left: a ChRF reduction of 3SAT to 3COLOR (this fulfils Eq. 2, not complexity reduction, see Sect. 3.1). In the middle (b) shows the process diagram for data mining CRISP-DM[3]. Right (c) shows supervised learning reformulated in the language of ChRF (see Section "Inductive ChRF").

We briefly mention metalevel possible view. Consider S_1 situation as above as a (real world) challenge instance and S_2 as a (model) response instance of a generalized situation S. Response S_2 meets challenge S_1 (is a good model for a real world challenge) when there is a ChRF reduction (φ^-, φ^+) fulfilling Eq. (2). We can say that a generalized situation $S_1 = (S_{11}, S_{12}, (\varphi_1^-, \varphi_1^+))$ is reduced to a generalized situation $S_2 = (S_{21}, S_{22}, (\varphi_2^-, \varphi_2^+))$ (saying that the model S_2 is better than model S_1) when there is a pair of mappings (Ψ^-, Ψ^+) enabling to transform solutions of S_2 to solutions of S_1. In such a way we can build a framework of *generalized Challenge-Response reductions gChRF*. This can be interesting both from formal point of view and in practical applications.

3.2 ChRF as Reduction of Real World Situations to Model Situations

We would like to use ChRF idea in practical situations. The main viewpoint is that in a situation when one needs help, a recommendation, we can reduce this to a model. So rephrasing, a Challenge-Response Reduction of a situation $S_{real} = (C_{real}, R_{real}, A_{real})$ to a model situation $S_{model} = (C_{model}, R_{model}, A_{model})$ consists of a pair of functions (φ^-, φ^+) such that $\varphi^-: C_{real} \to C_{model}$ and $\varphi^+: R_{model} \to R_{real}$ with a requirement that acceptable model responses are acceptable to original challenges (after reductions (φ^-, φ^+)). If A_{model} is an algorithm α^h, the respective code can look like:

---

[3] https://en.wikipedia.org/wiki/Cross-industry_standard_process_for_data_mining.

```
FOR each C^real from challenges
     CALL φ⁻ with C^real RETURNING C^model
     CALL α^h with C^model RETURNING R^model
     CALL φ⁺ with R^model RETURNING R^real
     CALL A_real with C^real and R^real RETURNING accepted
     IF accepted PRINT ''R^real is a response to C^real''
          ELSE PRINT ''there is no response to C^real''
     END IF
END FOR
```

We have already seen that pure mathematical understanding of Eq. (2) has to be adapted.

The second problem is how to understand quantifiers $(\forall c \in C_1)\ (\forall r \in R_2)$. We will see that these can be interpreted as aggregation in the sense of various metric used in experiments.

Inductive ChRF

Looking to Fig. 2 we can see some similarity between CRISP-DM model and ChRF approach to learning. Starting with the real situation first reduction can be to "business understanding". This can contain a challenge requiring reduction to "data understanding" and further to "data preparation". In [13] we introduced *Inductive ChRF* in which we look for a method $\alpha \in \Pi$ and a hyperparameter $h \in H^\alpha$ to evaluate α^h on training data $\overline{x}y$ comparing with $\overline{x}\hat{y}$. Here $\overline{x}y$ is an abbreviation of $c = \overline{x}, E(c) = y$ where E is the example set and $\hat{y} = \varphi^+(\alpha^h(\varphi^-(c)))$. The acceptability relation *evaluate($\overline{x}\hat{y}$)* can be defined by an instance metric e.g. $|y - \hat{y}|$ and the quantifier $(\forall c \in C_1)$ can be understood as an aggregation, e.g. by RMSE. The quality of our estimation is

$$\left\| (\forall c \in C_1)(A_1(c, \varphi^+(\alpha^h(\varphi^-(c))))) \right\| = \sqrt{\sum \frac{\left(E(c) - \varphi^+\left(\alpha^h\left(\varphi^-(c)\right)\right)\right)^2}{|C_1|}} \qquad (4)$$

The most usual case of finding an acceptable solution in a model situation is to find it by induction (data mining, learning…). We are not going into details of ChRF modeling of learning, tuning, cross validation etc.

Real world acceptability depends on user u. In the case of recommender systems, this can be either user's explicit rating or our interpretation of u's behavior (see Sect. 4). User's behavior can be e.g. purchase, click, time reading detail of an item, etc.

Note that this gives a dynamic model of ChR, because user's satisfaction has to be followed (e.g. by scripts), evaluated and taken into account in the next recommendation (more on this in Sect. 5).

4 Implicit Preference Relations in Recommendation

In this section we use results from [19] to make a step in extending ChRF. In previous sections, the overall object preference was a number obtained as an aggregation of the object's attribute preference score. The size of a number itself does not matter.

We use numbers as an ordinal scale and numbers code an ordering. For application in recommender systems, we need sometimes to aggregate several recommenders (algorithms). Sometimes these do not offer a rating (score), they give just a position (rank). Here we describe a real world experiment where a linear ordering form a recommender was enhanced by a partial ordering coming from preference interpretation of the user's implicit behavior.

The approach of [19] is illustrated in Fig. 3 left. Fix a user u. Assume we have an ordered list of objects $\overline{L_u}$, from a recommender. The idea is to use the information on the visibility of objects and the user's action (clicked, scrolled). In time T1 objects O1, O2, O3 and O4 were visible. He/she clicked on object O3 and did not act on remaining objects. This can be interpreted in a way that object O3 is more preferred than the other 3 objects. Nevertheless, after a scrolling (and much shorter visibility) objects O3 to O6 were visible and there was no further action. Now object O4 was visible much longer than e.g. O1. So some preference degree of O3 over O4 should be greater than that over O1. In [19] we designed some measures to express this intensity and output relation IPR[4]. As user behavior data are quite sparse we extended this relation by similarity of object and computed relation $\widehat{R_u}$ (it is a partial order, nevertheless has information on objects the user was searching, clicking, ignoring).

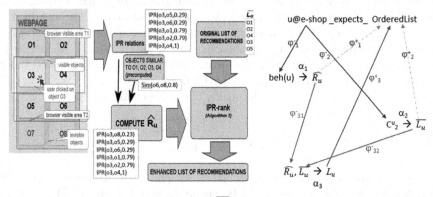

Fig. 3. Left, enhancing a recommender result $\overline{L_u}$ by implicit user's behavior on visible (after scrolling) and clicked objects (see Sect. 4, also [19]). Right, a new ChRF construction describing this sort of aggregation of two models (a merge of a partial order with a linear one by algorithm α_3).

In [19] we have designed several ways how to merge these two ordering, the linear ordering $\overline{L_u}$ and the partial ordering $\widehat{R_u}$ to get final ordering L_u. Then, in experiments we have evaluated how far is L_u better than $\overline{L_u}$, and which method gives the best results. Roughly speaking, when e.g. a contradiction between ordering of O3 and O1 in L_u and $\widehat{R_u}$ is discovered we can put O3 just before O1 in next iteration of L_u (or O1 just behind O3, or swap both...). Please consult the paper for more details.

---

[4] IPR source codes: https://github.com/lpeska/Implicit-Preference-Relations, for more resources see the paper.

Here we are interested in an extension of the ChRF where the model (algorithm α_3) giving L_u is a combination of algorithms α_1 and α_2, originally computing $\widehat{R_u}$ and $\overline{L_u}$.

To our surprise, original meet and join in the algebraic category of [24] and [1] (or corresponding lattice) do not apply. In Fig. 3 right, we propose a construction which takes responses of two models, presents them as a challenge of a model situation which could be considered as an aggregation of previous situations. It is an interesting problem if this construction has a category theoretic interpretation.

5 Predictability of On-line Recommendation

This is the last section devoted to recommender systems. We would like to illustrate here another possibility of interpreting universal quantification. The content is based on the paper [18][5]. The long standing problem is the connection between off-line recommendation (one based on historic production data) and on-line recommendation. Of course, we can be careful and use only A/B testing for changing our recommender. Still, each A/B test takes time, effort and can be discouraging for customers. So the idea is to provide A/B testing only with the promising candidate(s). Before choosing this candidate we have to solve the problem of algorithms and metrics by which we will evaluate which candidate solution is most promising.

We had true production data and also the access to provide online A/B testing. Therefore, off-line data played the role of a model and on-line production was the real world to be modeled. The implication $A_{model}(\ldots) \to A_{real}(\ldots)$ became $A_{off\text{-}line}(\ldots) \to A_{on\text{-}line}(\ldots)$ and this can be interpreted as our main task – how to evaluate online results based on offline achievements.

First problem occurs with users. It is difficult to identify users from off-line data and on-line testing (these can be quite disjoint sets). So, we have to quantify all users. Quantification over all objects is already a part of ChRF reduction formalization. For the beginning we chose several item-to-item recommendation algorithm sufficiently rich to represent content based attribute, textual description of objects and collaborative aspects of our data. So finally we had to quantify over all algorithms.

In Fig. 4, using notation of beginning, middle and end session we can see that the previous session's responses (visualized top-k recommendation) are challenges of the next session. User's acceptability is his/her perception of sessions, φ^- denotes our scripts recording user's behavior. The model computes next recommendation based on previous behavior and outputs top-k, which is visualized by φ^+ to next session.

This is another understanding of ChRF in a real world situation. In [18] we provided A/B testing with 12 most promising algorithms. Motivated by [10] we interpret quantifiers in implication describing ChR reduction from off-line to on-line by aggregation. It makes good sense because we would like to have an overall evaluation of "how good are algorithms (trained off-line with respect to some metric) in predicting user's on-line behavior". Most of aggregations were just averages. It is a challenge for future research and experiments to consider some other aggregations. In [18] we aggregated over all

---

[5] See https://github.com/lpeska/FUZZ-IEEE2020 for source codes, evaluation data and complete results are available from.

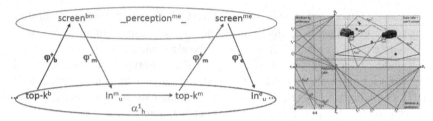

Fig. 4. Left, illustration of ChRF representation of three consecutive sessions as in Fig. 1, beginning can represent off-line data, later can represent on-line prediction. Right there is miniaturized Fig. 1 with 3 sessions and green background represents three sessions of real situations, whereas the red one illustrates the development of corresponding models.

algorithms and results were novelty metrics which are best predictors for on-line recommendation. One can imagine aggregating over metrics to get best algorithms and joining both could be interesting to test.

6   Object Detection from Visual Data

So far we have had more or less reliable data about real world situations either from training and/or behavioral data. Data reliability is obtained by human expert intervention designing data collection. In the final section we consider a situation where we do not have any human annotated training data. We will build on object detection model developed in [4]. Main goal of [4] was to automatically create a system for object detection in industrial premises without any human intervention. This has lead us to a concept of "pseudo ground truth". Pseudo ground truth PGT_3 is created by a heuristic process considering a correct object detection be the one where at least three models agreed (lower index 3 in PGT_3 refers to number of models required to agree on an instance).

From the point of view of ChRF, this situation is interesting. The real ChR situation is on camera screen. For the model situation we do not have any train and test data (correct in the sense, that object detection bounding box and class was annotated by a human). So, we have a pseudo-model situation and the main point is that the modelling algorithm is chosen without any human intervention, just considering a performance on pseudo-ground truth. So it can be deployed in situations where there is no staff for annotation. We discuss quality of our model to give acceptable response. For this purpose we annotated some video frames.

Figure 5 shows an example of a CCTV camera from an office environment. The picture shows the detections of 11 objects belonging to 3 classes - person, bottle and mouse. False positive predictions are marked in red.

Figure 6 shows performance of nine models we used for creation of the pseudo-ground truth.

Models are in columns, predictions are in rows (ids of detected persons correspond to those in Fig. 5). Last three rows are false positives.

First 9 columns (with names of deep neural network model) depict the size of the confidence score of respective predictions in the blue bar. We can see, that some models

Table 2. Full links and references to model abbreviations used in Fig. 6. References are to corresponding Arxiv papers, Model and/or library links to object detection software are listed at the end of References.

Abbrev	Model	Backbone	Model/library link	Model arxiv	Backbone arxiv
YOLO3	YOLO3	Darknet53	[26]	[20]	[20]
YOLO4	YOLO4	CSPDarknet53	[27]	[3]	[3]
RN50	Retinanet	ResNet50	[28]	[14]	[11]
R-RN101	Retinanet	ResNet101	[29]	[14]	[11]
FR-CNN	Faster R-CNN	ResNet152	[29]	[20]	[11]
CN-HG104	CenterNet	HourGlass104	[29]	[6]	[20]
CN-RN50	CenterNet	ResNet50	[29]	[6]	[11]
ED D3	EfficientDet D3	EfficientNet B3	[29]	[23]	[22]
ED D6	EfficientDet D6	EfficientNet B6	[29]	[23]	[22]

Fig. 5. Office scene with true (white bounding box) and false positive (red bounding box) object detection. Ids of persons will be used in text below (video source YouTube). (Color figure online)

did not detect an object at all, some detected with small confidence and some made a wrong prediction. GT column is a yes-no column (depicted in black) that shows objects to be used as pseudo-ground truth on this image. PGT_3 column depicts confidence the pseudo ground truth was obtained. Based on PGT_3, we chose the best model. Best model

(YOLO3) for a specific CCTV camera (this model also shows a false negative error rate). In addition to the best model, the method also determines the order of the models according to the expected performance. Column W * TOP3 shows the confidence we gained by weighing the 3 best models obtained by our method. The weights for these 3 models were determined using linear regression. However, the CenterNet-HG104 model was also included in the TOP3 models, which demonstrates a false positive prediction in the case of object I. This false positive prediction was also transferred to the W * ALL prediction. To complete, we also present the W * ALL column, which shows the confidence gained by weighing all 9 models. Again, these weights are determined by linear regression. The hope was that wrong influence of some models may have been eliminated. This elimination really came about, because it is visible that false positive predictions (J and K) from the Retinanet-RN50 model are not included.

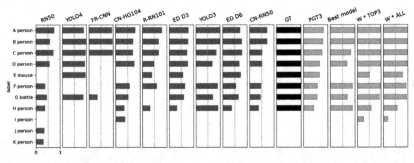

Fig. 6. Different confidence of models on respective (true/false) detections. See Table 2 for explanation of model abbreviations and links to software and papers. Rows denote object IDs recognized in Fig. 5.

This experiment shows a new ChRF reduction from real situation to model one. Various metrics can evaluate the overall quality of responses. Some show that false positives can be eliminated. Still there is a problem with false negatives – we leave it for future work.

7   Conclusions and Future Work

We considered real world recommender systems based on Fagin-Lotem-Naor data model with aggregation. Our main interest was to test Challenge-Response Framework in several real world situations. Results show that proper reduction to a model situation requires using different metrics and different aggregations in place of logical quantifiers and calculation of truth values. Finally, we mention several problems both in the formal model and practical use of ChRF.

Results show that ChRF is quite flexible when measured by appropriate metric. The role of aggregation in quantification goes beyond the classical understanding of aggregation in multicriterial modeling. Some future experiments could shed more light into this phenomenon. Maybe, fuzzy integrals could be a possible choice for these aggregations. Let us base our future experiments on real world production data and business relevant metrics.

References

1. Blass, A.: Questions and answers. A category arising in linear logic, complexity theory, and set theory. In: Girard, J.-Y., et al. (eds.) London Mathematical Society Lecture Note Series 22, pp. 61–81. Cambridge University Press, Cambridge (1995)
2. Blass, A.: Combinatorial cardinal characteristics of the continuum. In: Foreman, M., Kanamori, A. (eds.) Handbook of Set Theory, pp. 395–489. Springer, Heidelberg (2010). https://doi.org/10.1007/978-1-4020-5764-9_7
3. Bochkovskiy, A., et al.: YOLOv4: Optimal Speed and Accuracy of Object Detection. https://arxiv.org/abs/2004.10934. Accessed 15 July 2021
4. Brezani, S., Hrasko, R., Vojtas, P.: Smart extensions to regular cameras in the industrial environment. Preprint, Submitted to ISM 2021 (2021)
5. Brown, T.: Change by design: how design thinking transforms organizations and inspires innovation. HarperBusiness (2009)
6. Duan, K., et al.: CenterNet: Keypoint Triplets for Object Detection. https://arxiv.org/abs/1904.08189. Accessed 15 July 2021
7. Fagin, R., Lotem, A., Naor, M.: Optimal aggregation algorithms for middleware. J. Comput. Syst. Sci. **66**(41), 614–656 (2003)
8. Grabisch, M., Marichal, J., Mesiar, R., Pap, E.: Aggregation Functions (Encyclopedia of Mathematics and its Applications) Cambridge University Press (2009)
9. Hajek, P.: Metamathematics of Fuzzy Logic. Springer, Heidelberg (1998)
10. Hajek, P., Havranek, T.: Mechanizing Hypothesis Formation. Springer, Heidelberg (1978)
11. He, K., et al.: Deep Residual Learning for Image Recognition. https://arxiv.org/abs/1512.03385. Accessed 15 July 2021
12. Klement, E.-P., Mesiar, R., Pap, E.: Triangular Norms. Springer, Heidelberg (2000)
13. Kopecky, M., Vojtas, P.: Visual E-commerce values filtering framework with spatial database metric. Comput. Sci. Inf. Syst. **17**(3), 983–1006 (2020)
14. Lin, T.-Y., et al.: Focal Loss for Dense Object Detection. https://arxiv.org/abs/1708.02002. Accessed 15 July 2021
15. Navrat, P., Bielikova, M., Rozinajova, V.: Acquiring, organising and presenting information and knowledge from the web. Commun. Cogn. **40**(1–2), 37–44 (2007)
16. Peska, L., Eckhardt, A., Vojtas, P.: Interpreting Implicit User Behavior for E-shop Recommendation with Families of Fuzzy T-conorms, p. 36, preprint (2012)
17. Peska, L., Eckhardt, A., Vojtas, P.: Preferential interpretation of fuzzy sets in recommendation with real e-shop data experiments. Arch. Philos. Hist. Soft Comput. **2**, 14 (2015). https://www.unipapress.it/it/book/aphsc-2-%7C-2015_170
18. Peska, L., Vojtas, P.: Predictability of off-line to on-line recommender measures via scaled fuzzy implicators. In: FUZZ-IEEE 2020, pp. 1–8 (2020)
19. Peska, L., Vojtas, P.: Using implicit preference relations to improve recommender systems. J. Data Semant. **6**(1), 15–30 (2016). https://doi.org/10.1007/s13740-016-0061-8
20. Redmon, J., Farhadi, A.: YOLOv3: An Incremental Improvement. https://arxiv.org/abs/1804.02767. Accessed 15 July 2021
21. Ries, E.: The Lean Startup: How Today's Entrepreneurs Use Continuous Innovation to Create Radically Successful Businesses. Crown Publication (2011)
22. Tan, M., Le, Q.V.: EfficientNet: Rethinking Model Scaling for Convolutional Neural Networks. https://arxiv.org/abs/1905.11946. Accessed 15 July 2021
23. Tan, M., et al.: EfficientDet: Scalable and Efficient Object Detection. https://arxiv.org/abs/1911.09070. Accessed 15 July 2021
24. Vojtas, P.: Generalized Galois-Tukey connections between objects of real analysis. In: Israel Mathematical Conference Proceedings, vol. 6, pp. 619–643 (1993)

25. Vojtas, M., Vojtas, P.: Problem reduction as a general epistemic reasoning method. In: Extended abstract CLMPST 2019, EasyChair Preprint no. 1208. https://easychair.org/publications/preprint/HfsP. Accessed 10 June 2021
26. Object detection software. https://github.com/qqwweee/keras-yolo3. Accessed 15 July 2021
27. Object detection software. https://github.com/Tianxiaomo/pytorch-YOLOv4. Accessed 15 July 2021
28. Object detection software. https://github.com/fizyr/keras-retinanet. Accessed 15 July 2021
29. Object detection software. https://github.com/tensorflow/models/blob/master/research/object_detection/g3doc/tf2_detection_zoo.md. Accessed 15 July 2021

The Impact of User Demographics and Task Types on Cross-App Mobile Search

Mohammad Aliannejadi[1], Fabio Crestani[2]([⊠]), Theo Huibers[3], Monica Landoni[2], Emiliana Murgia[4], and Maria Soledad Pera[5]

[1] University of Amsterdam, Amsterdam, The Netherlands
m.aliannejadi@uva.nl
[2] Università della Svizzera Italiana, Lugano, Switzerland
{fabio.crestani,monica.landoni}@usi.ch
[3] University of Twente, Enschede, The Netherlands
t.w.c.huibers@utwente.nl
[4] Università degli Studi di Milano-Bicocca Milano, Milan, Italy
emiliana.murgia@unimib.it
[5] Boise State University, Boise, ID, USA
solepera@boisestate.edu

Abstract. Recent developments in the mobile app industry have resulted in various types of mobile apps, each targeting a different need and a specific audience. Consequently, users access distinct apps to complete their information need tasks. This leads to the use of various apps not only separately, but also collaboratively in the same session to achieve a single goal. Recent work has argued the need for a *unified mobile search* system that would act as metasearch on users' mobile devices. The system would identify the target apps for the user's query, submit the query to the apps, and present the results to the user in a unified way. In this work, we aim to deepen our understanding of user behavior while accessing information on their mobile phones by conducting an extensive analysis of various aspects related to the search process. In particular, we study the effect of task type and user demographics on their behavior in interacting with mobile apps. Our findings reveal trends and patterns that can inform the design of a more effective mobile information access environment.

Keywords: Mobile search · User evaluation

1 Introduction

The ever-increasing use of smartphones has made them pervasive in our lives, originating an abundance of mobile apps that users install and use [10]. Many of the apps that users interact with daily have their own data repository and feature their own search engine. This prompted researchers to study and report on the

© Springer Nature Switzerland AG 2021
T. Andreasen et al. (Eds.): FQAS 2021, LNAI 12871, pp. 223–234, 2021.
https://doi.org/10.1007/978-3-030-86967-0_17

need and significance of having a truly universal mobile search framework that would act as a metasearch engine on the device [3–5]. In this case, users could type their search queries in a unique search box and the framework would route the query to relevant apps that could retrieve useful results that would then be displayed in a unified interface. To inform the design of such an engine, it is critical to understand how users interact and access information using different apps. It is also imperative to understand user behavior while accessing different apps on their smartphones, as this plays a crucial role in improving the system.

The high significance of understanding user behavior in relation to various demographic attributes and the prominence of cross-app search in people's lives, motivated us to study how different users interact with different apps as they complete a search task. While the influence of user demographics on web search queries [36] and app usage [22,39] has been already investigated, to the best of our knowledge no work has looked at cross-app search queries. In this paper, we study the behavior of over 600 users in terms of mobile app usage over 200 search tasks to answer two research questions: *RQ1*: Do demographic factors condition app usage for search? and, *RQ2*: Do extrinsic factors impact app usage for search? We analyze the relationship between users' app selection behavior with respect to different demographics characteristics as well as other system-related aspects. In particular, we study age, education, device type, and task type. We observe that all of these dimensions impact the way users complete search tasks on their smartphones.

Trends and patterns emerging from the analysis we conducted reveal the impact that demographic factors have on users' selection to conduct information-seeking tasks; the device and the task type itself also direct app selection. Findings from this work could serve as groundwork informing the design of a personalized metasearch system for mobile devices; they also offer insights that recommender systems could leverage in terms of suggesting suitable apps given the task of choice, in addition to diversification of app selection to complete search tasks on mobile devices.

2   Related Work

In this section, we discuss existing literature that offers context to our work. We first emphasize the influence that demographic information has on several areas of study. We then briefly mention existing works focused on mobile app search.

Existing works have emphasized the importance of demographic information from various perspectives [16] such as web search [36], video consumption [35], music [20], and mobile app usage [22,39]. These studies reveal that understanding users' demographics and usage patterns is crucial to provide enhanced service and identify which users to target (e.g., showing ads about family vacations). Weber and Castillo [36] studied the behavior of different user segments on web search from various aspects (e.g., income level, education, ethnicity) looking at how demographic aspects affected their search queries and clicks. They demonstrated the high impact that demographics can have on user behavior.

This motivated a series of works aiming to predict user demographics based on user behavior, and in this context, mobile app usage has been extensively studied [22,39].

More closely focusing on mobile search, we start with the study in [24], which outlines differences on search behavior observed on mobiles vs desktop Web search. In a similar work, Song et al. [30] found a significant difference in search patterns done using iPhone, iPad, and desktop. We also highlight the work by Carrascal and Church [7], who examine users' engagement with mobile search and report that in a mobile context, users turn to more apps and that certain app categories are used more intensively. Kamvar et al. [18] did a large-scale mobile search query analysis, finding mobile search topics were less diverse. Similar studies done in [13] and [9] compared typed-in queries and spoken queries on mobile devices conducted comparative studies on mobile spoken and typed-in queries where they found similar conclusions, i.e., spoken queries are more similar to natural language. Tian et al. [32] look into how automatic task segmentation can directly improve mobile search. For instance, the authors discuss how after performing a certain task the probability to formulate a particular query increases [32,38].

This work is closely related to our previous studies on unified mobile search [3–5] where we introduced and studied research on unified mobile search and collected cross-app queries through crowdsourcing, as well as in situ user study. We based our work here on the data collected through an in situ user study and provide further analysis on how users with different demographics interact with applications while searching on mobile devices.

3   Methodology

In this section, we describe the data and experiments that we used to address our research questions.

3.1   Data

We use the UniMobile[1] dataset released by Aliannejadi et al. [4,8]. The dataset contains 5,812 cross-app mobile search queries for 206 search tasks spread across multiple task categories. The dataset also includes demographics surveys in which participants provided details about their background, search experience, and preferences. They also answered survey questions aimed at understanding how participants access the Internet and use their phones. In particular, in one question the participants specified the device that they most frequently used to access the Internet. Finally, participants shared whether they use their smartphones primarily for personal reasons or work-related reasons.

The data contains the queries submitted by 625 users located in the United States (400 identified themselves as female, the rest as male). 39% of the participants were aged between 25 to 34, followed by 24% between 35 and 44, and 20%

---

[1] https://github.com/aliannejadi/unimobile.

between 18 and 24. 17% of the participants were in other age groups. Most participants held a Bachelor's degree (38%), followed by "Some college, no degree" (26%), and Master's degree (16%). The other 20% had other levels of education (e.g., high school and doctorate).

The majority of participants used their smartphones as their primary Internet device (48%), followed by 31% using a Laptop computer, 14% Desktop computer, 5% tablets, and 2% other devices. Most participants stated that they used their smartphones more for personal reasons (71%), 19% about an equal amount for work and personal reasons, and 10% more for work-related reasons.

3.2   Experiments

Here, we describe the experiments we designed based on user demographics and task-related measures.

Age. To investigate the effect of users' age on their search behavior, in Fig. 1 we show the distribution of selected apps per age group. We count the total number of unique apps that each participant selects when completing different tasks and plot the distribution of each age group. We hypothesize that users of different age groups use a different range of apps to complete their daily search tasks.

Education. We examine the effect of education from three different perspectives. First, in Fig. 2a we show the distribution of the total number of unique apps per user. Our hypothesis is that users' educational background plays a role in their app selection. Second, in Fig. 2b we show the diversity of users selecting apps for different tasks. For each user, we count the number of times they select each app for different tasks. Then, we plot the unique app count per user group (and 95% confidence interval)[2]. We hypothesize that users' ability and/or tendency to diversify their app selection depends on their level of education. Third, we are interested in finding out if education impacts how much users would "follow the crowd." In other words, we observe whether a user selects an app that the majority of users have also selected for the same task (e.g., if 8 out of 10 users choose Google Search for a task, would a user choose the same app or not?). We show in Fig. 2c the number of apps that are not in line with the crowd per user (and 95% confidence interval). To determine popular apps for a given task, we first assume that the number of app selections follows a normal distribution. Then, we consider apps that fall into the 25th quantile as *rare*, i.e., non-popular. If a user chooses one of the popular apps for a given task, we treat this as a *follow-the-crowd* selection and dismiss it in our counts. Instead, if a user selects one of the "rare" apps, we include that in our computation.

Device. We plot in Fig. 3a app usage across devices used to access the Internet, whereas in Fig. 3b we capture how many apps users choose to complete different tasks with (and 95% confidence interval). Our hypothesis is that the preferred device to access the Internet influences the user's behavior.

---

[2] Estimated via empirical analysis of a Bootstrap sampling with 1,000 resamples.

Task. We study task impact in two different experiments. First, we compute how many unique apps participants choose to complete the same task. We group the search tasks by their category label (labeled by three expert annotators) and plot unique app distribution in Fig. 4. Second, we analyze Fig. 5, in which we depict how users' preference for smartphone use impacts their behavior. In this figure, we group users by their preferred use of smartphones, i.e., *personal* or *work* reasons.

Significance Testing. To determine significant differences we conduct the one-sided ANOVA ($p < 0.001$) test.

4   Results and Analysis

Here we discuss the results of the experiments described in Sect. 3.2, along with other factors that can offer context to our analysis. Unless otherwise noted, reported results are significant.

Age. As captured in Fig. 1, younger users (18 to 44) tend to use a broader selection of apps when searching for information. This was anticipated, as older adults (45 or older) are known to be less prone to downloading and using new apps [28]. Further, our results align with those reported by Gordon et al. [12], regarding older adults using fewer apps. Overall, the distribution of selected apps across different age groups serves as evidence to validate our hypothesis, as indeed users in varying age groups turn to a different range of apps to complete their daily search tasks.

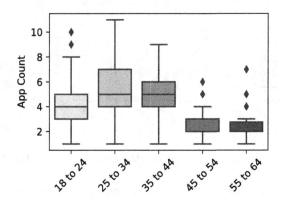

Fig. 1. Number of apps used to complete search tasks across different age groups.

Education. We posit that users' educational background could impact the manner in which they engage with mobile apps. It is evident from Fig. 2a that education background plays a role: users with a professional degree or doctorate mostly turn to a single app, a number that increases to 4 and 5 for users with a

Master's degree and Bachelor's degree, respectively. This could be due to multiple reasons such as less tendency to switch between apps, or having a "go-to" app for all tasks. For example, as reported by Wai et al. [33], bachelors are known to use a broad range of apps for learning purposes. Thus it is not unexpected to find that they choose more range of apps for searching, given their exposure to varied apps. Figure 2b helps us answer this question as it shows how often users with different educational backgrounds choose a certain app, thus indicating how diverse each group is in selecting apps. We see that indeed users with a Ph.D. degree tend to be less diverse in their selection of apps since they complete more tasks with the same app. On the other hand, we see that users with a Professional degree tend to submit fewer queries to the same app.

We also study how much one's educational background can impact the selection of *Rare Apps*, i.e., apps that other users choose less frequently to complete the same task. We see in Fig. 2c that the rate of choosing rare apps significantly correlates with educational background. In this case, the higher the education, the more rare apps the users select. This could be due to the complexity of the tasks undertaken by users who possess higher educational backgrounds. Together, Figs. 2a, b, and c complement each other to paint a picture of how many unique choices each user group has, and how is the distribution of queries that they submit. For example, Ph.D. and Professional users select a similar number of unique apps to complete their search tasks (Fig. 2a), however, most of the queries of Ph.D. participants are submitted to a few apps (Fig. 2b) and Ph.D. participants are very selective in the apps they choose as they have the highest rate of rare app usage (Fig. 2c).

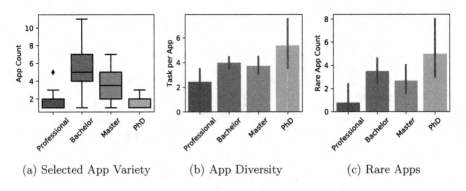

(a) Selected App Variety   (b) App Diversity   (c) Rare Apps

Fig. 2. Impact of educational background on app selection and usage.

Device. We turn to Fig. 3 for trends related to the primary device used for Internet access. It is evident from Fig. 3a that the device used to access the Internet significantly impacts the number of distinct apps users turn to seek information. For example, the highest number of unique apps chosen is among smartphone users, whereas the lowest is among Desktop users. This is expected, based on recent statistics indicating that users spend more time on smartphones than Desktops; 90% of the time spent on smartphones is on apps [1,17,29]. Moreover, we see in Fig. 3b that smartphone users show less tendency towards diversifying their app selections (i.e., they submit more queries to fewer apps), as opposed to other users. Perhaps this is because they are more used to minimizing their search effort. Also, such users often access their smartphones in various contexts with fragmented attention [2,15], which can affect their choice of apps.

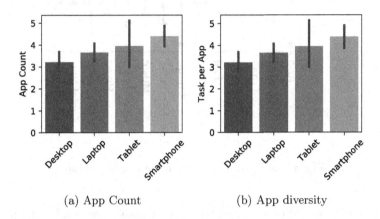

(a) App Count   (b) App diversity

Fig. 3. Impact of primary device used for Internet access on selected apps.

Task. We aim to understand two different aspects of the impact of task on user's behavior, i.e., personal vs. work reasons and task type. Figure 5 shows the impact of users' search app preferences when using their smartphones mainly for personal or work purposes. We see that the more participants use their phones for personal reasons, the more apps they choose to complete their search tasks. We attribute this to the variety of tasks that they can perform for personal reasons, which exceed those for work purposes that are generally more focused. Also, the existence of several personal apps such as instant messaging and social networking implicitly increases their choices. In order to understand this aspect better, we plot in Fig. 4 the number of selected apps per task category. In this figure, we see that task type significantly impacts the user's behavior in terms of the apps they choose to complete the task. Interestingly we see that News and General Information categories exhibit the least number of apps, suggesting the existence of dominant apps for these categories (i.e., Google Search). However, for other task types, we observe a higher number of apps. Also, we see a larger range of app count for some task types (e.g., File), suggesting that there is a personal effect involved while completing these types of tasks, some users choosing multiple apps for these tasks while other users selecting fewer apps.

5   Discussion and Implications

We conclude our study by further discussing our findings and the design implications we get from them. Our discussion covers specifically how task categorization

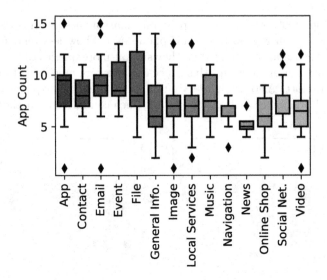

Fig. 4. Impact of task type on the number of apps.

and complexity should be incorporated into the design process. Furthermore, we argue that design for users of certain age groups should be considered. This can be in the form of enhanced app switching mechanisms or app recommender systems. Finally, we point out how various contextual factors can impact user's performance and the need for further study to uncover that.

It is of note that the current iteration of our work overlooks the two tail ends of the use spectrum, children and older adults. Both of these populations have varied levels of expertise and access when it comes to information seeking, smartphone use, and Internet access [14,31]. This would suggest the need to expand our study to understand all users, not just mainstream ones. Further, it is of interest to study search tasks categories across specific use cases, for example, apps used for health information seeking [25] and learning [11], as aspects inherent to the use case could open up other areas of analysis, complementing the dimensions considered in this study, to further understand search behavior across apps. Demographic factors such as age and education clearly influence mobile app choice for search. Recommender systems could support users in their choice of the app given a specific search task, yet making available demographic profiles to these recommender systems could result in posing "undesirable privacy risk" [34]; further recommendation algorithms should simultaneously account for apps' permissions and users' interests and needs [26], which is a non-trivial task. If we consider younger demographics, while recommender systems could indeed aid users' selection of suitable apps to turn to complete a given task, research has demonstrated that children favor knowing the source of the recommendations if they are to trust and take advantage of them [27]; in their case, additional developmental traits and external factors are also a must to consider for recommendation purposes [23], which results in complex design requirements. Therefore, we leave further exploration of this direction for future work.

As noted by Tian et al. [32], task categorization could be leveraged to improve mobile services. In our case, findings related to task categorization complemented by demographic information could provide predictive contexts to improve mobile search, allowing "for a more personalized and engaging experience" [32].

When exploring the design space defined by our analysis, we recognize a few dimensions worth of notice: the type and complexity of the task, the effort the user is willing to put in the discovery, assessment, selection, and in case combination of suitable apps to reduce task complexity (minimum, medium and high), and the motivation for running the search (work or not). The task complexity dimension is well studied in literature and classified as an objective factor in the definition by Wildemuth et al. [37], who state that the task complexity is determined by the uncertain nature of the task and of the information need behind it. Also, motivation is a well-researched dimension as it is closely linked with relevance, being a "characteristic of all of the subjective types of relevance." [6]. The app-related dimension is equally subjective and in need of further study as it accounts for a number of factors: the knowledge and degree of familiarity of the user with the available apps, the willingness to take control and engage in the selection and combination process of the apps providing the best performance, as well as the interest in finding particular apps specific to a task. That would push us to explore solutions where according to the complexity and type of the task together with the effort required to deal with it, and the motivations behind the search, users would be more or less inclined to give up control and instead trust a system to select and combine apps in order to get the best search performance.

The work reported in [32] goes in this direction when they report mobile user behaviors similar to those we have discussed here in terms of engagement with multiple apps, and suggest that in the future "intelligent switching interfaces"

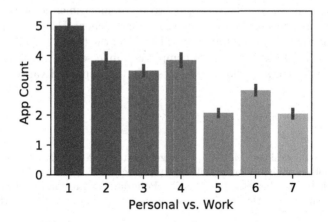

Fig. 5. App variety on smartphones across the personal-work spectrum. In this case, 1 indicates personal use more than work; in contrast, 7 denotes work use more than personal.

would provide mobile users better search experiences. Still, we believe more study is necessary in order to better understand which apps are better suitable for which tasks and group of users. A good starting point is a work by Liu et al. [21] who already provide some preliminary results to be expanded for aiming at a more encompassing taxonomy on demographic and task to predict user choice in the context of mobile search. While [19] let us explore the combination of tasks and demographics into context to inform future recommending systems.

6   Conclusions and Directions for Future Work

Based on our analysis we can answer both RQ1 and RQ2 positively and provide some useful insights into the demographic and the extrinsic factors that condition the use of apps for search. Respectively age and education and type of device and task. Some of our findings were to be expected, e.g. younger users tend to use a broader selection of apps when searching for information and the highest number of unique apps chosen is among smartphone users. Others, such that the higher the education, the more rare apps the users select, and that the more participants use their phones for personal reasons, the more apps they choose to complete their search tasks, provide an original insight. How these factors influence each other is still to be fully studied, as for instance smartphone users often access their devices with fragmented attention [15] and this affects the complexity of tasks they could engage with successfully. Therefore, we need to explore further the role played by task types in the selection of apps for search beyond the personal vs. work dichotomy, perhaps by focusing on task complexity instead. Starting from finding out why users do not trust apps for search to perform complex tasks and how we can change this attitude by providing users with better support when performing complex searches using smartphones.

We need to look more closely at differences across work-related tasks as these could be linked to time pressure, fragmented attention, overall higher task complexity, and less tolerance to failure. That in turn will modify the design space making time and relevance the two dominant dimensions while pushing for more control to be left to users that could benefit from a unified mobile search and recommendation framework. Hence, in the future, we plan to conduct a field study in which users would complete mobile search tasks under various conditions and contexts, allowing us to study the impact of various contextual factors.

References

1. Mobile vs. desktop internet usage (latest 2020 data). https://www.broadbandsearch.net/blog/mobile-desktop-internet-usage-statistics#
2. Aliannejadi, M., Harvey, M., Costa, L., Pointon, M., Crestani, F.: Understanding mobile search task relevance and user behaviour in context. In: CHIIR, pp. 143–151. ACM (2019)
3. Aliannejadi, M., Zamani, H., Crestani, F., Croft, W.B.: In situ and context-aware target apps selection for unified mobile search. In: CIKM, pp. 1383–1392. ACM (2018)

4. Aliannejadi, M., Zamani, H., Crestani, F., Croft, W.B.: Target apps selection: towards a unified search framework for mobile devices. In: SIGIR, pp. 215–224. ACM (2018)
5. Aliannejadi, M., Zamani, H., Crestani, F., Croft, W.B.: Context-aware target apps selection and recommendation for enhancing personal mobile assistants. CoRR abs/2101.03394 (2021)
6. Borlund, P.: The concept of relevance in IR. J. Am. Soc. Inform. Sci. Technol. **54**(10), 913–925 (2003)
7. Carrascal, J.P., Church, K.: An in-situ study of mobile app & mobile search interactions. In: Proceedings of the 33rd Annual ACM Conference on Human Factors in Computing Systems, pp. 2739–2748 (2015)
8. Costa, L., Aliannejadi, M., Crestani, F.: A tool for conducting user studies on mobile devices. In: CHIIR, pp. 462–466. ACM (2020)
9. Crestani, F., Du, H.: Written versus spoken queries: a qualitative and quantitative comparative analysis. JASIST **57**(7), 881–890 (2006)
10. Crestani, F., Mizzaro, S., Scagnetto, I.: Mobile Information Retrieval. Springer Briefs in Computer Science, Springer, Cham (2017). https://doi.org/10.1007/978-3-319-60777-1
11. Domingo, M.G., Garganté, A.B.: Exploring the use of educational technology in primary education: teachers' perception of mobile technology learning impacts and applications' use in the classroom. Comput. Hum. Behav. **56**, 21–28 (2016)
12. Gordon, M.L., Gatys, L., Guestrin, C., Bigham, J.P., Trister, A., Patel, K.: App usage predicts cognitive ability in older adults. In: Proceedings of the 2019 CHI Conference on Human Factors in Computing Systems, pp. 1–12 (2019)
13. Guy, I.: Searching by talking: analysis of voice queries on mobile web search. In: SIGIR, pp. 35–44 (2016)
14. Hargittai, E., Piper, A.M., Morris, M.R.: From internet access to internet skills: digital inequality among older adults. Univ. Access Inf. Soc. **18**(4), 881–890 (2018). https://doi.org/10.1007/s10209-018-0617-5
15. Harvey, M., Pointon, M.: Searching on the go: the effects of fragmented attention on mobile web search tasks. In: SIGIR, pp. 155–164. ACM (2017)
16. Hinds, J., Joinson, A.N.: What demographic attributes do our digital footprints reveal? A systematic review. PLoS ONE **13**(11), e0207112 (2018)
17. Johnson, J.: Daily time spent online by device 2021, January 2021. https://www.statista.com/statistics/319732/daily-time-spent-online-device/
18. Kamvar, M., Baluja, S.: A large scale study of wireless search behavior: google mobile search. In: CHI, pp. 701–709 (2006)
19. Karatzoglou, A., Baltrunas, L., Church, K., Böhmer, M.: Climbing the app wall: enabling mobile app discovery through context-aware recommendations. In: Proceedings of the 21st ACM International Conference on Information and Knowledge Management, pp. 2527–2530 (2012)
20. Krismayer, T., Schedl, M., Knees, P., Rabiser, R.: Predicting user demographics from music listening information. Multimed. Tools Appl. **78**(3), 2897–2920 (2018). https://doi.org/10.1007/s11042-018-5980-y
21. Liu, B., Wu, Y., Gong, N.Z., Wu, J., Xiong, H., Ester, M.: Structural analysis of user choices for mobile app recommendation. ACM Trans. Knowl. Discov. Data (TKDD) **11**(2), 1–23 (2016)
22. Malmi, E., Weber, I.: You are what apps you use: demographic prediction based on user's apps. In: ICWSM, pp. 635–638. AAAI Press (2016)

23. Murgia, E., Landoni, M., Huibers, T., Fails, J.A., Pera, M.S.: The seven layers of complexity of recommender systems for children in educational contexts. In: Proceedings of the 2019 ComplexRec Workshop: Co-Located with the 13th ACM Conference on Recommender Systems (2019). http://ceur-ws.org/Vol-2449/paper1.pdf

24. Ong, K., Järvelin, K., Sanderson, M., Scholer, F.: Using information scent to understand mobile and desktop web search behavior. In: Proceedings of the 40th International ACM SIGIR Conference on Research and Development in Information Retrieval, pp. 295–304 (2017)

25. Pandey, A., Hasan, S., Dubey, D., Sarangi, S.: Smartphone apps as a source of cancer information: changing trends in health information-seeking behavior. J. Cancer Educ. **28**(1), 138–142 (2013)

26. Peng, M., Zeng, G., Sun, Z., Huang, J., Wang, H., Tian, G.: Personalized app recommendation based on app permissions. World Wide Web **21**(1), 89–104 (2017). https://doi.org/10.1007/s11280-017-0456-y

27. Pera, M.S., Murgia, E., Landoni, M., Huibers, T.: With a little help from my friends: use of recommendations at school. In: Proceedings of ACM RecSys 2019 Late-Breaking Results: Co-Located with the 13th ACM Conference on Recommender Systems, pp. 61–65 (2019)

28. Rosales, A., Fernández-Ardèvol, M.: Smartphone usage diversity among older people. In: Sayago, S. (ed.) Perspectives on Human-Computer Interaction Research with Older People. HIS, pp. 51–66. Springer, Cham (2019). https://doi.org/10.1007/978-3-030-06076-3_4

29. Saccomani, P.: People spent 90% of their mobile time using apps in 2019, February 2021. https://www.mobiloud.com/blog/mobile-apps-vs-the-mobile-web

30. Song, Y., Ma, H., Wang, H., Wang, K.: Exploring and exploiting user search behavior on mobile and tablet devices to improve search relevance. In: WWW, pp. 1201–1212 (2013)

31. Starkey, L., Eppel, E.A., Sylvester, A.: How do 10-year-old New Zealanders participate in a digital world? Inf. Commun. Soc. **22**(13), 1929–1944 (2019)

32. Tian, Y., Zhou, K., Lalmas, M., Pelleg, D.: Identifying tasks from mobile app usage patterns. In: Proceedings of the 43rd International ACM SIGIR Conference on Research and Development in Information Retrieval, pp. 2357–2366 (2020)

33. Wai, I.S.H., Ng, S.S.Y., Chiu, D.K., Ho, K.K., Lo, P.: Exploring undergraduate students' usage pattern of mobile apps for education. J. Librariansh. Inf. Sci. **50**(1), 34–47 (2018)

34. Wang, C., Zheng, Y., Jiang, J., Ren, K.: Toward privacy-preserving personalized recommendation services. Engineering **4**(1), 21–28 (2018)

35. Wang, Y., Xiao, Y., Ma, C., Xiao, Z.: Improving users' demographic prediction via the videos they talk about. In: EMNLP, pp. 1359–1368. The Association for Computational Linguistics (2016)

36. Weber, I., Castillo, C.: The demographics of web search. In: SIGIR, pp. 523–530. ACM (2010)

37. Wildemuth, B., Freund, L., Toms, E.G.: Untangling search task complexity and difficulty in the context of interactive information retrieval studies. J. Doc. **70**, 23 (2014)

38. Zhang, A., et al.: Towards mobile query auto-completion: an efficient mobile application-aware approach. In: Proceedings of the 25th International Conference on World Wide Web, pp. 579–590 (2016)

39. Zhong, E., Tan, B., Mo, K., Yang, Q.: User demographics prediction based on mobile data. Pervasive Mob. Comput. **9**(6), 823–837 (2013)

Author Index

Printed in the United States
by Baker & Taylor Publisher Services